THE FEMALE RE

OR

MISCELLANEOUS PIECES,

IN PROSE AND VERSE;

SELECTED FROM THE BEST WRITERS,

AND DISPOSED UNDER PROPER HEADS;

FOR THE IMPROVEMENT OF YOUNG WOMEN.

By Mr. CRESSWICK, TEACHER OF ELOCUTION.

TO WHICH IS PREFIXED

A PREFACE, CONTAINING SOME HINTS ON FEMALE EDUCATION.

———

LONDON:
PRINTED FOR J. JOHNSON, ST. PAUL'S CHURCH-YARD.
1789.

PREFACE.

It is universally allowed that many poems, tales, and allegories, are scattered through our best authors, particularly calculated to affect a young heart and improve an opening understanding, which the gay and thoughtless seldom have patience to look for, or discernment to select; and many collections have been made, in order to present in one point of view the most useful passages of many volumes, where various other subjects are mixed that were only written for minds matured by experience.

Before the publication of Dr. Enfield's Speaker*, a methodical order in the arrangement of the pieces selected was not attempted, or even thought of, though it is evidently the only way to render a book of this kind extensively useful; as whatever tends to impress habits of order on the expanding mind may be reckoned the most beneficial part of education: for by

* As this work and the sequel to it are generally used in schools, the editor has avoided selecting pieces that are in either of them.

this means the surest foundation of virtue is settled without a struggle, and strong restraints knit together before vice has introduced confusion.

In the present volume, which is principally intended for the improvement of females, the subjects are not only arranged in separate books, but are carefully disposed in a series that tends to make them illustrate each other; linking the detached pieces seemed to give an interest to the whole, which even the slightest connexion will not fail to produce.

The main object of this work is to imprint some useful lessons on the mind, and cultivate the taste at the same time—to infuse a relish for a pure and simple style, by presenting natural and touching descriptions from the Scriptures, Shakspeare, &c. Simplicity and sincerity generally go hand in hand, as both proceed from a love of truth.

In subordination to this design, passages varying in style, in verse and prose, have been chosen to enable a scholar to learn to read well: and, at a time when female accomplishments are deemed of more consequence than they ever were, the most essential demands some attention.

Female

Females are not educated to become public speakers or players; though many young ladies are now led by fashion to exhibit their persons on a stage, sacrificing to mere vanity that diffidence and reserve which characterizes youth, and is the most graceful ornament of the sex.

But if it be allowed to be a breach of modesty for a woman to obtrude her person or talents on the public when necessity does not justify and spur her on, yet to be able to read with propriety is certainly a very desirable attainment; to facilitate this task, and exercise the voice, many dialogues have been selected; but not always the most beautiful with respect to composition, as the taste should very gradually be formed. A contrary method may teach young people what to say; but probably will prevent their ever learning to think. It would be needless to repeat here the trite remark which proves an undeniable fact—that the ignorant never read with propriety; and they must ever be accounted ignorant who are suddenly made wise by the experience of others, never brought to a test by their own feeble unexercised reason.

Some little helps to elocution are necessary even for those who never aspire at being orators; but teachers should be very careful not to make scholars practise rules they cannot understand, as monotony is less disgusting than affectation.

In the beginning only prevent their acquiring bad habits; instruct them in the common methods of observing stops and articulating each syllable; and as the mind is stored with arranged knowledge they will insensibly read well, interested by the sentiments they understand. To guard against a dull indifferent tone, they should be allowed to read amusing tales, allegories, &c. Reasoning must be tedious and irksome to those whose passions have never led them to reason; and examples of virtue will ever most forcibly illustrate precepts of morality.

In this selection many tales and fables will be found, as it seems to be following the simple order of nature, to permit young people to peruse works addressed to the imagination, which tend to awaken the affections and fix good habits more firmly in the mind than cold arguments and mere declamation.

It is scarcely necessary to make any
apology

apology for introducing the book which contains devotional pieces. A late amiable writer* has asserted that, amidst the scenes of silent unobserved distress, in which women are very frequently involved, religion is their only solace and support. They cannot, when oppressed by sorrow, or harassed by wordly cares, fly to business or those tumultuous pleasures which dissipate, if they do not calm, the mind: condemned to fight on even ground and listen to the very echo of their grief, piety alone can still the murmurs of discontent, and give stability to their principles: but piety is not to be acquired in the hour of trouble; it must have been a cherished inmate of the soul, or it will not afford consolation when every other source fails.

To fix devotional habits in a young mind, forms must in some degree be attended to. Those who constantly make a point of repeating a prayer at a stated time, though it may be termed mechanical devotion, yet learn to consider it as a duty; and piety may imperceptibly warm the heart that was at first unmoved by the task. It is however to be lamented that so

---

* Dr. Gregory.

great a stress is laid on the mere act as to lead many to imagine that they have made their peace with God, and may securely rely on his favour, only because they punctually read over a long prayer, and observe the ceremonies enjoined by religion to keep alive the vital spirit, which, amongst frail mortals, stands in need of a bodily support to give it permanency and effect. Obedience is the only daily incense pleasing to the Supreme Being. Yet many women who constantly address him do not attempt to govern their tempers, or render their dependents comfortable, though they think they are not like other women on this very account; they go to church twice a week and give alms.

Every thing then which tends to strengthen sentiments of piety, founded on morality, not introduced in a gloomy dress, must be useful: and even the imagination and affections should not be allowed to take another course; for a character will never have any firmness or uniformity which is not governed by one main spring.

The distinction between social and private prayers has been observed in those inserted in this volume; for private converse, even with our heavenly Father, without being familiar, ought to be more interesting than the petitions offered up by a common general voice.

In the preface to a book designed for females we may, with the greatest propriety, introduce a quotation from an essay which does honour to a female pen*:

"Philosophy represents the Deity in too abstracted a manner to engage our affections.

"A Being without hatred and without fondness, going on in one steady course of even benevolence, neither delighted with praises, nor moved by importunity, does not interest us so much as a character open to the feelings of indignation, the soft relentings of mercy, and the partialities of particular affections. We require some common nature, or at least the appearance of it, on which to build our intercourse. It is also a fault of which philosophers are often guilty, that they dwell too much in generals. Accustomed to reduce every thing to the operation of general laws, they turn our attention to larger views, attempt to grasp the whole order of the universe; and, in the zeal of a systematic spirit, seldom leave room for those

* Miss Aikin.

particular

particular and personal mercies which are the food of gratitude. They trace the great outline of nature, but neglect the colouring which gives warmth and beauty to the piece. As in poetry it is not vague and general description, but a few striking circumstances clearly related and strongly worked up; as in a landscape it is not such a vast extensive range of country as pains the eye to stretch to its limits, but a beautiful well-defined prospect, which gives the most pleasure—so neither are those unbounded views, in which philosophy delights, so much calculated to touch the heart as home views and nearer objects. The philosopher offers up general praises on the altar of universal nature; the devout man, on the altar of his heart, presents his own sighs, his own thanksgivings, his own earnest desires; the former worship is more grand, the latter more personal and affecting.

"He has impressed me with the idea of trust and confidence, and my heart flies to him in dangers; of mercy to forgive, and I melt before him in penitence; of bounty to bestow, and I ask of him all I want or wish for. I may make use of an inaccurate expression, I may paint him to my imagination too much in the fashion of humanity; but, while my heart is pure, while I depart not from the line of moral duty, the error is not dangerous. Too critical a spirit is the bane of every thing great or pathetic. In our creeds let us be guarded, let us there weigh every syllable; but, in compositions addressed to the heart, let us give freer scope to the language of the affections, and the overflowing of a warm and generous disposition."

It has been a custom too prevalent to make children learn by rote long passages from authors, to whose very expressions they could not annex an idea, not considering how vain, and indeed cruel it is, to compel them to repeat a round of unintelligible words. Parents are often led astray by the selfish desire of having a wonderful child to exhibit; but these monsters very seldom make sensible men or women: the wheels are impaired by being set in motion before the time pointed out by nature, and both mind and body are ever after feeble. If, however, a girl be inclined to commit poems, &c. to memory, let me warn the fond mother not to persuade her to display this trifling attainment in company; for the young and thoughtless

less will seldom endeavour, by virtue and propriety of behaviour, to deserve praise, when they can obtain it at such an easy rate. Nay, if they wished them to learn to read well, they would not require them to run over emphatical expressions with the same voice: to teach them just tones, as far as a parrot can be taught, is still worse; for it will infallibly render them affected; and though we do not see the wires we discern that they are mere puppets. Should it then be thought necessary to exercise the memory, pray chuse a simple tale or fable, and many children will find them so entertaining that they will instinctively vary their tones; but let them only be repeated to a mother or governess; if you do not mean to light a spark, you will not easily extinguish, when it has quietly spread through the whole mass.

When a girl arrives at a more advanced age, it would be still more useful to make her read a short lesson, and then transcribe it from her memory; and afterwards let her copy the original, and lead her to remark the mistakes she has made. This method would exercise the memory, and form the judgment at the same time: she would learn to write correctly, and retain the precepts which

which in some measure she has composed herself, and a kind of emulation would be excited from which no bad consequences could possibly flow. If this employment is allowed to occupy two mornings every week, at the end of four or five years the understanding will have received great strength, and the pupil will express herself both in speaking and writing, provided she has a tolerable capacity, with a degree of propriety that will astonish those that have not adopted the same plan. She will understand English, and express her sentiments in her native tongue; instead of which our young ladies of fashion write a mixture of French and Italian, and speak the same jargon.

If my young readers, for whom this collection is principally intended, would listen to me a few moments, I would endeavour to prove to them that the most sedulous attention to the person will never improve it, whilst a cultivated mind renders the most graceful form more pleasing:—What do I say?—there is no grace without it; nor any beauty, that will charm for half an hour, which does not arise from an artless display of virtue or sense.—But it is not necessary to speak to display mental charms—the eye will quickly inform us if an active soul resides within; and a blush is far more eloquent than the best turned period.

Exterior accomplishments are not to be obtained by imitation, they must result from the mind, or the deception is soon detected, and admiration gives place to contempt. If you wish to be loved by your relations and friends, prove that you can love them by governing your temper; good humour and cheerful gaiety will then enliven every feature and dimple your cheeks—but this my young friends is not the work of a day. An attention to truth gives dignity to the manners: and a dependence on Providence banishes those fears which render many girls very ridiculous, and make them appear as insignificant as they are helpless; if they do not endeavour to conquer them they will forfeit the esteem of those whose protection they most want—the good and the wise.

Another observation I must here be allowed to dwell on; supposing a young lady has received the best education, she has advanced but a few steps towards the improvement of her mind and heart—that is the business of her whole life; she must not mistake and call blossoms fruit, for the

summer

summer often proves the hopes of spring fallacious; and it must ripen the most promising to give it real value. The plenty of autumn only rewards the industrious, and industry is never irksome when it becomes habitual.

As we are created accountable creatures we must run the race ourselves, and by our own exertions acquire virtue: the utmost our friends can do is to point out the right road, and clear away some of the loose rubbish which might at first retard our progress.—If, conquering indolence and a desire of present enjoyment, we push forward, not only the tranquil joy of an approving conscience will cheer us here, but we shall anticipate in some degree, while we advance to it, that happiness of which we can form no conception in our present state, except when we have some faint glimpse from the pleasures arising from benevolence, and the hope of attaining more perfect knowledge.—We are indeed all children educated by a beneficent Father for his kingdom—some are nearer the awful close than others, to their advice the young should listen—for respectable is the hoary head when found in the path of virtue.

THE CONTENTS.

SELECT DESULTORY THOUGHTS: ADDRESSED TO FEMALES.

BOOK I.
NARRATIVE PIECES.

		Page
The Importance of Religion to Minds of Sensibility	*Mirror*	1
Continuation of the Story of La Roche	*Ibid*	5
Conclusion of the Story of La Roche	*Ibid*	9
The History of Joseph	*Genesis*	14
Joseph's Interview with his Brethren	*Ibid*	16
Filial Attention	*Mirror*	22
Filial Piety and Affection of a Daughter		26
Filial Obedience rewarded	*Jeremiah*	27
History of Inkle and Yarico	*Spectator*	29
Crazy Kate	*Cowper*	31
The Folly of being led by the Fashion	*World*	32
The Absurdity of Extremes	*Ibid*	35
The Contrast	*Young*	36
On the Loss of Beauty	*Rambler*	37
The Discovery of America	*Voltaire*	47
The Influence of Science on the Manners of Men	*Robertson*	50

BOOK II.
DIDACTIC AND MORAL PIECES.

Female Passion for Dress and Show	*Spectator*	52
On Cleanliness	*Ibid*	54
The Art of improving Beauty	*Ibid*	57
The Art of being Pretty	*Adventurer*	60
Dress	*Original Stories*	63
The same Subject	*Gregory*	64
The same Subject	*Wollstonecraft*	64
Dress subservient to useful Purposes	*Mrs. Trimmer*	65
Ode to a young Lady on Dress	*Shenstone*	65
On Employment	*Lady Pennington*	66
Benevolent Employments	*Mrs. Trimmer*	68
The same Subject continued	*Ibid*	72
On Waste of Time	*Cowper*	74
Indolence		

CONTENTS

		Page
Indolence and Want of Thought	L. Chesterfield	75
Bad Effects of Indolence	Connoisseur	76
On the Government of the Temper	Mrs. Chapone. Proverbs	80
On Obedience	Proverbs	81
On Humility	St. Mark. St. Matthew	83
On Politeness	Miss Talbot	84
False Sensibility	Mrs Chapone	86
False Notions of Sentiment	Lounger	88
The Poet, the Oyster, and Sensitive Plant, a Fable	Cowper	89
Vanity and Affectation	Lord Halifax	91
Dissimulation	Blair	96
The Natural Beauty	Johnson	98
A Definition of Taste	Gregory	99
True Elegance	Clio	100
Ridicule	Ibid	102
Music	Gregory	103
An Association of Ideas produced by Rural Sounds	Cowper	104
Essay on Talkativeness	Rack	106
On Telling of Secrets	Adventurer. James	113
Justice defined	Goldsmith	115
On Covetousness	St. Luke	116
True Pleasure defined	Seed	117
True End of Life	Johnson	118
A Letter on Letter Writing	Bp. Atterbury	118
The Advantages arising from Reading		120

BOOK III.

ALLEGORIES AND PATHETIC PIECES.

A Vision	Guardian	121
Carazan, a Vision: on social Love	Adventurer	126
Verses supposed to be written by Alex. Selkirk	Cowper	130
An Allegory	Rambler	133
Pity: an Allegory	Aikins's Mis.	138
Esther's Interview with the King	Esther	140
St. Paul taking Leave of his Friends	The Acts	141
Lazarus raised from the Dead	St. John	143
The Widow's Son raised from the Dead	St. Luke	146
Christ's Agony.---Peter's Denial of Christ	St. Matthew	147
The Death of Christ, and the Penitent Thief	St. Luke	151
Character of Christ	Isaiah	152
The Ignorance and Weakness of Man	Job	153
The Ignorance of Man	Merrick	156
A Grateful Effusion	Isaiah	157
Peter's want of Faith	St. Matthew	159
A Paraphrase on the latter Part of St. Matt. ch. vi.	Thomson	160
The Peace of God	Isaiah	161
Dying Friends	Young	162

CONTENTS.

		Page
Hymn on Death	Mrs. Barbauld	163
On the Resurrection	Ibid	165
On the last Judgment	Revelation. St. Matthew	166
The Judgments of God	Isaiah. Jeremiah	169
The Lamentations of the Jews in Captivity	Psalms	171
Negro Woman	Mrs. Barbauld	172
A prophetic Description of the Destruction of Babylon	Revelation	173
The Punishment of the Wicked foretold	Isaiah	174
Divine Mercy	Isaiah. St. Luke. St. Matthew	174
Esau deprived of his Father's Blessing	Genesis	175
David's Lamentation for the Death of his Son	Samuel	178
Gloster, Edgar, and Old Man	Shakspeare	180
Kent and Gentleman	Ibid	186
Cordelia, Kent, and Physician	Ibid	188
Hubert and Executioners	Ibid	192
King Philip, Constance, and Pandulpho	Ibid	199
Lady Macbeth	Ibid	202
William and Margaret		208
Sonnet to Sleep	Charlotte Smith	211
The Friar of Orders Grey		212
A Mouse's Petition	Miss Aikin	216
The Dying Kid	Shenstone	218
Sonnet to a Nightingale	Charlotte Smith	219
Song from the Lapland Tongue	Steele	220
A Fragment	Aikins's Miscel.	221

BOOK IV.

DIALOGUES, CONVERSATIONS, AND FABLES.

Lord and Lady Townley	Cumberland	226
Conversation between Colonel Rivers and his Daughter, on her intended Elopement	Ibid.	233
Bevil and Indiana	Steele	236
Orlando and Rosalind	Shakspeare	240
Prospero and Miranda	Ibid	246
Prospero, Miranda, Ferdinand, and Ariel, (singing invisible)	Ibid	251
Ferdinand (bearing a log)	Ibid	256
Prospero and Ariel	Ibid	259
Miranda, Ferdinand, &c.	Ibid	262
Imogen and Pisanio	Ibid	263
Imogen, (in Boy's Clothes)	Ibid	265
Bellarius and Guiderius	Ibid	269
Dirge in Cymbeline	Collins	271
Queen and Lady	Shakspeare	272
Conversation between Adam and Eve on going to rest	Milton	273
The Camelion. A Fable	Merrick	276

		Page
The Sparrow and Diamond		278
The Monkies. A Tale	*Merrick*	280
The Nightingale and Glow-worm. A Fable	*Moore*	281
The Goose and the Swans. A Fable	*Ibid*	283
The Pin and the Needle. A Fable	*Gay*	286
The Two Bees. A Fable		287
Indirect Disputes	*Adventurer*	288
A Conversation on Truth	*Original Stories*	291
Lying Punished	*Ibid*	293

BOOK V.

DESCRIPTIVE PIECES.

The Character of Queen Elizabeth	*Hume*	295
The Character of Mary Queen of Scots	*Robertson*	297
A Portrait of Mankind influenced by Vanity	*Sterne*	300
The Planetary and Terrestrial Worlds comparatively considered	*Spectator*	301
A Devotional Psalm		304
The Pleasures of the Country	*Cowper*	305
Men and Animals compared	*Gregory*	307
Tenderness for Animals	*Cowper*	309
An Evening's Invocation to Winter	*Ibid*	312
The Empress of Russia's Palace of Ice	*Cowper*	315
The Post Boy	*Ibid*	317
An Invocation to the Stars	*Ibid*	318
Written at Midnight during a Thunder-storm	*Miss Carter*	319
Ode on Æolus's Harp	*Thomson*	320
On Slavery	*Cowper*	321
The Bastile	*Ibid*	322
On Humanity	*Cowper*	326
Poverty and Luxury contrasted	*Goldsmith*	327
A Character	*Miss Aikin*	330
A Character	*Ibid*	331
A Comparison	*Cowper*	331
A Comparison	*Ibid*	332
On a Lady's Writing	*Miss Aikin*	332
Female Amusements	*Thomson*	332
True Gaiety	*Cowper*	333
To Stella visiting me in my Sickness	*Swift*	333
Dorina, Lucy. A Conversation	*Mad. Genlis*	3 7
Dorina, Toinetta, Lucy	*Ibid*	342
Lucy, Dorina	*Ibid*	347
Portrait of a modern fine Lady	*Address to Mothers*	348
Stella's Birth-day	*Swift*	351
Ornaments	*Shakspeare*	353

BOOK VI.

DEVOTIONAL PIECES, AND REFLECTIONS ON RELIGIOUS SUBJECTS.

		Page
Passages from Miss Aikin, Dr. Gregory, Proverbs		354
Piety	Young. Proverbs. M. Wollstonecraft. St. James	357
Charity	St. Paul	358
The Widow's Mite	St. Luke	359
Christ's Sermon	St. Matthew	360
On Christian Virtues	Madame Genlis	363
Mutual Forbearance	St. Matthew	367
On the Government of Servants	Mrs. Chapone. Mrs. Trimmer	368
Providence compared to an indulgent Mother	Richardson	369
St. Paul's Address to the Athenians	The Acts	370
On Prayer	St. Matthew. St. John	371
On Prayer	Original Stories. St. James	375
A Prophetic Effusion	Isaiah	373
A private Morning Prayer	O.	378
A private Evening Prayer	Ibid	379
A social Morning Prayer	Ibid	381
A social Evening Prayer	Ibid	382
The Morning Hymn	Milton	383
An Address to the Deity	Miss Aikin	385
An Address to the Deity	Thomson	388
Character of a good Man	Psalms	388
An Address to the Deity	Young	389
David's Confidence in God's Grace	Psalms	390
An Address to the Deity	Young	390
The Presence of God	Psalms	390
The Power of God	Ibid	391
The Goodness of God	Ecclesiastes	393

SELECT DESULTORY THOUGHTS;

ADDRESSED TO FEMALES.

As the two sexes have very different parts to act in life nature has marked their characters very differently, in a way that best qualifies them to fulfil their respective duties in society.
GREGORY.

WHILST men are proud of power, of wealth, dignity, learning, or abilities, young women are usually ambitious of nothing more than to be admired for their persons, their dress, or their most trivial accomplishments. The homage of men is their grand object: but they only desire them to be in love with their persons, careless how despicable their minds appear, even to those their pretended adorers.
MRS. CHAPONE.

ALL finery is a sign of littleness.   LAVATER.

THE principal virtues or vices of a woman must be of a private and domestic kind. Within the circle of her own family and dependants lies her sphere of action—the scene of almost all those tasks and trials which must determine her character and her fate here and hereafter.

Reflect, for a moment, how much the happiness of her husband, children, and servants, must depend on her temper, and you will see that the greatest good or evil which she ever may have in her power to do may arise from her correcting or indulging its infirmities.

MRS. CHAPONE.

The imperfection of our nature is such, that scarce a day can pass in which we have not committed some error; for which reason the people most amiable, and most beloved, will always be those who, by confessing the wrongs they have done, shew their candour and goodness of heart. This sublime quality always appertains to the generous and the feeling; while little and confined minds, enslaved by false shame, as mean as it is foolish, would rather aggravate their faults than retract them or say a word in expiation.

MADAME GENLIS.

In order to render yourself amiable in society, correct every appearance of harshness in behaviour. Let that courtesy distinguish your demeanour which springs not so much from studied politeness as from a mild and gentle heart. Follow the customs of the world in matters indifferent; but stop when they become sinful. Let your manners be simple and natural, and of course they will be engaging. Affectation is certain deformity. By forming yourselves on fantastic models, and vying with one another in every reigning folly, the young begin with being ridiculous, and end in being vicious and immoral.

GREGORY.

All affectation is the vain and ridiculous attempt of poverty to appear rich.

LAVATER.

A CONSTANT

A CONSTANT attention to the management of the temper produces gentleness and humility, and is practised on all occasions, as it is not done "to be seen of men." This meek spirit arises from good sense and resolution; and should not be confounded with indolence and timidity, weaknesses of mind, which often pass for good-nature.

O.

WHO forces herself on others is to herself a load. Impetuous curiosity is empty and inconstant: prying intrusion may be suspected of whatever is little.

LAVATER.

WHO can listen without constraint whilst an important thing is telling, can keep a secret when told.

IBID.

WHO, inattentive to answers, accumulates questions, will not be informed; and who means not to be informed, asks like a fool.

IBID.

WHO begins with severity in judging of another, ends commonly with falsehood.

IBID.

WHO, without pressing temptation, tells a lie, will, without pressing temptation, act ignobly and meanly.

IBID.

THE most exuberant encomiast turns easily into the most inveterate censor.

IBID.

SHE, who sets out with the praise of a friend, stumbles as she proceeds on a *but*, and ends in a rigid censure, call what you choose but honest.

IBID.

Beware of making confidants of your servants. Dignity not properly understood very readily degenerates into pride, which enters into no friendships, because it cannot bear an equal, and is so fond of flattery as to grasp at it even from servants and dependants. The most intimate confidants, therefore, of proud people are valets-de-chambre and waiting-women. Shew the utmost humanity to your servants; make their situation as comfortable to them as possible: but if you make them your confidants you spoil them and debase yourselves.

GREGORY.

The behaviour of girls to servants is generally in extremes, too familiar or too haughty. Indeed the one often produces the other as a check when the freedoms are troublesome.

O.

Though the domestics of the rich are ignorant, yet, from frequently hearing their masters, they get a more refined, or rather a more affected, manner of speaking than the peasants, yet full as defective. The chief vice in their dialect is a meanness of expression and puerility of ideas, rather than words. I am not afraid that, by conversing with peasants, you should learn to say, *I connot, I munnot, I wunnot*:—these expressions are so different from those you are accustomed to hear, there is little fear of your adopting them; but, on the contrary, the language of servants is in words something so like your own, that there is great reason to apprehend you might adopt it imperceptibly. But there is another thing which is yet far more to be feared; domestics have in general vices and defects, which are the consequences of the servile state

they

they have chosen. If an ignorant man be not laborious, if he leads a life of idleness, and loiters away his time, it is hardly possible he should be virtuous.
MADAME GENLIS.

The first and most respectable part that enters into the composition of elegance is the lofty consciousness of worth or virtue, which sustains an habitual decency and becoming pride.
CLIO.

From the combination of these fine parts—grandeur of soul, complacency, and ease—arise the enchantments of elegance; but the appearance of the two last are oftener found together, and then they form politeness.
IBID.

Decency is the habit which a noble train of thinking fixes upon the mind; and it is related to religion, because religion more than any other object ennobles our ideas.
GREGORY.

Who is respectable, when thinking himself alone and free from observation, will be so before the eye of the world.
LAVATER.

Men who are occupied only by dreams of enriching themselves think all delicacy the prejudice of education: it is very difficult for such persons to preserve noble sentiments; their probity is strictly reduced to common honesty; and such kind of probity can never confer a desirable reputation.
MADAME GENLIS.

What pleases us generally appears beautiful. Complaisance, that is so engaging, gives an agreeableness to the whole person, and creates a beauty that nature gave not to the features; it submits, it promises, it applauds in the countenance; the heart lays itself in smiles at your feet; and a voice that is indulgent and tender is always heard with pleasure.
GREGORY.

There is a certain gentleness of spirit and manners extremely engaging in your sex, not that indiscriminate attention, that unmeaning simper, which smiles on all alike. This arises either from an affectation of softness or from perfect insipidity.
IBID.

Who censures with modesty will praise with sincerity.
LAVATER.

Cultivate an enlarged charity for all mankind, however they may differ from you in their religious opinions: that difference may probably arise from causes in which you had no share, and from which you can derive no merit.
GREGORY.

Never indulge yourselves in ridicule on religious subjects; nor give countenance to it in others, by seeming diverted with what they say. This, to people of good-breeding, will be a sufficient check.
IBID.

Our capacities are too confined to comprehend all the truths which are demonstrable; and it would be absurd to affirm a thing does not exist, because it is beyond the limits of our understandings. Let us not adopt errors, but

but let us not give way to that vain and ridiculous presumption which rejects with disdain, and without examination, every thing that reason cannot conceive.

MADAME GENLIS.

HUMOUR is a quality that will make your company much solicited; but be cautious how you indulge it. It is often a great enemy to delicacy, and still a greater one to dignity of character. It may sometimes gain you applause, but will never procure you respect.

GREGORY.

THERE is a species of refinement in luxury just beginning to prevail among the gentlemen of this country, to which our ladies are yet as great strangers as any women upon earth; I hope for the honour of the sex they may continue so: I mean—the luxury of eating. It is a despicable vice in men, but in women it is beyond expression indelicate and disgusting.

IBID.

IN every instance the abuse of pleasure is its destruction; and those who satiate desire extinguish it. Remember, therefore, that superfluity and excess, far from contributing to, exterminate happiness: remember that luxury dazzles none but fools, and does not produce one real delight; for nothing is more troublesome than magnificence.

MADAME GENLIS.

WHEN passion forms projects it is blind to all obstacles, will hear no objections; but, fearing all reasons which may deter it from what it is previously determined to do, it never discovers its own folly and imprudence till they are past remedy.

IBID.

The bulk of mankind are incapable of thinking or judging for themselves on any subject. There are a few leading spirits whom the rest must follow. This makes systems so universally acceptable. If they cannot teach people to think and to feel, they teach them what to say, which answers all the purposes of the most universally ruling passion among mankind—vanity.

GREGORY.

Who can look quietly at nothing will never do any thing worthy of imitation.

LAVATER.

I would have every one try to form an opinion of an author themselves, though modesty may restrain them from mentioning it. Many are so anxious to have the reputation of taste that they only praise the authors whose merit is indisputable. I am sick of hearing of the sublimity of Milton, the elegance and harmony of Pope, and the original untaught genius of Shakspeare. These cursory remarks are made by some who know nothing of nature, and could not enter into the spirit of those authors, or understand them.

O.

We expect none of those properties from children which are commonly the fruits of experience. Thus, for example, we think it natural enough that they should sometimes be inconsistent, wild, or idle: but we expect they should occasionally give indications of all the virtues that originate in the heart, are natural to it, born with it, and only require cultivation. A child, therefore, who should give proofs of cowardice, cruelty, or ingratitude, might be thought a monster, if its vices were not the consequences of a bad education.

MADAME GENLIS.

The human genius, with the best assistance and the finest examples, breaks forth but slowly; and the greatest men have but gradually acquired a just taste and chaste simple conceptions of beauty. At an immature age the sense of beauty is weak and confused, and requires an excess of colouring to catch its attention: it then prefers extravagance and rant to justness; a gross false wit to the engaging light of nature; and the showy, rich, and glaring, to the fine and amiable. This is the childhood of taste; but as the human genius strengthens and grows to maturity, if it be assisted by a happy education, the sense of universal beauty awakes; it begins to be disgusted with that false and misshapen deceptions that pleased before, and rests with delight on elegant simplicity, on pictures of easy and unaffected grandeur.

CLIO.

Have you ever seen the miser make a present, and have you not observed how much his pomp and emphasis have proved the action came not from his heart, but was the mere effect of vanity; and, in fact, it had cost him so much to perform it that his ostentation was almost pardonable? Remark, on the contrary, with what noble simplicity a generous person gives. Thus it is that common minds are vain of their good actions, and think them extremely meritorious because they find them so painful; while great souls have no such pride, being, by their own natural dignity, inclined to complaisant and virtuous actions.

MADAME GENLIS.

It is not from want of capacity that so many women are such trifling insipid companions—so ill qualified for the

friendship

friendship and conversation of a sensible man—or for the task of governing and instructing a family; it is much oftener from the neglect of exercising the talents which they really have, and from omitting to cultivate a taste for intellectual improvement: by this neglect they lose the sincerest of all pleasures; a pleasure which would remain when almost every other forsakes them—which neither fortune nor age can deprive them of—and which would be a comfort and resource in almost every possible situation of life.
Mrs. Chapone.

How is it possible to give any marking proofs of fortitude, if we are habitually feeble? She, who suffers her imagination to have dominion over her, can neither drive from her memory what is dangerous to recollect, nor reject thoughts she ought not to entertain; and can such a person always be supposed rational? The faculty of thinking should be turned to the improvement of the heart and mind; but we pervert this noble faculty when we suffer our imagination to dwell upon objects beneath, unworthy of, or derogatory to, ourselves; therefore there is no doubt but the most secret thoughts of a wise man are far more pure and sublime than his words.
Madame Genlis.

When our thoughts are vague and unconnected, our ideas become as troublesome to ourselves as they would be to others, were we to vent these vague thoughts in conversation: while, on the contrary, we amuse ourselves when the imagination is not idle, but, instead of common and frivolous things, is employed on interesting subjects.
Ibid.

A soul

A soul without reflection, like a pile without inhabitant, to ruin runs.
YOUNG.

Modesty, which I think so essential in your sex, will naturally dispose you to be rather silent in company, especially in a large one. People of sense and discernment will never mistake such silence for dulness. One may take a share in conversation without uttering a syllable. The expression of the countenance shews it, and this never escapes an observing eye.
GREGORY.

Modesty is silent when it would not be improper to speak: the humble, without being called upon, never recollects to say any thing of herself.
LAVATER.

I should be glad that you had an easy dignity in your behaviour at public places, but not that confident ease, that unabashed countenance, which seems to set the company at defiance. If, while a gentleman is speaking to you, one of superior rank addresses you, do not let your eager attention and visible preference betray the flutter of your heart. Let your pride on this occasion preserve you from that meanness into which your vanity would sink you. Consider that you expose yourselves to the ridicule of the company, and affront one gentleman only to swell the triumph of another, who perhaps thinks he does you honour in speaking to you.

Converse with men even of the first rank with that dignified modesty which may prevent the approach of the most distant familiarity, and consequently prevent them from feeling themselves your superiors.
GREGORY.

In

In your father's house it is certainly proper for you to pay civility to the guests, and to talk to them in your turn with modesty and respect—if they encourage you to it. Young ladies, of near your own age, who visit there, fall of course to your share to entertain. But, whilst you exert yourself to make their visit agreeable to them, you must not forget what is due to the elder part of the company; nor, by whispering and laughing apart, give them cause to suspect, what is too often true, that they themselves are the subjects of your mirth. It is so shocking an outrage against society to talk of, or laugh at, any person in his own presence, that one would think it could only be committed by the vulgar. I am sorry however to say that I have too often observed it amongst young ladies, who little deserved that title whilst they indulged their overflowing spirits in defiance of decency and good-nature. The desire of laughing will make such inconsiderate young persons find a subject of ridicule, even in the most respectable of characters.

Mrs. Chapone.

Indiscretion, rashness, falsehood, levity, and malice, produce each other.

Lavater.

Consider that it is a sure indication of good sense to be diffident of it. We then, and not till then, are growing wise, when we begin to discern how weak and unwise we are. An absolute perfection of understanding is impossible: he makes the nearest approaches to it who has the sense to discern, and the humility to acknowledge, its imperfections.

imperfections. Modesty always sits graceful upon youth; it covers a multitude of faults, and doubles the lustre of every virtue which it seems to hide: the perfections of men being like those flowers which appear more beautiful when their leaves are a little contracted and folded up, than when they are full blown, and display themselves without any reserve to the view.   SEED.

Those qualities which are only brilliant have ever more enemies than admirers; but those which are the offspring of the heart obtain the suffrages of all. You cannot outshine other men without wounding their pride; whilst you astonish them, you often irritate; and, whenever you are personal, you are assuming.   MADAME GENLIS.

If you have any acquired talent of entertainment, such as music, painting, or the like, your own family are those before whom you should most wish to excel, and for whom you should always be ready to exert yourself; not suffering the accomplishments which you have gained, perhaps by their means, and at their expense, to lie dormant, till the arrival of a stranger gives you spirit in the performance. Where this last is the case you may be sure vanity is the only motive of the exertion. A stranger will praise you more: but how little sensibility has that heart which is not more gratified by the silent pleasure painted on the countenance of a partial parent, or of an affectionate brother, than by the empty compliments of a visiter, who is perhaps inwardly more disposed to criticize and ridicule than to admire you!   MRS. CHAPONE.

We should be astonished to see a woman pass her life in playing on the guittar, and designing flowers; but no one will blame you when you use such things only as recreations, by way of agreeably saving time, which would otherwise be lost, and without being proud of such trifling accomplishments.
MADAME GENLIS.

Give instruction to a wise man and he will be yet wiser: teach a just man, and he will increase in learning. The fear of the Lord is the beginning of wisdom, and the knowledge of the holy is understanding.
PROVERBS.

Whoso loveth instruction loveth knowledge, but he that hateth reproof is brutish.
IBID.

If you wish to acquire a command over your passions accustom yourself to regulate your imagination at your pleasure, and to banish any certain train of thoughts when you wish so to do.
MADAME GENLIS.

He who courageously submits to his fate, and suffers without murmuring, is certainly a most respectable being; and it must be a mean and insensible mind that can refuse its pity to a man who, obliged to endure, hardens himself in sorrow, and supports pain nobly. Such virtuous resignation should excite our admiration, and render sympathy more tender and active. Besides, it is very natural to shrink from beholding misery in others, which we ourselves could support without complaining. This is a sublime sensation, and common to all superior minds, of which we have daily a thousand proofs. For example; I can see myself bled, and hold the bason, and yet I am affected when I look at the lancet wounding the vein of another.
IBID.

Cold

Cold grows less intense when you have been long in the air; thus it is with all physical evils: we inure ourselves to all those that may be supported without death being the consequence; habit makes the most frightful and dangerous objects familiar, and robs even affliction of its sting. This is a truth which it is very necessary well to comprehend, because it teaches us to face the pains and misfortunes attendant on human nature.

            Ibid.

Remember that the coldest hearts, nay the hardest, cannot forbear admiring such virtue; but that, while they stop at this involuntary and barren homage, the feeling mind burns with emulation.

            Ibid.

The more you can forget others who suffer, and dwell upon yourself who suffer not, the more contemptible is your self-love.

           Lavater.

It is not always natural to prefer ourselves to others; and she who thinks only of and for herself, and who is not affected by the misfortunes of others, is a vicious and degraded being.

          Madame Genlis.

We cannot hide from ourselves what is in its own nature blameable: in vain would specious reasons gloss over actions, and call them noble, delicate, refined: the heart and the conscience give such reasonings the lie!

            Ibid.

Happy

Happy is the man that findeth wisdom, and the man that getteth understanding.
PROVERBS.

Life is short, its duration uncertain; and extravagance only would patiently expect a desired blessing, which activity and address might presently obtain.
LAVATER.

Virtue is not to be considered in the light of mere innocence, or abstaining from harm, but as the exertion of our faculties in doing good.
CONNOISSEUR.

There is not a more pleasing exercise of the mind than gratitude. It is accompanied with such inward satisfaction, that the duty is sufficiently rewarded by the performance. It is not like the practice of many other virtues, difficult and painful, but attended with so much pleasure, that were there no positive command which enjoined it, nor any recompense laid up for it hereafter—a generous mind would indulge in it for the natural gratification that accompanies it.
SPECTATOR.

Ingratitude is reckoned among some nations a capital crime; for they reason thus, that whoever makes ill returns to his benefactor must needs be a common enemy to the rest of mankind, from whom he hath received no obligation, and therefore such a man is not fit to live.
SWIFT.

There are few good dispositions of any kind with which the improvement of taste is not more or less connected. A cultivated taste increases sensibility to all the tender and humane passions, by giving them frequent exercise, while it tends to weaken the more violent and fierce emotions.
BLAIR.

BOOK I.

NARRATIVE PIECES.

THE IMPORTANCE OF RELIGION TO MINDS OF SENSIBILITY.

More than forty years ago an English philosopher, whose works have since been read and admired by all Europe, resided at a little town in France. Some disappointments in his native country had first driven him abroad, and he was afterwards induced to remain there, from having found, in this retreat, where the connexions even of nation and language were avoided, a perfect seclusion and retirement highly favourable to the developement of abstract subjects, in which he excelled all the writers of his time.

One morning, while he sat busied in those speculations which afterwards astonished the world, an old female domestic, who served him for a house-keeper, brought him word that an elderly gentleman and his daughter had arrived in the village the preceding evening, on their way to some distant country, and that the father had been suddenly seized in the night with a dangerous disorder, which the people of the inn where they lodged feared would prove mortal: that she had been sent for, as having some knowledge in medicine, the village-surgeon being then absent; and that it was truly piteous to see the good

good old man, who seemed not so much afflicted by his own distress, as by that which it caused to his daughter. Her master laid aside the volume in his hand, and broke off the chain of ideas it had inspired. His night-gown was exchanged for a coat, and he followed his governante to the sick man's apartment.

'Twas the best in the little inn where they lay, but a paultry one notwithstanding. Mr. —— was obliged to stoop as he entered it. It was floored with earth, and above were the joints not plastered, and hung with cobwebs.—On a flock bed, at one end, lay the old man he came to visit; at the foot of it sat his daughter. She was dressed in a clean white bed-gown; her dark locks hung loosely over it as she bent forward, watching the languid looks of her father. Mr. —— and his housekeeper had stood some moments in the room without the lady's being sensible of their entering it.—' Mademoi-
' selle!' said the old woman at last, in a soft tone.—She turned and showed one of the finest faces in the world.— It was touched, not spoiled, with sorrow; and when she perceived a stranger, whom the old woman now introduced to her, a blush at first, and then the gentle ceremonial of native politeness, which the affliction of the time tempered, but did not extinguish, crossed it for a moment, and changed its expression. It was sweetness all, however, and our philosopher felt it strongly. It was not a time for words; he offered his services in a few sincere ones. ' Monsieur lies miserably ill here,' said the governante; ' if he could possibly be moved any where.'— ' If he could be moved to our house,' said her master.— He had a spare bed for a friend, and there was a garret room unoccupied, next to the governate's. It was contrived accordingly. The scruples of the stranger, who

could

could look scruples, though he could not speak them, were overcome, and the bashful reluctance of his daughter gave way to her belief of its use to her father. The sick man was wrapped in blankets, and carried across the street to the English gentleman's. The old woman helped his daughter to nurse him there. The surgeon, who arrived soon after, prescribed a little, and nature did much for him: in a week he was able to thank his benefactor.

By that time his host had learned the name and character of his guest. He was a Protestant clergyman of Switzerland, called La Roche, a widower, who had lately buried his wife, after a long and lingering illness, for which travelling had been prescribed; and was now returning home, after an ineffectual and melancholy journey with his only child, the daughter we have mentioned.

He was a devout man, as became his profession. He possessed devotion in all its warmth, but with none of its asperity; I mean that asperity which men, called devout, sometimes indulge in. Mr. ———, though he felt no devotion, never quarrelled with it in others.—His governante joined the old man and his daughter in the prayers and thanksgivings which they put up on his recovery; for she too was a heretic, in the phrase of the village.— The philosopher walked out, with his long staff and his dog, and left them to their prayers and thanksgivings.— 'My master,' said the old woman, 'alas! he is not a 'Christian; but he is the best of unbelievers.'—'Not a 'Christian!' exclaimed Mademoiselle La Roche, 'yet 'he saved my father! Heaven bless him for it; I would 'he were a Christian!'—'There is a pride in human 'knowledge, my child,' said her father, 'which often 'blinds men to the sublime truths of revelation; hence 'opposers

'opposers of Christianity are found among men of vir-
'tuous lives as well as among those of dissipated and
'licentious characters. Nay, sometimes I have known
'the latter more easily converted to the true faith than
'the former, because the fume of passion is more easily
'dissipated than the mist of false theory and delusive spe-
'culation.'—' But Mr. ———,' said his daughter, ' alas!
'my father, he shall be a Christian before he dies.'—She
was interrupted by the arrival of the landlord—he took
her hand with an air of kindness—she drew it away from
him in silence; threw down her eyes to the ground, and
left the room.—' I have been thanking God,' said the
good La Roche, ' for my recovery.'—' That is right,'
replied his landlord.—' I would not wish,' continued the
old man hesitatingly, ' to think otherwise; did I not
'look up with gratitude to that Being, I should barely
'be satisfied with my recovery, as a continuation of life,
'which, it may be, is not a real good:—Alas! I may
'live to wish I had died, that you had left me to die,
'Sir, instead of kindly relieving me (he clasped Mr.
'———'s hand);—but, when I look upon this renovated
'being as the gift of the Almighty, I feel a far different
'sentiment—my heart dilates with gratitude and love to
'him: it is prepared for doing his will, not as a duty
'but as a pleasure, and regards every breach of it, not
'with disapprobation, but with horror.'—' You say
'right, my dear Sir,' replied the philosopher; ' but you
'are not yet re-established enough to talk much—you
'must take care of your health, and neither study nor
'preach for some time. I have been thinking over a
'scheme that struck me to-day, when you mentioned your
'intended departure. I never was in Switzerland; I
'have a great mind to accompany your daughter and
'yo

'you into that country.—I will help to take care of you 'by the road; for, as I was your first physician, I hold 'myself responsible for your cure.' La Roche's eyes glistened at the proposal; his daughter was called in and told of it. She was equally pleased with her father; for they really loved their landlord—not perhaps the less for his infidelity; at least that circumstance mixed a sort of pity with their regard for him—their souls were not of a mould for harsher feelings, hatred never dwelt in them.

CONTINUATION OF THE STORY OF LA ROCHE.

They travelled by short stages; for the philosopher was as good as his word, in taking care that the old man should not be fatigued. The party had time to be well acquainted with one another, and their friendship was increased by acquaintance. La Roche found a degree of simplicity and gentleness in his companion, which is not always annexed to the character of a learned or a wise man. His daughter, who was prepared to be afraid of him, was equally undeceived.

On his part he was charmed with the society of the good clergyman and his lovely daughter. He found in them the guileless manner of the earliest times, with the culture and accomplishment of the most refined ones. Every better feeling, warm and vivid; every ungentle one, repressed or overcome. He was not addicted to love; but he felt himself happy in being the friend of Mademoiselle La Roche, and sometimes envied her father the possession of such a child.

After a journey of eleven days they arrived at the dwelling of La Roche. It was situated in one of those vallies of the canton of Berne, where Nature seems to repose, as it were, in quiet, and has enclosed her retreat with mountains inaccessible. A stream, that spent its fury in the hills above, ran in front of the house; and a broken waterfall was seen through the wood that covered its sides; below it circled round a tufted plain, and formed a lake in front of a village, at the end of which appeared the spire of La Roche's church, rising above a clump of beeches.

Mr. ——— enjoyed the beauty of the scene; but, to his companions, it recalled the memory of a wife and parent they had lost. The old man's sorrow was silent; his daughter sobbed and wept. Her father took her hand, kissed it twice, pressed it to his bosom, threw up his eyes to heaven; and, having wiped off a tear that was just about to drop from each, began to point out to his guest some of the most striking objects which the prospect afforded. The philosopher interpreted all this; and he could but slightly censure the creed from which it arose.

They had not been long arrived when a number of La Roche's parishioners, who had heard of his return, came to the house to see and welcome him. The honest folks were awkward, but sincere, in their professions of regard. They made some attempts at condolence: it was too delicate for their handling; but La Roche took it in good part. ‘ It ‘ has pleased God,’ said he; and they saw he had settled the matter with himself.—Philosophy could not have done so much with a thousand words.

It was now evening, and the good peasants were about to depart, when a clock was heard to strike seven, and the hour was followed by a particular chime. The country folks, who had come to welcome their pastor, turned their looks towards him at the sound; he explained their meaning to his guest. ‘ That is the signal,’ said he, ‘ for our
‘ evening

'evening exercise; this is one of the nights of the week
'in which some of my parishioners are wont to join in it;
'a little rustic saloon serves for the chapel of our family,
'and such of the good people as are with us: if you chuse
'rather to walk out I will furnish you with an attendant;
'or here are a few old books that may afford you some
'entertainment within.'—'By no means,' answered the
philosopher; 'I will attend Ma'moiselle at her devotions.'
'She is our organist,' said La Roche; 'our neighbour-
'hood is the country of musical mechanism; and I have a
'small organ fitted up for the purpose of assisting our sing-
'ing.' ''Tis an additional inducement,' replied the other;
and they walked into the room together. At the end stood
the organ mentioned by La Roche; before it was a curtain,
which his daughter drew aside; and, placing herself on a
seat within, and drawing the curtain close, so as to save
her the aukwardness of an exhibition, began a voluntary,
solemn and beautiful in the highest degree. Mr. ———
was no musician; but he was not altogether insensible to
music. This fastened on his mind more strongly from its
beauty being unexpected. The solemn prelude introduced
a hymn, in which such of the audience as could sing im-
mediately joined; the words were mostly taken from holy
writ; it spoke the praises of God, and his care of good
men. Something was said of the death of the just; of such
as die in the Lord. The organ was touched with a hand
less firm; it paused; it ceased; and the sobbing of Ma'moi-
selle La Roche was heard in its stead. Her father gave a
sign for stopping the psalmody, and rose to pray. He was
discomposed at first, and his voice faltered as he spoke;
but his heart was in his words, and his warmth overcame
his embarrassment. He addressed a Being whom he loved,

B 4 and

and he spoke for those he loved. His parishioners catched the ardour of the good old man; even the philosopher felt himself moved, and forgot for a moment to think why he should not.

La Roche's religion was that of sentiment, not theory; and his guest was averse from disputation: their discourse, therefore, did not lead to questions concerning the belief of either; yet would the old man sometimes speak of his, from the fulness of a heart impressed with its force, and wishing to spread the pleasure he enjoyed in it. The ideas of his God and his Saviour were so congenial to his mind that every emotion of it naturally awaked them. A philosopher might have called him an enthusiast; but, if he possessed the fervour of enthusiasts, he was guiltless of their bigotry. 'Our Father which art in heaven!' might the good man say, for he felt it; and all mankind were his brethren.

'You regret, my friend,' said he to Mr. ———, 'when
'my daughter and I talk of the exquisite pleasure derived
'from music, you regret your want of musical powers and
'musical feelings; it is a department of soul, you say,
'which Nature has almost denied you, which, from the
'effects you see it have on others, you are sure must be
'highly delightful. Why should not the same thing be said
'of religion? Trust me, I feel it in the same way—an
'energy, an inspiration, which I would not lose for all the
'blessings of sense, or enjoyments of the world; yet, so
'far from lessening my relish of the pleasures of life, me-
'thinks I feel it heighten them all. The thought of re-
'ceiving it from God adds the blessing of sentiment to
'that of sensation in every good thing I possess; and
'when calamities overtake me, and I have had my share,

'it

' it confers a dignity on my affliction, so lifts me above
' the world. Man, I know, is but a worm; yet methinks I
' am then allied to God!' It would have been inhuman in
our philosopher to have clouded, even with a doubt, the
sunshine of this belief.

It was with regret he left a society in which he found
himself so happy; but he settled with La Roche and his
daughter a plan of correspondence; and they took his promise, that, if ever he came within fifty leagues of their
dwelling, he should travel those fifty leagues to visit them.

CONCLUSION OF THE STORY OF LA ROCHE.

ABOUT three years after our philosopher was on a visit
at Geneva. The promise he made to La Roche and his
daughter on his former visit was recalled to his mind by
the view of that range of mountains on a part of which
they had often looked together. There was a reproach,
too, conveyed along with the recollection, for his having
failed to write to either for several months past. The truth
was, that indolence was the habit most natural to him,
from which he was not easily roused by the claims of correspondence either of his friends or of his enemies: when
the latter drew their pens in controversy, they were often
unanswered as well as the former. While he was hesitating
about a visit to La Roche, which he wished to make, but
found the effort rather too much for him, he received a
letter from the old man, which had been forwarded to him
from Paris, where he had then his fixed residence. It contained a gentle complaint of Mr. ———'s want of punctu-

ality, but an assurance of continued gratitude for his former good offices; and, as a friend whom the writer considered interested in his family, it informed him of the approaching nuptials of Ma'moiselle La Roche, with a young man, a relation of her own, and formerly a pupil of her father's, of the most amiable dispositions, and respectable character. Attached from their earliest years, they had been separated by his joining one of the subsidiary regiments of the canton, then in the service of a foreign power. In this situation he had distinguished himself as much for courage and military skill as for the other endowments which he had cultivated at home. The term of his service was now expired, and they expected him to return in a few weeks, when the old man hoped, as he expressed it in his letter, to join their hands, and see them happy before he died.

Our philosopher felt himself interested in this event, and determined to see his old friend and his daughter happy.

On the last day of his journey different accidents had retarded his progress: he was benighted before he reached the quarter in which La Roche resided. His guide, however, was well acquainted with the road; and he found himself at last in view of the lake, which I have before described, in the neighbourhood of La Roche's dwelling. A light gleamed on the water, that seemed to proceed from the house; it moved slowly along as he proceeded up the side of the lake, and at last he saw it glimmer through the trees, and stop at some distance from the place where he then was. He supposed it some piece of bridal merriment, and pushed on his horse that he might be a spectator of the scene; but he was a good deal shocked, on approaching the spot, to find it proceed from the torch of a

person

person clothed in the dress of an attendant on a funeral, and accompanied by several others, who, like him, seemed to have been employed in the rites of sepulture.

On Mr. ———'s making inquiry who was the person they had been burying, one of them, with an accent more mournful than is common to their profession, answered, 'Then you knew not Mademoiselle, Sir!—you never be-'held a lovelier—' 'La Roche!' exclaimed he in reply. 'Alas! it was she indeed!' The appearance of surprise and grief which his countenance assumed attracted the notice of the peasant with whom he talked. He came up closer to Mr. ———; 'I perceive, Sir, you were ac-'quainted with Mademoiselle La Roche.'—'Acquainted 'with her!—Good God!—when—how—where did she 'die?—where is her father?'—'She died, Sir, of heart-'break, I believe. The young gentleman to whom she 'was soon to have been married was killed in a duel by a 'French officer, his intimate companion, and to whom, 'before their quarrel, he had often done the greatest 'favours. Her worthy father bears her death, as he has 'often told us, as a Christian should; he is even so compos-'ed as to be now in his pulpit, ready to deliver a few ex-'hortations to his parishioners, as is the custom with us on 'such occasions. Follow me, Sir, and you shall hear him.' He followed the man without answering.

The church was dimly lighted, except near the pulpit, where the venerable La Roche was seated. His people were now lifting up their voices in a psalm to that Being whom their pastor had taught them ever to bless and to revere. La Roche sat, his figure bending gently forward, his eyes half closed, lifted up in silent devotion. A lamp, placed near him, threw its light strongly on his head, and marked the shadowy lines of age across the paleness of his brow, thinly covered with gray hairs.

The music ceased; La Roche sat for a moment, and Nature wrung a few tears from him. His people were loud in their grief. Mr. ——— was not less affected than they. La Roche arose; 'Father of Mercies,' said he, 'forgive
'these tears; assist thy servant to lift up his soul to thee;
'to lift to thee the souls of thy people! My friends! it is
'good so to do: at all seasons it is good; but in the days of
'our distress, what a privilege it is! Well said the sacred
'book, " Trust in the Lord; at all times trust in the
" Lord." When every other support fails us, when the
'fountains of worldly comfort are dried up, let us then
'seek those living waters which flow from the throne of
'God. It is only from the belief of the goodness and wis-
'dom of a Supreme Being that our calamities can be
'borne in that manner which becomes a man. Human
'wisdom is here of little use; for, in proportion as it be-
'stows comfort, it represses feeling, without which we
'may cease to be hurt by calamity, but we shall also cease
'to enjoy happiness. I will not bid you be insensible, my
'friends; I cannot, I cannot if I would.' His tears flowed afresh. 'I feel too much myself, and I am not ashamed
'of my feelings; but therefore may I the more willingly
'be heard; therefore have I prayed God to give me
'strength to speak to you; to direct you to him, not with
'empty words, but with these tears; not from speculation,
'but from experience, that while you see me suffer you
'may know my consolation.

'You behold the mourner of his only child, the last
'earthly stay and blessing of his declining years! Such a
'child too! It becomes not me to speak of her virtues;
'yet

'yet it is but gratitude to mention them, because they
'were exerted towards myself. Not many days ago you
'saw her young, beautiful, virtuous, and happy: ye who
'are parents will judge of my felicity then; ye will judge
'of my affliction now. But I look towards him who struck
'me; I see the hand of a father amidst the chastenings of
'my God. Oh! could I make you feel what it is to pour
'out the heart when it is pressed down with many sor-
'rows, to pour it out with confidence to him, in whose
'hands are life and death, on whose power waits all that
'the first enjoys, and in contemplation of whom disappears
'all that the last can inflict: for we are not as those who
'die without hope: we know that our Redeemer liveth;
'that we shall live with him, with our friends his servants,
'in that blessed land where sorrow is unknown, and happi-
'ness is endless as it is perfect. Go, then, mourn not for
'me; I have not lost my child: but a little while, and we
'shall meet again never to be separated. But ye are all
'my children. Would ye that I should grieve without
'comfort? So live as she lived, that when your death
'cometh it may be the death of the righteous, and your
'latter end be like his.'

Such was the exhortation of La Roche: his audience an-
swered it with their tears. The good old man dried up his
at the altar of the Lord; his countenance had lost its sad-
ness, and assumed the glow of faith and hope. Mr. ——
followed him into his house. The inspiration of the pul-
pit was past: at the sight of him the scenes they had last
met in rushed again on his mind. La Roche threw his
arms round his neck and watered it with his tears. The
other was equally affected. They went together in silence
into the parlour, where the evening service was wont to
be

be performed. The curtains of the organ were open, La Roche ſtarted back at the ſight,—' Oh! my friend!" ſaid he, and his tears burſt forth again. Mr. —— had now recollected himſelf; he ſtepped forward and drew the curtains cloſe—the old man wiped off his tears, and, taking his friend's hand, ' You ſee my weakneſs," ſaid he, ' 'tis
' the weakneſs of humanity, but my comfort is not there-
' fore loſt.'—' I heard you,' ſaid the other, ' in the pul-
' pit; I rejoice that ſuch conſolation is yours.'—' It is
' my friend,' ſaid he, ' and I truſt I ſhall ever hold it faſt;
' if there are any who doubt our faith, let them think of
' what importance religion is to calamity, and forbear to
' weaken its force; if they cannot reſtore our happineſs,
' let them not take away the ſolace of our affliction.'

Mirror.

THE HISTORY OF JOSEPH.

And Iſrael ſaid unto Joſeph, Do not thy brethren feed the flock in Shechem? Come, and I will ſend thee unto them. And he ſaid unto him, Here am I. And he ſaid to him, Go, I pray thee, ſee whether it be well with thy brethren, and well with the flocks, and bring me word again. So he ſent him out of the vale of Hebron, and he came to Shechem; and a certain man found him, and behold he was wandering in the field: and the man aſked him, ſaying, What ſeekeſt thou? And he ſaid, I ſeek my brethren; tell me, I pray thee, where they feed their flocks? And the man ſaid, They are departed hence: for I heard them ſay, Let us go to Dothan. And Joſeph went after his brethren, and found them in Dothan.

And

And when they saw him afar off, even before he came near unto them, they conspired against him to slay him. And they said one to another, Behold, this dreamer cometh, come now therefore, and let us slay him, and cast him into some pit, and we will say some evil beast hath devoured him; and we shall see what will become of his dreams. And Reuben heard it, and he delivered him out of their hands; and said, Let us not kill him. And Reuben said unto them, Shed no blood, but cast him into this pit that is in the wilderness, and lay no hand upon him; that he might rid him out of their hands to deliver him to his father again. And it came to pass when Joseph came unto his brethren, that they stripped Joseph out of his coat, his coat of many colours that was on him. And they took him and cast him into a pit: and the pit was empty, there was no water in it. And they sat down to eat bread: and they lifted up their eyes and looked, and behold, a company of Ishmaelites came from Gilead, with their camels bearing spicery, and balm, and myrrh, going to carry it down to Egypt. And Judah said unto his brethren, What profit is it if we slay our brother, and conceal his blood? come, and let us sell him to the Ishmaelites, and let not our hand be upon him; for he is our brother and our flesh: and his brethren were content. Then there passed by Midianites, merchant-men: and they drew and lifted up Joseph out of the pit, and sold Joseph to the Ishmaelites for twenty pieces of silver; and they brought Joseph into Egypt. And Reuben returned unto the pit; and he rent his clothes. And he returned unto his brethren, and said, The child is not; and I, whither shall I go? And they took Joseph's coat of many colours, and killed a kid of the goats, and dipped the coat in the
blood;

blood; and they brought it to their father, and said, This have we found, know now whether it be thy son's coat or no? And he knew it, and said, It is my son's coat; an evil beast hath devoured him: Joseph is without doubt rent in pieces. And Jacob rent his clothes, and put sackcloth upon his loins, and mourned for his son many days. And all his sons and all his daughters rose up to comfort him: but he refused to be comforted; and he said, for I will go down into the grave unto my son mourning: thus his father wept for him.

And the Midianites sold him into Egypt unto Potiphar, an officer of Pharaoh, and captain of the guard.

JOSEPH's INTERVIEW WITH HIS BRETHREN.

AND they made ready the present against Joseph came at noon: for they heard that they should eat bread there. And when Joseph came home they brought him the present which was in their hand unto the house, and bowed themselves to him to the earth. And he asked them of their welfare, and said, Is your father well, the old man of whom ye spake? Is he yet alive? And they answered, Thy servant our father is in good health, he is yet alive; and they bowed down their heads and made obeisance. And he lifted up his eyes and saw his brother Benjamin, his mother's son, and said, Is this your younger brother, of whom ye spake unto me? and he said, God be gracious unto thee, my son. And Joseph made haste; for his bowels did yearn upon his brother; and he sought where to weep; and he entered into his chamber and wept there. And

And he washed his face, and went out and refrained himself, and said, Set on bread. And they set on for him by himself, and for them by themselves, and for the Egyptians which did eat with him by themselves; because the Egyptians might not eat bread with the Hebrews, for that is an abomination unto the Egyptians. And they set before the first-born according to his birth-right, and the youngest according to his youth; and the men marvelled one at another: and he took and sent messes unto them from before him, but Benjamin's mess was five times so much as any of theirs. And they drank and were merry with him.

And he commanded the steward of his house, saying, Fill the men's sacks with food, as much as they can carry, and put every man's money in his sack's mouth. And put my cup, the silver cup, in the sack's mouth of the youngest, and his corn-money. And he did according to the word that Joseph had spoken. As soon as the morning was light the men were sent away, they and their asses. And when they were gone out of the city, and not yet far off, Joseph said unto his steward, Up, follow after the men; and when thou dost overtake them say unto them, Wherefore have ye rewarded evil for good? Is not this it in which my Lord drinketh, and whereby indeed he divineth? ye have done evil in so doing. And he overtook them, and he spake unto them these same words. And they said unto him, Wherefore saith my Lord these words? God forbid that thy servants should do according to this thing; behold the money which we found in our sacks' mouths we brought again unto thee out of the land of Canaan; how then should we steal out of thy lord's house silver or gold? With whomsoever of thy servants it

be

be found, both let him die, and we also will be my lord's bondmen. And he said, Now let it be according unto your words; he with whom it is found shall be my servant, and ye shall be blameless. Then they speedily took down every man his sack to the ground, and opened every man his sack. And he searched, and began at the eldest and left at the youngest; and the cup was found in Benjamin's sack. Then they rent their clothes, and laded every man his ass, and returned to the city. And Judah and his brethren came to Joseph's house; (for he was yet there) and they fell before him on the ground. And Joseph said unto them, What deed is this that ye have done; wot ye not that such a man as I can certainly divine?

And Judah said, What shall we say unto my lord? what shall we speak, or how shall we clear ourselves? God hath found out the iniquity of thy servants; behold, we are my lord's servants, both we and he also with whom the cup is found. And he said, God forbid that I should do so; but the man in whose hand the cup is found he shall be my servant; and, as for you, get you up in peace unto your father. Then Judah came near unto him, and said, Oh, my lord, let thy servant, I pray thee, speak a word in my lord's ears, and let not thine anger burn against thy servant, for thou art even as Pharaoh. My lord asked his servants, saying, Have ye a father or a brother? and we said unto my lord, We have a father, an old man, and a child of his old age, a little one; and his brother is dead, and he alone is left of his mother, and his father loveth him. And thou saidst unto thy servants, Bring him down unto me that I may set mine eyes upon him. And we said unto my lord, The lad cannot leave his father, for if he should leave his father his father would die. And thou

saidst

saidst unto thy servants, Except your youngest brother come down with you ye shall see my face no more. And it came to pass, when we came up unto thy servant my father, we told him the words of my lord. And our father said, Go again and buy us a little food. And we said, We cannot go down; if our youngest brother be with us then will we go down; for we may not see the man's face except our youngest brother be with us. And thy servant my father said unto us, Ye know that my wife bare me two sons; and the one went out from me, and I said, surely he is torn in pieces: and I saw him not since: and if you take this also from me, and mischief befal him, ye shall bring down my gray hairs with sorrow to the grave. Now, therefore, when I come to thy servant my father, and the lad be not with us, (seeing that his life is bound up in the lad's life;) it shall come to pass, when he seeth that the lad is not with us, that he will die; and thy servants shall bring down the gray hairs of thy servant our father with sorrow to the grave; for thy servant became surety for the lad unto my father, saying, If I bring him not unto thee, then I shall bear the blame to my father for ever. Now, therefore, I pray thee let thy servant abide instead of the lad a bondman to my lord, and let the lad go up with his brethren: for how shall I go up to my father and the lad be not with me, lest peradventure I see the evil that shall come upon my father?

Then Joseph could not refrain himself before all them that stood by him; and he cried, Cause every man to go out from me. And there stood no man with him, while Joseph made himself known unto his brethren. And he wept aloud; and the Egyptians and the house of Pharaoh heard. And Joseph said unto his brethren, I am Joseph;

Joseph; Doth my father yet live? And his brethren could not answer him, for they were troubled at his presence. And Joseph said unto his brethren, Come near to me, I pray you: and they came near; and he said, I am Joseph your brother, whom you sold into Egypt; now, therefore, be not grieved nor angry with yourselves that ye sold me hither, for God did send me before you to preserve life; for these two years hath the famine been in the land, and yet there are five years in the which there shall neither be earing nor harvest. And God sent me before you to preserve you a posterity in the earth, and to save your lives by a great deliverance. So now it was not you that sent me hither, but God; and he hath made me a father to Pharaoh, and lord of all his house, and a ruler throughout all the land of Egypt.

Haste ye, and go up to my father, and say unto him, Thus saith thy son Joseph, God hath made me lord of all Egypt; come down unto me, tarry not: and thou shalt dwell in the land of Goshen, and thou shalt be near unto me, thou and thy children, and thy children's children, and thy flocks, and thy herds, and all that thou hast, and there will I nourish thee; (for yet there are five years of famine;) lest thou, and thy household, and all that thou hast, come to poverty. And, behold, your eyes see, and the eyes of my brother Benjamin, that it is my mouth that speaketh unto you: and ye shall tell my father of all my glory in Egypt, and of all that ye have seen: and ye shall haste, and bring down my father hither. And he fell upon his brother Benjamin's neck and wept; and Benjamin wept upon his neck. Moreover, he kissed all his brethren, and wept upon them; and after that his brethren talked with him. And the fame thereof was

heard

heard in Pharaoh's house, saying, Joseph's brethren are come. And it pleased Pharaoh well, and his servants. And Pharaoh said unto Joseph, Say unto thy brethren, This do ye; lade your beasts and go, get ye into the land of Canaan; and take your father, and your households, and come unto me, and I will give you the good of the land of Egypt, and ye shall eat the fat of the land. Now thou art commanded, this do ye; take ye waggons out of the land of Egypt for your little ones, and for your wives, and bring your father, and come. Also regard not your stuff, for the good of the land of Egypt is yours. And the children of Israel did so; and Joseph gave them waggons, according to the commandment of Pharaoh, and gave them provision for the way. To all of them he gave each man changes of raiment; but to Benjamin he gave three hundred pieces of silver and five changes of raiment: and to his father he sent after this manner; ten asses laden with the good things of Egypt, and ten she-asses laden with corn and bread, and meat for his father by the way. So he sent his brethren away, and they departed; and he said unto them, See that ye fall not out by the way.

And they went up out of Egypt, and came into the land of Canaan unto Jacob their father, and told him, saying, Joseph is yet alive, and he is governor over all the land of Egypt. And Jacob's heart fainted, for he believed them not; and they told him all the words of Joseph which he said unto them: and when he saw the waggons which Joseph had sent to carry him, the spirit of Jacob their father revived: and Israel said, It is enough; Joseph my son is yet alive, I will go and see him before I die.

Genesis.

BILIAL

FILIAL ATTENTION.

The incidents attending domestic and private situations are of all others the most apt to affect the heart. Descriptions of national events are too general to be very interesting, and the calamities befalling kings and princes too far removed from common life to make a deep impression. With the virtues of such personages, it is nearly the same as with their sufferings: the heroic qualities which history ascribes to great and illustrious names, play around the imagination, but rarely touch the feelings, or direct the conduct: the humbler merits of ordinary life are those to which we feel a nearer relation; from which, therefore, precept is more powerfully enforced, and example more readily drawn.

Mr. Hargrave is one of my earliest friends: being many years younger than he I have ever been accustomed to regard him both as my guard and my friend; and the reverence with which I looked on him in the one character, never took from the tender and affectionate warmth I felt for him in the other. After having been for some time a good deal in the world, he retired to the country, where he lived with elegance and ease. His wife, a very amiable woman, died soon after her marriage, leaving only one child, a girl; to the care of whose education Mr. Hargrave, after her mother's death, devoted his whole attention. Nature had done much for her; and the instruction she received from an accomplished father gave her every grace which can adorn the female character.

Emily

Emily Hargrave was now in her twentieth year. Her father was advanced in life, and he began to feel the weaknesses of age coming fast upon him. Independent of the gratification which he used to receive from the observation of his daughter's virtues and accomplishments, he had come to feel a pleasure somewhat more selfish from the advantage which those virtues were of to himself. Her care and dutiful attention were almost become necessary to him; and the principal pleasure he received was from her company and conversation. Emily was sensible of this; and, though she was at pains to conceal her solicitude, it was plain that her whole care centered in him.

It was impossible that a girl so amiable as Emily Hargrave could fail to attract attention. Several young men of character and fortune became her professed admirers. But, though she had a sweetness which gave her a benevolent affability to all, she was of a mind too delicate to be easily satisfied in the choice of a husband. In her present circumstances, she had another objection to every change of situation. She felt too much anxiety about her father to think of any thing which could call off her attention from him, and make it proper to place any of it elsewhere. With the greatest delicacy, therefore, and with that propriety with which her conduct was always attended, she checked every advance that was made her; while, at the same time, she was at the utmost pains to conceal from her father the voluntary sacrifice she was resolved to make on his account.

About a month ago, I paid a visit to Mr. Hargrave's family. I found him more changed than I had expected: the imbecilities of age, which were beginning to approach the last time I had seen him, had now made great advances.

advances. Formerly Mr. Hargrave used to be the delight of every company, and he never spoke without instructing or entertaining. Now he spoke little; when he did, it was with feebleness both of voice and manner. Feeling his memory declining, sensible that he was not so acute as he once was, and unable to keep up his attention to a continued discourse, though his understanding was still perfectly good, he was afraid to venture his opinion, or to take any decided measure. He was too conscious of his own infirmities; and that consciousness led him to think that his failure was greater than it really was. In this situation his whole dependance was upon Emily, and she was his only support. Never, indeed, did I see any thing more lovely, more engaging. To all her other charms, the anxious solicitude she felt for her father had stamped upon her countenance

> 'That expression sweet of melancholy
> 'Which captivates the soul.'

There is something in the female character which requires support. That gentleness, that delicate softness, approaching to timidity, which forms its most amiable feature, makes it stand in need of assistance. That support and assistance Emily had received in the completest manner from her father. What an alteration now! Instead of receiving support herself, she was obliged to give it; she was under the necessity of assisting, of counselling, and of strengthening the timid resolutions of him who had been, in her earlier years, her instructor and her guide; and to whom, next to Heaven, she had ever looked up. Emily felt all this; but feeling took not from her the power of acting.

Hargrave is abundantly sensible of his daughter's goodness. Her consciousness of this, and of how much importance

ance her attentions are to her father, gives her the best consolation.

While I was at his house he hardly ever spoke of himself. Once, indeed, I remember he said to me, 'I am be-'come a strange being; even the goodness of that girl 'distresses me; it is too much for me to bear; it is,' added he, in a very faint and broken voice, 'like to over-'whelm me.'

I have often remarked that there is a perseverance in virtue, and a real magnanimity in the other sex, which is scarcely to be equalled in ours. In the virtue of men there are generally some considerations not altogether pure attending it; which, though they may not detract from, must certainly diminish our wonder at their conduct. The heroic actions of men are commonly performed upon the great theatre, and the performers have the applauses of an attending and admiring world to animate and support them. When Regulus suffered all the tortures which cruelty could invent rather than give up his honour or his country, he was supported by the conscious admiration of those countrymen whom he had left, and of those enemies in whose hands he was. When Cato stabbed himself rather than give up the cause of liberty, he felt a pride which told him, that 'Cato's would be no less honoured 'than Cæsar's sword.' And when ' the self-devoted Decii 'died,' independent of their love for Rome, they had every motive of applause to animate their conduct. But, when Emily Hargrave sacrifices every thing to filial goodness and filial affection, she can have no concomitant motive; she can have no external circumstance to animate her. Her silent and secret virtue is the pure and unmingled effect of tenderness, of affection, and of duty.—

MIRROUR.

THE FILIAL PIETY AND AFFECTION OF A DAUGHTER.

One of the Roman judges had given up to the Triumvir a woman of some rank, condemned for a capital crime, to be executed in the prison. He who had the charge of the execution, in consideration of her birth, did not immediately put her to death: he even ventured to let her daughter have access to her in the prison, carefully searching her, however, as she went in, lest she should carry with her any sustenance; concluding that in a few days the mother must of course perish for want, and that the severity of putting a woman of quality to a violent death, by the hand of the executioner, might thus be avoided. Some days passing in this manner the Triumvir began to wonder that the daughter still came to visit her mother, and could by no means comprehend how the latter should live so long. Watching, therefore, carefully what passed in the interview between them, he found, to his great astonishment, that the life of the mother had been all this time supported by the milk of the daughter, who came to the prison every day to give her mother her breasts to suck. The strange contrivance between them was represented to the judges, and procured a pardon for the mother. Nor was it thought sufficient to give to so dutiful a daughter the forfeited life of her condemned mother; but they were both maintained afterwards by a pension settled on them for life; and the ground upon which the prison stood was consecrated, and a temple to Filial Piety built upon it.

FILIAL OBEDIENCE REWARDED.

The word which came unto Jeremiah from the Lord, in the days of Jehoiakim the son of Josiah king of Judah, saying, Go into the house of the Rechabites, and speak unto them, and bring them into the house of the Lord, into one of the chambers, and give them wine to drink. Then I took Jaazaniah, the son of Jeremiah the son of Habaziniah, and his brethren, and all his sons, and the whole house of the Rechabites; and I brought them into the house of the Lord; into the chamber of the sons of Hanon the son of Igdaliah, a man of God; which was by the chamber of the princes, which was above the chamber of Maaseiah the son of Shallum the keeper of the door; and I set before the sons of the house of the Rechabites pots full of wine, and cups, and I said unto them, Drink ye wine. But they said, We will drink no wine: for Jonadab the son of Rachab our father commanded us, saying, Ye shall drink no wine, neither ye, nor your sons for ever: neither shall ye build house, nor sow seed, nor plant vineyard, nor have any: but all your days ye shall dwell in tents; that ye may live many days in the land where ye be strangers. Thus have we obeyed the voice of Jonadab the son of Rechab our father, in all that he hath charged us, to drink no wine all our days, we, our wives, our sons, nor our daughters: nor to build houses for us to dwell in: neither have we vineyard, nor field, nor seed: but we have dwelt in tents, and have obeyed and done according to all that Jonadab our father commanded us. But it came to pass, when Nebuchadnezzar king of Babylon came up into the land, that we said, Come, and let us go to

Jerusalem

Jerusalem for fear of the army of the Chaldeans, and for fear of the army of the Syrians. So we dwelt at Jerusalem.

Then came the word of the Lord unto Jeremiah, saying, thus saith the Lord of hosts, the God of Israel; Go, and tell the men of Judah, and the inhabitants of Jerusalem, Will ye not receive instruction to hearken to my words? saith the Lord. The words of Jonadab the son of Rechab, that he commanded his sons not to drink wine, are performed: for unto this day they drink none, but obey their father's commandment: notwithstanding, I have spoken unto you rising early and speaking; but ye hearkened not unto me. I have sent also unto you all my servants the prophets, rising up early, and sending them, saying, Return ye now every man from his evil way, and amend your doings, and go not after other gods to serve them, and ye shall dwell in the land which I have given to you and to your fathers; but ye have not inclined your ear, nor hearkened unto me. Because the sons of Jonadab the son of Rechab have performed the commandment of their father, which he commanded them; but this people hath not hearkened unto me: therefore thus saith the Lord God of hosts, the God of Israel; Behold, I will bring upon Judah, and upon all the inhabitants of Jerusalem, all the evil that I have pronounced against them; because I have spoken unto them but they have not heard, and I have called unto them but they have not answered. And Jeremiah said unto the house of the Rechabites, Thus saith the Lord of hosts, the God of Israel; Because ye have obeyed the commandment of Jonadab your father, and kept all his precepts, and done according unto all that he hath commanded you:
therefore

therefore thus saith the Lord of hosts, the God of Israel; Jonadab the son of Rechab shall not want a man to stand before me for ever.

JEREMIAH.

THE HISTORY OF INKLE AND YARICO.

Mr. Thomas Inkle, of London, aged twenty years, embarked in the Downs, in the good ship called the Achilles, bound for the West-Indies, on the 16th of June, 1647, in order to improve his fortune by trade and merchandize. Our adventurer was the third son of an eminent citizen, who had taken particular care to instil into his mind an early love of gain, by making him a perfect master of numbers, and consequently giving him a quick view of loss and advantage, and preventing the natural impulses of his passions by prepossessions towards his interest. With a mind thus turned, young Inkle had a person every way agreeable; as ruddy vigour in his countenance, strength in his limbs, with ringlets of fair hair loosely flowing on his shoulders. It happened, in the course of the voyage, that the Achilles, in some distress, put into a creek on the main of America in search of provisions: the youth, who is the hero of my story, among others, went ashore on this occasion. From their first landing they were observed by a party of Indians, who hid themselves in the woods for that purpose. The English unadvisedly marched a great distance from the shore into the country, and were intercepted by the natives, who slew the greatest number of them. Our adventurer escaped among others, by flying into a forest. Upon his coming into a remote and pathless part of the wood, he threw himself, tired and breathless, on a little hillock, when an Indian maid rushed from a thicket behind him. After the first surprise they appeared mutually agreeable to each other. If the European was highly charmed with the limbs, features, and wild graces of the naked American, the American was no less taken with the dress, complexion, and shape of an European, covered from head to foot. The Indian grew immediately enamoured of him, and consequently solicitous for his preservation: she therefore conveyed him to a cave, where she gave him a delicious repast of fruits, and led him to a stream to slake his thirst. She was, it seems, a person of distinction, for she every day came to him in a different dress, of the most beautiful shells, bugles, and beads. She likewise brought him a great many spoils, which her other lovers had presented to her; so that his cave was richly adorned with all the spotted skins of beasts, and most party-coloured feathers of fowls, which that world afforded. To make his confinement more tolerable, she would carry him in the dusk of the evening, or by the favour of moonlight, to unfrequented groves and solitudes, and shew him where to lie down in safety, and sleep amidst the falls of waters, and melody of nightingales. Her part was to watch him while asleep, for fear of her countrymen, and wake him on occasions to consult his safety. In this manner did they pass away their time, till they had learned a language of their own, in which the voyager communicated to his mistress how happy he should be to have her in his country, where she should be clothed in such silks as his waistcoat was made of, and be carried in houses drawn by horses, without being exposed to wind or weather.

ther. All this he promised her the enjoyment of, without such fears and alarms as they were there tormented with. In this tender correspondence they lived for several months, when Yarico, instructed by her lover, discovered a vessel on the coast, to which she made signals; and in the night, with the utmost joy and satisfaction, accompanied him to the ship's crew of his countrymen, bound for Barbadoes. When a vessel from the main arrives in that island, it seems the planters come down to the shore, where there is an immediate market for the Indian, and other slaves, as with us of horses and oxen.

To be short, Mr. Thomas Inkle, now coming to English territories, began seriously to reflect upon his loss of time, and to weigh with himself how many days interest of his money he had lost during his stay with Yarico. This thought made the young man very pensive and careful what account he should be able to give his friends of his voyage. Upon which considerations the prudent and frugal young man sold Yarico to a Barbadian merchant; notwithstanding that the poor girl, to incline him to commiserate her condition, told him she was with child by him: but he only made use of that information to rise in his demands upon the purchaser.

SPECTATOR.

CRAZY KATE.

There often wanders one, whom better days
Saw better clad, in cloak of satin trimm'd
With lace, and hat with splendid ribband bound.
A serving maid was she, and fell in love

With one who left her, went to sea, and died.
Her fancy followed him through foaming waves
To distant shores, and she would sit and weep
At what a sailor suffers. Fancy too,
Delusive most where warmest wishes are,
Would oft anticipate his glad return,
And dream of transports she was not to know.
She heard the doleful tidings of his death,
And never smil'd again. And now she roams
The dreary waste; there spends the livelong day;
And there, unless when charity forbids,
The livelong night. A tatter'd apron hides,
Worn as a cloak, and hardly hides, a gown
More tatter'd still; and both but ill conceal
A bosom heav'd with never-ceasing sighs.
She begs an idle pin of all she meets,
And hoards them in her sleeve; but needful food,
Though press'd with hunger oft, or comlier clothes,
Though pinch'd with cold, asks never.—Kate is craz'd.

COWPER.

THE FOLLY OF BEING LED BY THE FASHION.

THE princess Parizade, the happiest as well as the most beautiful of her sex, lived with her two beloved brothers in a splendid palace, situated in the midst of a delightful park, and the most exquisite gardens, in the East. It happened one day, while the princes were hunting, that an old woman came to the gate, and desired admittance to the oratory, that she might say her prayers. The princess no
sooner

sooner knew of her request than she granted it; giving orders to her attendants, that, after the good woman's prayers were ended, they should shew her all the apartments of the palace, and then bring her into the hall where she herself was sitting. Every thing was performed as directed; and the princess, having regaled her guest with some fruits and sweetmeats, among many other questions, asked her what she thought of the palace.

'Madam,' answered the old woman, 'your palace
' is beautiful, regular, and magnificently furnished; its
' situation is delightful, and its gardens are beyond com-
' pare. But yet, if you will give me leave to speak
' freely, there are three things wanting to make it per-
' fect.'—' My good mother,' interrupted the princess
Parizade, ' what are those three things? I conjure you
' to tell me what they are; and if there be a possibility
' of obtaining them, neither difficulties nor dangers shall
' stop me in the attempt.'—' Madam,' replied the old
woman, ' the first of these three things is the Talking
' Bird, the second is the Singing Tree, and the third is
' the Yellow or Golden Water.'—' Ah, my good mo-
' ther,' cried the princess, ' how much am I obliged to
' you for the knowledge of these things! They are no
' doubt the greatest curiosities in the world, and unless
' you can tell me where they are to be found I am the
' most unhappy of women.' The old woman satisfied the princess in that material point, and then took her leave.

The story goes on to inform us that when the two princes returned from hunting they found the princess Parizade so wrapped up in thought, that they imagined some great misfortune had befallen her, which, when they had conjured her to acquaint them with, she only lifted up her eyes to look upon them, and then fixed them again upon the ground, telling them nothing difturbed her. The entreaties of the two princes, however, at laft prevailed, and the princefs addreffed them in the following manner.

'You have often told me, my dear brothers, and I have always believed that this houfe, which our father built, was complete in every thing; but I have learnt this day that it wants three things; thefe are the Talking Bird, the Singing Tree, and the Yellow Water. An old woman has made this difcovery to me, and told me the place where they are to be found, and the way thither. Perhaps you may look upon thefe rarities as trifles; but, think what you pleafe, I am fully perfuaded that they are abfolutely neceffary; and, whether you value them or not, I cannot be eafy without them.'

The fequel tells us that, after the princefs Parizade had expreffed herfelf with this proper fpirit upon the occafion, the brothers, in pity to her wants, went in purfuit of thefe *neceffaries*; and that, failing in the enterprife, they were one after another turned into ftone.

The application of this tale is fo univerfal, that enumerating particulars is almoft unneceffary labour. The whole fafhionable world are fo many Parizades; and things not only ufelefs in their natures, but alfo ugly in themfelves, from being once termed *charming* by fome fafhionable leaders of modern tafte, are now become fo *neceffary* that nobody can do without them.

WORLD.

THE ABSURDITY OF EXTREMES.

I am an humble cousin to two sisters, who, though they are good-humoured, good sort of people, and (all things considered) behave to me tolerably well; yet their manners and dispositions are so extremely opposite, that the task of pleasing them is rendered very difficult and troublesome. The elder of my cousins is a very lively girl, and so great an enemy to all kinds of form, that you seldom see her with so much as a pin in her gown; while the younger, who thinks in her heart that her sister is no better than a *slattern*, runs into the contrary extreme, and is in every thing she does an absolute *fid-fad*. She takes up almost as much time to put on her gown as her sister does to dirty one. The elder is too thoughtless to remember what she is to do, and the other is so tedious in doing it that the time is always elapsed in which it was necessary for it to be done. If you lend any thing to the elder you are sure of having it lost, or if you would borrow any thing of the younger it is odds but she refuses it, from an opinion that you will be less careful of it than herself. Whatsoever work is done by one sister is too slight to hang together for an hour's wear; and whatsoever is undertaken by the other is generally too nice and curious to be finished.

As they are constantly bed-fellows, the first sleep of the elder is sure to be broken by the younger, whose usual time of undressing and folding up her clothes is at least an hour and a half, allowing a third part of that time for hindrances occasioned by her elder sister's things, which lie scattered every where in her way.

If they had lovers I know exactly how it would be: the elder would lose her's by saying *Yes* too soon, and the younger by saying *No* too often. If they were wives the one would be too hasty to do any thing right, and the other too tedious to do any thing pleasing: or, were they mothers, the daughters of the elder would be playing at taw with the boys, and the sons of the younger dressing dolls with the misses.

WORLD.

THE CONTRAST.

Morose is sunk with shame, whene'er surpris'd
In linen clean, or peruke undisguis'd.
No sublunary chance his vestments fear;
Valu'd, like leopards, as their spots appear.
A fam'd surtout he wears, which once was blue,
And his foot swims in a capacious shoe:
One day his wife (for who can wives reclaim)
Levell'd her barb'rous needle at his fame:
But open force was vain: by night she went,
And, while he slept, surpris'd the darling rent:
Where yawn'd the frieze is now become a doubt;
' And glory, at one entrance, quite shut out.'
He scorns Florella, and Florella him;
This hates the filthy creature, that the prim:
Thus in each other both these fools despise
Their own dear selves, with undiscerning eyes;
Their methods various, but alike their aim,
The sloven and the foppling are the same.

YOUNG.

ON THE LOSS OF BEAUTY.

SIR,

You have very lately observed that, in the numerous subdivisions of the world, every class and order of mankind have joys and sorrows of their own; we all feel hourly pain and pleasure from events which pass unheeded before other eyes, but can scarcely communicate our perceptions to minds pre-occupied by different objects, any more than the delight of well-disposed colours or harmonious sounds can be imparted to such as want the senses of hearing or of light.

I am so strongly convinced of the justness of this remark, and have on so many occasions discovered with how little attention pride looks upon calamity of which she thinks herself not in danger, and indolence listens to complaint when it is not echoed by her own remembrance; that, though I am about to lay the occurrences of my life before you, I question whether you will condescend to peruse my narrative, or without the help of some female speculatist be able to understand it.

I was born a beauty. From the dawn of reason I had my regard turned wholly upon myself, nor can recollect any thing earlier than praise and admiration. My mother, whose face had luckily advanced her to a condition above her birth, thought no evil so great as deformity. She had not the power of imagining any other defect than a cloudy complexion, or disproportionate features; and therefore contemplated me as an assemblage of all that could raise envy or desire, and depicted with triumphant fondness the extent of my conquests and the number of my slaves.

She never mentioned any of my young acquaintance before me, but to remark how much they fell below my perfection; how one would have had a fine face, but that her eyes were without lustre; how another struck the sight at a distance, but wanted my hair and teeth at a nearer view; another disgraced an elegant shape with a brown skin; some had short fingers, and others dimples in a wrong place.

As she expected no happiness or advantage but from beauty, she thought nothing but beauty worth her care; and her maternal kindness was chiefly exercised in contrivances to protect me from any accident that might deface me with a scar, or stain me with a freckle: she never thought me sufficiently shaded from the sun, or screened from the fire. She was severe or indulgent with no other intention than the preservation of my form; she excused me from work lest I should learn to hang down my head, or harden my finger with a needle. She snatched away my book because a young lady in the neighbourhood had made her eyes red with reading by a candle; but she would scarcely suffer me to eat lest I should spoil my shape, nor walk lest I should swell my ancle with a sprain. At night I was accurately surveyed from head to foot, lest I should have suffered any diminution of my charms in the adventures of the day; and was never permitted to sleep till I had passed through the cosmetic discipline, part of which was regular lustration performed with bean-flour water and May-dews; my hair was perfumed with variety of unguents, by some of which it was to be thickened, and by others to be curled. The softness of my hands was

secured

secured by medicated gloves, and my bosom rubbed with a pomade prepared by my mother, of virtue to discuss pimples and clear discolorations.

I was always called up early, because the morning air gives a freshness to the cheeks; but I was placed behind a curtain in my mother's chamber, because the neck is easily tanned by the rising sun. I was then dressed with a thousand precautions, and again heard my own praises, and triumphed in the compliments and prognostications of all that approached me.

My mother was not so much prepossessed with an opinion of my natural excellencies as not to think some cultivation necessary to their completion. She took care that I should want none of the accomplishments included in female education, or considered as necessary in fashionable life. I was looked upon in my ninth year as the chief ornament of the dancing-master's ball; and Mr. Ariot used to reproach his other scholars with my performances on the harpsichord. At twelve I was remarkable for playing my cards with great elegance of manner and accuracy of judgment.

At last the time came when my mother thought me perfect in my exercises, and qualified to display in the open world those accomplishments which had yet only been discovered in select parties or domestic assemblies. Preparations were therefore made for my appearance on a public night, which she considered as the most important and critical moment of my life. She cannot be charged with neglecting any means of recommendation, or leaving any thing to chance which prudence could ascertain. Every ornament was tried in every position, every friend was consulted about the colour of my dress, and the mantua-makers were harassed with directions and alterations.

At

At last the night arrived from which my future life was to be reckoned. I was dressed and sent to conquer, with a heart beating like that of an old knight-errant at his first sally. Scholars have told me of a Spartan matron, who, when she armed her son for battle, bade him bring back his shield, or be brought upon it. My venerable parent dismissed me to a field, in her opinion, of equal glory, with a command to shew that I was her daughter, and not to return without a lover.

I went, and was received, like other pleasing novelties, with a tumult of applause. Every man who valued himself upon the graces of his person, or the elegance of his address, crowded about me, and wit and splendour contended for my notice. I was delightfully fatigued with incessant civilities, which were made more pleasing by the apparent envy of those whom my presence exposed to neglect, and returned with an attendant equal in rank and wealth to my utmost wishes; and from this time stood in the first rank of beauty; was followed by gazers in the Mall, celebrated in the papers of the day, imitated by all who endeavoured to rise into fashion, and censured by those whom age or disappointment forced to retire.

My mother, who pleased herself with the hopes of seeing my exaltation, dressed me with all the exuberance of finery; and, when I represented to her that a fortune might be expected proportionate to my appearance, told me that she should scorn the reptile who could inquire after the fortune of a girl like me. She advised me to prosecute my victories, and time would certainly bring a captive who might deserve the honour of being enchained for ever.

My lovers were indeed so numerous that I had no other care than that of determining to whom I should seem to give

give the preference. But, having been steadily and industriously instructed to preserve my heart from any impressions which might hinder me from consulting my interest, I acted with less embarrassment, because my choice was regulated by principles more clear and certain than the caprice of approbation. When I singled out one from the rest as more worthy of encouragement, I proceeded in my measures by the rules of art; and yet, when the ardour of the first visits was spent, generally found a sudden declension of my influence. I felt in myself the want of some power to diversify amusement and enliven conversation, and could not but suspect that my mind failed in performing the promises of my face. This opinion was soon confirmed by one of my lovers, who married Lavinia, with less beauty and fortune than mine, because he thought a wife ought to have qualities which might make her amiable when her bloom was past.

The vanity of my mother would not suffer her to discover any defect in one that had been formed by her instructions, and had all the excellence which she herself could boast. She told me that nothing so much hindered the advancement of women as literature and wit, which generally frightened away those who could make the best settlements, and drew about them a needy tribe of poets and philosophers, that filled their heads with wild notions of content and contemplation, and virtuous obscurity. She therefore enjoined me to improve my minuet step with a new French dancing-master, and wait the event of the next birth-night.

I had now almost completed my nineteenth year. If my charms had lost any of their softness, it was more than compensated by additional dignity; and if the attractions
of

of innocence were impaired, their place was supplied by the arts of allurement. I was therefore preparing for a new attack, without any abatement of my confidence, when, in the midst of my hopes and schemes, I was seized by that dreadful malady which has so often put a sudden end to the tyranny of beauty. I recovered my health after a long confinement; but when I looked again on that face which had often been flushed with transport at its own reflection, and saw all that I had learned to value, all that I had endeavoured to improve, all that had procured me honours or praises, irrevocably destroyed, I sunk at once into melancholy and despondence. My pain was not much consoled or alleviated by my mother, who grieved that I had not lost my life together with my beauty; and declared that she thought a young woman divested of her charms had nothing for which those who loved her could desire to save her from the grave.

Having thus continued my relation to the period from which my life took a new course, I shall conclude it in another letter, if by publishing this you shew any regard for the correspondence of,

Sir, &c.

VICTORIA.

Sir,

You have shewn, by the publication of my letter, that you think the life of Victoria not wholly unworthy of the notice of a philosopher; I shall therefore continue my narrative, without any apology for unimportance which you have dignified, or for inaccuracies which you are to correct.

When

When my life appeared to be no longer in danger, and as much of my strength was recovered as enabled me to bear the agitation of a coach, I was placed at a lodging in a neighbouring village, to which my mother dismissed me with a faint embrace, having repeated her command not to expose my face too soon to the sun or wind, and told me that with care I might perhaps become tolerable again. The prospect of being tolerable had very little power to elevate the imagination of one who had so long been accustomed to praise and ecstasy; but it was some satisfaction to be separated from my mother, who was incessantly ringing the knell of departed beauty, and never entered my room without the whine of condolence or the growl of anger. She often wandered over my face, as travellers over the ruins of a celebrated city, to note every place which had once been remarkable for a happy feature. She condescended to visit my retirement; but always left me more melancholy: for, after a thousand trifling inquiries about my diet, and a minute examination of my looks, she generally concluded, with a sigh, that I should never more be fit to be seen.

At last I was permitted to return home, but found no great improvement of my condition; for I was imprisoned in my chamber as a criminal whose appearance would disgrace my friends, and condemned to be tortured into new beauty. Every experiment which the officiousness of folly could communicate, or the credulity of ignorance admit, was tried upon me. Sometimes I was covered with emollients, by which it was expected that all the scars would be filled, and my cheeks plumped up to their former smoothness; and sometimes I was punished with artificial excoriations, in hopes of gaining new graces with a new skin.

The

The cosmetic science was exhausted upon me: but who can repair the ruins of nature? My mother was forced to give me rest at last, and abandon me to the fate of a fallen toast, whose fortune she considered as a hopeless game, no longer worthy of solicitude or attention.

The condition of a young woman who has never thought or heard of any other excellence than beauty, and whom the sudden blast of disease wrinkles in her bloom, is indeed sufficiently calamitous. She is at once deprived of all that gave her eminence or power; of all that elated her pride, or animated her activity; all that filled her days with pleasure and her nights with hope; all that gave gladness to the present hour, or brightened her prospects of futurity. It is perhaps not in the power of a man whose attention has been divided by a diversity of pursuits, and who has not been accustomed to derive from others much of his happiness, to image to himself such helpless destitution, such dismal inanity. Every object of pleasing contemplation is at once snatched away, and the soul finds every receptacle of ideas empty, or filled only with the memory of joys that can return no more. All is gloomy privation, or impotent desire; the faculties of anticipation slumber in despondency, or the powers of pleasure mutiny for employment.

I was so little able to find entertainment for myself, that I was forced in a short time to venture abroad, as the solitary savage is driven by hunger from his cavern. I entered with all the humility of disgrace into assemblies where I had lately sparkled with gaiety and towered with triumph. I was not wholly without hope that dejection had misrepresented me to myself, and that the remains of my former face might yet have some attraction and influence: but the first circle of visits convinced me that my reign was at an end; that life and death were no longer in my hands;

that

that I was no more to practise the glance of command, or the frown of prohibition; to receive the tribute of sighs and praises, or be soothed by the gentle murmurs of amorous timidity. My opinion was now unheard, and the meanness of my sentiments were easily discovered when the eyes were no longer engaged against the judgment; and it was observed, by those who had formerly been charmed with my vivacious loquacity, that my understanding was impaired as well as my face, and that I was no longer qualified to fill a place in any company but a party at cards.

It is scarcely to be imagined how soon the mind sinks to a level with the condition. I, who had long considered all who approached me as vassals condemned to regulate their pleasures by my eyes, and harass their inventions for my entertainment, was in less than three weeks reduced to receive a ticket with professions of obligation, to catch with eagerness at a compliment, and to watch with all the anxiousness of dependence, lest any little civility that was paid me should pass unacknowledged.

Though the negligence of the men was not very pleasing when compared with vows and adorations, yet it was far more supportable than the insolence of my own sex. For the first ten months after my return into the world, I never entered a single house in which the memory of my downfal was not revived. At one place I was congratulated on my escape with life; at another I heard of the benefits of early inoculation; by some I have been told in express terms that I am not without my charms; others have whispered at my entrance ' This is the celebrated beauty.' One told me of a wash that would smooth the skin; and another offered me her chair, that I might not front the light. Some soothed me with the observation that none can tell how soon my case may be her own; and some

thought

thought it proper to receive me with mournful tenderness, formal condolence, and confolatory blandifhments.

Thus was I every day haraffed with all the ftratagems of well-bred malignity: yet infolence was more tolerable than folitude; and I therefore perfifted to keep my time at the doors of my acquaintance, without gratifying them with any appearance of refentment or depreffion. I expected that their exultation would in time vapour away; that the joy of their fuperiority would end with its novelty; and that I fhould be fuffered to glide along in my prefent form among the numberlefs multitude whom Nature never intended to excite envy or admiration, nor enabled to delight the eye or inflame the heart.

This was naturally to be expected, and this I began to experience. But when I was no longer agitated by the perpetual ardour of refiftance and effort of perfeverance, I found more fenfibly the want of thofe entertainments which had formerly delighted me: the day rofe upon me without an engagement, and the evening clofed in its natural gloom without fummoning me to a concert or a ball. None had any care to find amufements for me, and I had no power of amufing myfelf. Idlenefs expofed me to melancholy, and life began to languifh in motionlefs indifference.

Mifery and fhame are nearly allied. It was not without many ftruggles that I prevailed on myfelf to confefs my uneafinefs to Euphemia, the only friend who had not pained me with comfort or with pity. I at laft laid my calamities before her, rather to eafe my heart than receive affiftance. ' We muft diftinguifh,' faid fhe, ' my
' Victoria, thofe evils which are impofed by Providence
' from thofe to which we ourfelves give the power of hurt-
' ing us. Of your calamity a fmall part is the infliction
' of

'of Heaven; the reſt is little more than the corroſion
'of idle diſcontent. You have loſt that which may indeed
'ſometimes contribute to happineſs, but to which happi-
'neſs is by no means inſeparably annexed. You have loſt
'what the greater number of the human race never have
'poſſeſſed; what thoſe on whom it is beſtowed for the moſt
'part poſſeſs in vain; and what you, while it was in your
'power, knew not how to uſe: you have only loſt early
'what the laws of Nature forbid you to keep long, and
'have loſt it while your mind is yet flexible, and while
'you have time to ſubſtitute more valuable and more
'durable excellencies. Conſider yourſelf, my Victoria,
'as being born to know, to reaſon, and to act: riſe at
'once from your dream of melancholy to wiſdom and to
'piety: you will find that there are other charms than
'thoſe of beauty, and other joys than the praiſe of
'fools.'

I am, Sir, &c.

VICTORIA,

RAMBLER.

THE DISCOVERY OF AMERICA.

It is to the diſcoveries of the Portugueſe in the Old World that we are indebted for the New, if we may call the conqueſt of America an obligation, which proved ſo fatal to its inhabitants, and at times to the conquerors themſelves.

This was doubtleſs the moſt important event that ever happened on our globe, one half of which had been hitherto ſtrangers to the other. Whatever had been eſteemed moſt great or noble before seemed absorbed in this kind of new creation. We still mention with respectful admiration the names of the Argonauts, who did not perform the hundredth part of what was done by the sailors under Gama and Albuquerque. How many altars would have been raised by the ancients to a Greek who had discovered America! and yet Bartholomew and Christopher Columbus were not thus rewarded.

Columbus, struck with the wonderful expeditions of the Portuguese, imagined that something greater might be done; and, from a bare inspection of the map of our world, concluded that there must be another, which might be found by sailing always west. He had courage equal to his genius, or indeed superior, seeing he had to struggle with the prejudices of his contemporaries and the repulses of several princes to whom he tendered his services. Genoa, which was his native country, treated his schemes as visionary, and by that means lost the only opportunity that could have offered of aggrandizing her power. Henry VII. king of England, who was too greedy of money to hazard any on this noble attempt, would not listen to the proposals made by Columbus's brother; and Columbus himself was rejected by John II. of Portugal, whose attention was wholly employed upon the coast of Africa. He had no prospect of success in applying to the French, whose marine lay totally neglected, and their affairs more confused than ever, during the minority of Charles VIII. The emperor Maximilian had neither ports for shipping, money to fit out a fleet, nor sufficient courage to engage in a scheme of this nature. The Venetians, indeed, might have undertaken it: but whether the natural aversion of the Genoese to these people would not suffer Columbus to apply to the rivals of his country, or that the Venetians
had

had no idea of any thing more important than the trade they carried on from Alexandria and in the Levant. Columbus at length fixed his hopes on the court of Spain.

Ferdinand, king of Arragon, and Isabella, queen of Castile, had by their marriage united Spain under one dominion, excepting only the kingdom of Grenada, which was still in the possession of the Moors, but which Ferdinand soon after took from them. The union of these two princes had prepared the way for the greatness of Spain, which was afterwards begun by Columbus; he was however obliged to undergo eight years of incessant application before Isabella's court would consent to accept of the inestimable benefit this great man offered it. The bane of all great projects is the want of money. The Spanish court was poor; and the prior Perez, and two merchants named Pinzans, were obliged to advance seventeen thousand ducats towards fitting out the armament. Columbus procured a patent from the court, and at length set sail from the port of Palas in Andalusia, with three ships, on August 23, in the year 1492.

It was not above a month after his departure from the Canary islands, where he had come to an anchor to get refreshment, when Columbus discovered the first island in America; and during this short run he suffered more from the murmurings and discontent of the people of his fleet than he had ever done from the refusals of the princes he had applied to. This island, which he discovered and named St. Salvador, lies about a thousand leagues from the Canaries. Presently after he likewise discovered the Lucayan islands, together with those of Cuba and Hispaniola, now called St. Domingo.

Ferdinand and Isabella were in the utmost surprise to see him return, at the end of nine months, with some of the American natives of Hispaniola, several rarities from that country, and a quantity of gold, with which he presented their majesties.

VOLTAIRE.

THE INFLUENCE OF SCIENCE ON THE MANNERS OF MEN.

The progress of science and the cultivation of literature had considerable effect in changing the manners of the European nations, and introduced that civility and refinement by which they are now distinguished. At the time when their empire was overturned, the Romans, though they had lost that correct taste which has rendered the productions of their ancestors the standards of excellence and models for imitation to succeeding ages, still preserved their love of letters, and cultivated the arts with great ardour. But rude barbarians were so far from being struck with any admiration of these unknown accomplishments, that they despised them. They were not arrived at that state of society in which those faculties of the human mind that have beauty and elegance for their objects begin to unfold themselves. They were strangers to all those wants and desires which are the parents of ingenious invention; and, as they did not comprehend either the merit or utility of the Roman arts, they destroyed the monuments of them with industry not inferior to that with which their posterity have since studied to preserve or to recover them. The convulsions occasioned by their settlement in the empire, the frequent as well as violent revolutions in every kingdom which they established, together with the interior defects in the form of government which they introduced, banished security and leisure; prevented the growth of taste or the culture of science; and kept Europe, during several centuries, in a state of ignorance. But as soon as liberty and independence began to be felt by every part of the community, and communicated some taste of the advantages arising from commerce, from public order, and from personal security, the human mind became conscious of powers which it did not formerly perceive, and fond of occupations or pursuits of which it was formerly incapable. Towards the beginning of the twelfth century we discern the first symptoms of its awaking from that lethargy in which it had long been sunk, and observe it turning with curiosity and attention towards new objects.

ROBERTSON.

BOOK II.

DIDACTIC AND MORAL PIECES.

FEMALE PASSION FOR DRESS AND SHEW.

When I was in France I used to gaze with great astonishment at the splendid equipages and party-coloured habits of that fantastic nation. I was one day in particular contemplating a lady that sat in a coach adorned with gilded Cupids, and finely painted with the loves of Venus and Adonis. The coach was drawn by six milk-white horses, and loaden behind with the same number of powdered footmen. Just before the lady were a couple of beautiful pages that were stuck among the harness, and, by their gay dresses and smiling features, looked like the elder brothers of the little boys that were carved and painted in every corner of the coach.

The lady was the unfortunate Cleanthe, who afterwards gave an occasion to a pretty melancholy novel. She had for several years received the addresses of a gentleman, whom, after a long and intimate acquaintance, she forsook upon account of this shining equipage, which had been offered to her by one of great riches, but a crazy constitution. The circumstances in which I saw her were, it seems, the disguises only of a broken heart and a kind of pageantry to cover distress; for, in two months after, she was carried to her grave with the same pomp and magnificence; being sent thither partly by the loss of one lover, and partly by the possession of another.

I have often reflected with myself on this unaccountable humour in woman kind, of being smitten with every thing that is showy and superficial, and on the numberless evils that befall the sex from this light fantastical disposition. I myself remember a young lady that was very warmly solicited by a couple of importunate rivals, who, for several months together, did all they could to recommend themselves by complacency of behaviour and agreeableness of conversation. At length, when the competition was doubtful, and the lady undetermined in her choice, one of the young lovers very luckily bethought himself of adding a supernumerary lace to his liveries, which had so soon an effect that he married her the very week after.

The usual conversation of ordinary women very much cherishes this natural weakness of being taken with outside and appearance. Talk of a new-married couple, and you immediately hear whether they keep their coach and six, or eat in plate; mention the name of an absent lady, and it is ten to one but you learn something of her gown and petticoat; a ball is a great help to discourse, and a birth-day furnishes conversation for a twelvemonth after; a furbelow of precious stones, a hat buttoned with a diamond, a brocade waistcoat or petticoat, are standing topics. In short, they consider only the drapery of the species, and never cast away a thought on those ornaments of the mind that make persons illustrious in themselves and useful to others. When women are thus perpetually dazzling one another's imaginations, and filling their heads with nothing but colours, it is no wonder that they are more attentive to the superficial parts of life than the solid and substantial blessings of it. A girl who has been trained up in this kind of conversation is in danger of every embroidered coat that comes in her way. In a word, lace and ribbons, silver and gold galloons, with the like glittering gewgaws, are so many lures to women of weak minds or low educations, and, when artificially displayed, are able to fetch down the most airy coquet from the wildest of her flights.

True happiness is of a retired nature, and an enemy to pomp and noise: it arises, in the first place, from the enjoyment of one's self; and, in the next, from the friendship and conversation of a few select companions. It loves shade and solitude, and naturally haunts groves and fountains, fields and meadows. In short, it feels every thing it wants within itself, and receives no addition from multitudes of witnesses and spectators. On the contrary, false happiness loves to be in a crowd, and to draw the eyes of the world upon her. She does not receive any satisfaction from the applauses which she gives herself, but from the admiration which she raises in others. She flourishes in courts and palaces, theatres and assemblies, and has no existence but when she is looked upon.

SPECTATOR.

ON CLEANLINESS.

I HAD occasion to go a few miles out of town, some days since, in a stage-coach, where I had for my fellow-travellers a dirty beau and a pretty young quaker woman. Having no inclination to talk much at that time, I placed myself backward,

backward, with a design to survey them, and pick a speculation out of my two companions. Their different figures were sufficient of themselves to draw my attention. The gentleman was dressed in a suit, the ground whereof had been black, as I perceived from some few spaces that had escaped the powder, which was incorporated with the greatest part of his coat; his perriwig, which cost no small sum, was after so slovenly a manner cast over his shoulders that it seemed not to have been combed since the year 1712; his linen, which was not much concealed, was daubed with plain spanish from the chin to the lowest button; and the diamond upon his finger (which naturally dreaded the water) put me in mind how it sparkled amidst the rubbish of the mine where it was first discovered. On the other hand, the pretty quaker appeared all the elegance of cleanliness; not a speck was to be found on her. A clear, lean, oval face, just edged about with little thin plaits of the purest cambric, received great advantage from the shade of her black hood, as did the whiteness of her arms from that sober-coloured stuff in which she had clothed herself. The plainness of her dress was very well suited to the simplicity of her phrases; all which put together, though they could not give a great opinion of her religion, indicated her innocence.

This adventure occasioned my throwing together a few hints upon *cleanliness*, which I shall consider as one of the half-virtues, as Aristotle calls them, and shall recommend it under the three following heads: as it is a mark of politeness; as it produces love; and as it bears an analogy to purity of mind.

First, it is a mark of politeness. It is universally agreed that no one unadorned with this virtue can go into company

pany without giving a manifest offence. The easier or higher any one's fortune is this duty rises proportionably. The different nations of the world are as much distinguished by their cleanliness as by their arts and sciences. The more any country is civilized the more they consult this part of politeness. We need but compare our ideas of a female Hottentot and an English beauty to be satisfied of the truth of what hath been advanced.

In the next place, cleanliness may be said to be the foster-mother of love. Beauty, indeed, most commonly produces that passion in the mind; but cleanliness preserves it. An indifferent face and person, kept in perpetual neatness, has won many a heart from a pretty slattern. Age itself is not unamiable while it is preserved clean and unsullied: like a piece of metal constantly kept smooth and bright, we look on it with more pleasure than on a new vessel that is cankered with rust.

I might observe farther, that as cleanliness renders us agreeable to others, so it makes us easy to ourselves; that it is an excellent preservative of health; and that several vices, destructive both to mind and body, are inconsistent with the habit of it. But these reflections I shall leave to the leisure of my readers, and shall observe, in the third place, that it bears a great analogy with purity of mind, and naturally inspires refined sentiments and passions.

We find from experience, that, through the prevalence of custom, the most vicious actions lose their horror by being made familiar to us. On the contrary, those who live in the neighbourhood of good examples fly from the first appearances of what is shocking. It fares with us much after the same manner as to our ideas. Our senses, which are the inlets to all the images conveyed to the mind, can only transmit the impression of such things as

usually

usually surround them: so that pure and unsullied thoughts are naturally suggested to the mind by those objects that perpetually encompass us, when they are beautiful and elegant in their kind.

In the east, where the warmth of the climate makes cleanliness more immediately necessary than in colder countries, it is made one part of their religion. The Jewish law (and the Mahometan, which in some things copies after it) is filled with bathings, purifications, and other rites of the like nature. Though there is the above named convenient reason to be assigned for these ceremonies, the chief intention undoubtedly was to typify inward purity and cleanliness of heart by those outward washings. We read several injunctions of this kind in the book of Deuteronomy, which confirm the truth, and which are but ill accounted for by saying, as some do, that they were only instituted for convenience in the desart, which otherwise could not have been habitable for so many years.

SPECTATOR.

THE ART OF IMPROVING BEAUTY.

MONSIEUR St. Evremont has concluded one of his essays with affirming that the last sighs of a handsome woman are not so much for the loss of her life as of her beauty. Perhaps this raillery is pursued too far; yet it is turned upon a very obvious remark, that a woman's strongest passion is for her own beauty, and that she values it as her favourite distinction. From hence it is that all arts which tend to improve or preserve it meet with so general a reception amongst the sex. To say nothing of many false helps, and contraband wares of beauty, which are daily vended in this great mart, there is not a maiden gentlewoman of a good family in any county of South Britain, who has not heard of the virtues of May-dew, or is not furnished with some receipt or other in favour of her complexion; and I have known a physician of learning and sense, after eight years study at the university, and a course of travels into most countries of Europe, owe the first raising of his fortunes to a cosmetic wash.

This has given me occasion to consider how so universal a disposition in woman-kind, which springs from a laudable motive, the desire of pleasing, and proceeds upon an opinion, not altogether groundless, that nature may be helped by art, may be turned to their advantage: and methinks it would be an acceptable service to take them out of the hands of quacks and pretenders, and to prevent their imposing upon themselves, by discovering to them the true secret and art of improving beauty.

In order to this, before I touch upon it directly, it will be necessary to lay down a few preliminary maxims, viz.

> That no woman can be handsome by the force of features alone, any more than she can be witty only by the help of speech.
>
> That pride destroys all symmetry and grace, and affectation is a more terrible enemy to fine faces than the small-pox.
>
> That no woman is capable of being beautiful who is not incapable of being false.
>
> And, that what would be odious in a friend is deformity in a mistress.

From these few principles, thus laid down, it will be easy to prove that the true art of assisting beauty consists in embellishing the whole person by the proper ornaments of virtuous

tuous and commendable qualities. By this help alone it is that those who are the favourite work of Nature, or, as Mr. Dryden expresses it, the porcelain clay of human kind, become animated, and are in a capacity of exerting their charms: and those who seem to have been neglected by her, like models wrought in haste, are capable, in a great measure, of finishing what she has left imperfect.

It is, methinks, a low and degraded idea of that sex, which was created to refine the joys and soften the cares of humanity by the most agreeable participation, to consider them merely as objects of sight. This is abridging them of their natural extent of power to put them on a level with their pictures at Kneller's. How much nobler is the contemplation of beauty heightened by virtue, and commanding our esteem and love, while it draws our observation! How faint and spiritless are the charms of a coquet, when compared with the real loveliness of Sophronia's innocence, piety, good-humour, and truth; virtues which add a new softness to her sex, and even beautify her beauty! Colours artfully spread upon canvas may entertain the eye but not affect the heart; and she who takes no care to add to the natural graces of her person any excelling qualities may be allowed still to amuse as a picture, but not to triumph as a beauty.

When Adam is introduced by Milton describing Eve in Paradise, and relating to the angel the impressions he felt upon seeing her at her first creation, he does not represent her like a Grecian Venus, by her shape or features, but by the lustre of her mind, which shone in them, and gave them their power of charming.

> Grace was in all her steps, heav'n in her eye,
> In all her gestures dignity and love!

Without this irradiating power the proudest fair one ought to know, whatever her dress may tell her to the contrary, that her most perfect features are uninformed and dead.

SPECTATOR.

THE ART OF BEING PRETTY.

Though the danger of disappointment is always in proportion to the height of expectation, yet I this day claim the attention of the ladies, and profess to teach an art by which all may obtain what has hitherto been deemed the prerogative of a few; an art by which their predominant passion may be gratified, and their conquests not only extended but secured; " The art of being pretty."

I shall principally consider that species of beauty which is expressed in the countenance; for this alone is peculiar to human beings, and is not less complicated than their nature. In the countenance there are but two requisites to perfect beauty, which are wholly produced by external causes, colour and proportion: and it will appear that, even in common estimation, these are not the chief; but that, though there may be beauty without them, yet there cannot be beauty without something more.

The finest features, ranged in the most exact symmetry, and heightened by the most blooming complexion, must be animated before they can strike; and, when they are animated, will generally excite the same passions which they express. If they are fixed in the dead calm of insensibility, they will be examined without emotion; and, if they do not express kindness, they will be beheld without love. Looks of contempt, disdain, or malevolence, will be reflected,

flected, as from a mirror, by every countenance on which they are turned.

Among particular graces the dimple has always been allowed the pre-eminence; and the reason is evident: dimples are produced by a smile, and a smile is an expression of complacency; so the contraction of the brows into a frown, as it is an indication of a contrary temper, has always been deemed a capital defect.

Beauty, however, does not always consist in smiles, but varies as expressions of meekness and kindness vary with their objects: it is extremely forcible in the silent complaint of patient sufferance, the tender solicitude of friendship, and the glow of filial obedience; and in tears, whether of joy, of pity, or of grief, it is almost irresistible.

This is the charm which captivates without the aid of Nature, and without which her utmost bounty is ineffectual. But it cannot be assumed as a mask to conceal insensibility or malevolence; it must be the genuine effect of corresponding sentiments, or it will impress upon the countenance a new and more disgusting deformity, affectation; it will produce the grin, the simper, the stare, the languish, the pout, and innumerable other grimaces, that render folly ridiculous, and change pity to contempt. By some, indeed, this species of hypocrisy has been practised with such skill as to deceive superficial observers, though it can deceive even these but for a moment. Looks which do not correspond with the heart cannot be assumed without labour, nor continued without pain: the motive to relinquish them must therefore soon preponderate, and the aspect and apparel of the visit will be laid by together; the smiles and languishments of art will vanish, and the fierceness of rage, or the gloom of discontent, will either obscure

scure or destroy all the elegance of symmetry and complexion.

The artificial aspect is, indeed, as wretched a substitute for the expression of sentiment as the smear of paint for the blushes of health: it is not only equally transient, and equally liable to detection; but, as paint leaves the countenance yet more withered and ghastly, the passions burst out with more violence after restraint, the features become more distorted, and excite more determined aversion.

Beauty, therefore, depends principally upon the mind, and consequently may be influenced by education. It has been remarked that the predominant passion may generally be discovered in the countenance; because the muscles by which it is expressed, being almost perpetually contracted, lose their tone, and never totally relax; so that the expression remains when the passion is suspended: thus an angry, a disdainful, a subtle, and a suspicious temper, is displayed in characters that are almost universally understood. It is equally true of the pleasing and the softer passions, that they leave their signatures upon the countenance when they cease to act: the prevalence of these passions therefore produces a mechanical effect upon the aspect, and gives a turn and cast to the features, which make a more favourable and forcible impression upon the mind of others than any charm produced by mere external causes.

Let it therefore be remembered that none can be disciples of the Graces but in the school of Virtue; and that those who wish to be lovely must learn to be good.

ADVENTURER.

DRESS.

DRESS.

In dress it is not little minute things but the *whole* that should be attended to; never desire to excel in trifles; if you do, there is an end to virtuous emulation; the mind cannot attend to both; if the main pursuit is trivial the character will of course be insignificant. Habitual neatness is laudable; but if you wish to be reckoned a well and elegantly-dressed girl, and feel that praises on account of it give you pleasure, you are vain; and a laudable ambition will not dwell with vanity.

Servants, and those women whose minds have had a very limited range, place all their happiness in ornaments, and frequently neglect the only essential in dress, neatness.

Fathers and men in general complain of this inattention; they have always to wait for the females. Learn to avoid an error which cannot be of little consequence, as it sometimes weakens esteem. When we frequently make allowances for another in trifling matters, notions of inferiority take root in the mind, and too often produce contempt. Respect for the understanding must be the basis of constancy; the tenderness which flows from pity is liable to perish insensibly, to consume itself; even the virtues of the heart, if they degenerate into weakness, sink a character in our estimation. Besides, a kind of gross familiarity takes place of decent affection, and the delicacy of the female character is sullied, if not lost.

ORIGINAL STORIES.

THE SAME SUBJECT.

Do not confine your attention to dress to your public appearances. Accustom yourselves to an habitual neatness, so that in the most careless undress, in your most unguarded hours, you may have no reason to be ashamed of your appearance. You will not easily believe how much we consider your dress as expressive of your characters. Vanity, levity, slovenliness, folly, appear through it. An elegant simplicity is an equal proof of taste and delicacy.

GREGORY.

THE SAME SUBJECT.

By far too much of a girl's time is taken up in dress. This is an exterior accomplishment; but I chose to consider it by itself. The body hides the mind, and it is in its turn obscured by the drapery. I hate to see the frame of a picture so glaring as to catch the eye and divide the attention: dress ought to adorn the person, and not rival it. It may be simple, elegant, and becoming, without being expensive; and ridiculous fashions disregarded, while singularity is avoided. The beauty of dress (I shall raise astonishment by saying so) is its not being conspicuous one way or the other; when it neither distorts or hides the human form by unnatural protuberances. If ornaments are much studied a consciousness of being well dressed will appear in the face; and surely this mean pride does not give much sublimity to it. ' Out of the abun-
' dance of the heart the mouth speaketh.' And how much conversation does dress furnish which surely cannot be very improving or entertaining.

M. WOLLSTONECRAFT.

DRESS SUBSERVIENT TO USEFUL PURPOSES.

Working for the poor is a species of charity which forms a part of the prerogative of our sex, and gives to those who have leisure for it an opportunity of doing much good with very little trouble and expense. Were it more generally practised by young people it would moderate that inordinate love of dress, which renders many, who cannot afford to employ milliners and mantua-makers, literally slaves to fashion: they would be ashamed to covet such a variety of ornaments when they beheld what trifles gratify others of the same species with themselves. Besides, the having caps and other things *gratis* would be an inducement to the poor to dress suitably to their condition: and then people in the middling stations of life might support a sufficient degree of gentility to secure respect, without being driven to extravagance.

Mrs. Trimmer.

ODE TO A YOUNG LADY ON DRESS.

Survey, my fair, that lucid stream
Adown the smiling valley stray;
Wou'd art attempt or fancy dream
To regulate its winding way?

So pleas'd I view thy shining hair
In loose dishevell'd ringlets flow;
Not all thy art, not all thy care,
Can there one single grace bestow.

Survey

Survey again that verdant hill,
With native plants enamell'd o'er;
Say, can the painter's utmost skill
Instruct one flow'r to please us more?

As vain it were, with artful dye,
To change the bloom thy cheeks disclose;
And, oh! may Laura, ere she try,
With fresh vermilion paint the rose.

Hark! how the woodlark's tuneful throat
Can ev'ry study'd grace excel;
Let art constrain the rambling note,
And will she Laura please so well?

Oh! ever keep thy native ease,
By no pedantic law confin'd;
For Laura's voice is form'd to please
If Laura's words be not unkind.

SHENSTONE.

ON EMPLOYMENT.

I shall first give you my advice concerning employment, it being of great moment to set out in life in such a method as may be useful to yourself and beneficial to others. Time is invaluable, its loss irretrievable! the remembrance of having made an ill use of it must be one of the sharpest tortures of those who are on the brink of eternity! and what can yield a more unpleasing retrospect than whole years idled away in an irrational insignificant manner! examples of which are continually before our eyes. Look on every day as a blank sheet of paper put into your hands

hands to be filled up; remember the characters will remain to endless ages, and can never be expunged; be careful therefore not to write any thing but what you may read with pleasure a thousand years hence. I would not be understood in a sense so strict as might debar you from any innocent amusement suitable to your age, and agreeable to your inclination; diversions properly regulated are not only allowable, they are absolutely necessary to youth, and are never criminal but when taken to excess; that is, when they engross the whole thought, are made the chief business of life, give a distaste to every valuable employment; and, by a sort of infatuation, leave the mind in a state of restless impatience from the conclusion of one till the commencement of another: this is the unfortunate disposition of many; guard most carefully against it; for nothing can be attended with more pernicious consequences; a little observation will convince you that there is not amongst the human species a set of more miserable beings than those who cannot live out of a constant succession of diversions: these people have no comprehension of the more satisfactory pleasures to be found in retirement; thought is insupportable to them, and consequently solitude must be intolerable; they are a burden to themselves, and a pest to their acquaintance, by vainly seeking for happiness in company where they are seldom acceptable; I say vainly, for true happiness exists only in the mind; nothing foreign can give it: the utmost to be attained by what is called a gay life is a short forgetfulness of misery, to be felt with accumulated anguish in every interval of reflection. This restless temper is frequently the product of a too eager pursuit of pleasure in the early part of life, to the neglect of those valuable improvements which would lay the foundation of a more solid and permanent felicity.

Youth

Youth is the season for diversions, but it is also the season for acquiring knowledge, for fixing useful habits, and laying in a stock of such well-chosen materials as may grow into a serene happiness that will increase with every added year of life, and bloom in the fullest perfection at the decline of it.

LADY PENNINGTON.

BENEVOLENT EMPLOYMENTS.

I BEG leave to recommend a branch of charity which is too much neglected amongst us; I mean that of visiting poor persons in sickness and affliction at their own houses.

The pleasure which accompanies benevolent actions, almost every woman, when in health, can in some measure purchase for herself; and the calls on our humanity are more frequent than on that of the other sex, as there are a variety of distresses which we only can personally relieve.

Let us begin with childing-women. We will suppose that the poor, inured to hardships from their infancy, have in general more strength than persons in superior stations to support the evils which are, in some degree, the allotted portions of all mothers: but they certainly are not exempted from the curse denounced on their sex—they feel it in its full force, 'In sorrow, (in accumulated sorrow) they bring forth children.' It is therefore an act of compassion, becoming all women who have ability to do it, to mitigate the dreadful sufferings which fall to the lot of many of their fellow-creatures. It must be acknowledged that ladies in general are ready to afford pecuniary assistance whenever a poor woman can find a friend to represent her horrid situation; but instead of sending money, which may be misapplied by a drunken or sordid nurse, or even by a sottish husband, it would answer a better purpose
if

if some, who can judge by sympathy of the feelings of these poor wretches, would enter their miserable dwellings, and view them in their uncomfortable beds.

Workhouses, crowded as they at present are, must be very uncomfortable at a time when repose is so essentially necessary: and there would be no occasion for the expedient of sending poor creatures to such places, from country towns and villages at least, if all women who can afford it would contribute their mite only to the laudable purpose of assisting them at those seasons with such necessaries as every housekeeper can furnish in one way or other: beer-caudle, which is made at a trifling expense, serves both for food and medicine; and, if made with no other spice but a little ginger, is so great a restorative, that women who are supplied with it will struggle through a variety of inconveniencies, and soon recover their strength.

A childbed basket, containing a pair of blankets, two pair of sheets, a bed-gown, &c. may be furnished for less than four pounds; which, if lent for three weeks only, would accommodate ten or twelve women in a year. The only objections that can, I think, be made to it, are that women would feel the want of these necessaries afterwards, and that it will be difficult to get them back again. To obviate the first, care should be taken, in the purchase of the various articles, that they are of the same materials as poor people buy for themselves; and to guard against the latter, that they are lent to women who may be depended upon; and such persons there doubtless are in every town and village, who would rejoice at the benefit, and make a proper use of it. I am of opinion that Schools of Industry would soon supersede the necessity of childbed-baskets; but, till they do, the latter will be very useful; and I have heard of their having been provided with success. If ladies use the precaution above-mentioned, and also visit the poor women while they lie-in, and see that they do not suffer for want of nourishment, there will be less temptation for their making away with the contents of the basket. If a set of apparel, for the baby to be christened in, were given as a reward for those who return the other things with punctuality, it would be a great encouragement; and the making of these would be a very agreeable employment to the younger ladies, who, I will engage to say, would have inexpressible delight in seeing a little creature incorporated into that church of which it is their own highest privilege to be members, neatly clothed by their charity and industry.

As they advance in years young ladies may, with great propriety, accompany their mothers in their visits to poor lying-in women; by which means they will have opportunities of making observations which may help to direct them afterwards in the management of their own children, whom (when convinced of the absurdity of feeding them too often, &c.) they will not abandon to the care of an ignorant nurse, to be crammed every half-hour with improper food; which is the fate of many a little innocent, whose mother has neglected to inform herself, before its birth, of the principles of rational nursing.

I may also add that, by observing the almost universal success of poor women in suckling their own children, and the satisfaction usually attending it, young ladies would be prepossessed in favour of this duty; and would not, when mothers themselves, so readily yield, as numbers do, to imaginary impossibilities of succeeding in the exercise of that delightful office, which seems to have been designed by Providence as the bond of reciprocal affection, the cement of family concord.

It

It is an old adage, but a very juſt one when properly applied, that 'Charity begins at home;' I hope therefore it will not be thought foreign to the deſign of my work to recommend to ladies the practice of nurſing their own children. Little do many young mothers think to what miſeries they expoſe their helpleſs offspring, by ſending them from under the paternal roof to cottages where they frequently endure all the hardſhips of a ſtate of poverty: little do they think that they are ſuppreſſing ſome of the moſt pleaſing emotions that the female heart is ſuſceptible of enjoying—emotions which would amply repay their utmoſt fatigues! that they are breaking one of the ſtrongeſt bands of domeſtic happineſs, by removing from view that dear pledge which was granted to increaſe conjugal love between them and their huſbands, and attach them to their own homes. If pleaſure is the object, where can a woman find one, in the whole circle of public amuſements, to compenſate for the loſs of that a fond mother feels while ſhe nouriſhes her infant with the food which is its natural right, and ſees a ſucceſſion of human beings thriving in their native ſoil under her own immediate culture? The maternal affections expand daily; filial love ariſes in the infant mind as an innate principle; the father is animated to ſuſtain his toils by the ſight of thoſe dear objects which render them neceſſary; his cares are lightened by the hopes which their progreſſive improvement excites in his heart; and their innocent ſports and prattle enliven his hours of leiſure, and ſupply the moſt ſalutary recreation to his mind.

It is a falſe ſhame which reſtrains young ladies from informing their minds in reſpect to the nurſing of children. They apprehend that their attention to theſe matters will be conſtrued into a haſty deſire of quitting the ſingle ſtate.

None

None but illiberal people will entertain such an opinion, especially if they shew, by applying their knowledge to the benefit of the poor, that they have a more immediate purpose in view.

THE SAME SUBJECT CONTINUED.

Another occasion, when poor people stand in particular need of the attention and assistance of their superiors, is when they have the small-pox in their families. Clean linen is then of the most salutary service, and the older it is the more comfortable; for if it lasts till the disease is over that is enough, as it would be advisable to destroy it afterwards. Numbers of poor creatures die of the effluvia of their own bodies, or at least suffer greatly for want of the refreshment which clean linen affords: and some endure extreme agony in having their things torn off, after having lain in them a considerable time; and the contagion is certainly spread by want of cleanliness. It is inconceivable, to those who have not been eye-witnesses of them, what absurdities the generality of poor people commit in the management of the small-pox; it would therefore be a great act of charity, to endeavour to introduce a more rational method among them. I am persuaded that the fatality of this disease (under Providence) would be greatly lessened among the poor, could they be restrained from injurious practices, and excited to cleanliness.

The welfare of a neighbourhood frequently depends on attention to little circumstances; for not only the small-pox, but other distempers, sometimes become putrid by improper treatment.

It often happens that, after severe illnesses, poor people languish for want of kitchen-physic, as it is called. Many thing things may be made for them in families with very little expense, which would be more beneficial than the intrinsic worth of them in money: for it is to be considered that poor people make these things at a greater charge than others, because they buy every article at the worst hand, and are perhaps obliged to have a fire on purpose to dress them: they must purchase meat when their stomach will bear only broth, which might be supplied by a neighbour, who has a joint of veal or mutton boiled, without any addition to the household expenses: other things that come under the denomination of kitchen-physic, such as white-wine whey, &c. it is likely they could not procure at all; and if they could, the fatigue of making them, should they know how, would be very likely to destroy the relish of them when done; for every one who has been an invalid knows that appetite is often excited by the production of an unexpected dainty; and frequently changed into aversion, when those longings which sick persons in general are subject to are not immediately gratified.

When our blessed Saviour multiplied the loaves and fishes he commanded his disciples ' to gather up the frag-' ments, that nothing might be lost.' Whoever is by the bounty of Providence enabled to spread a plentiful table, must unavoidably have fragments; these should in like manner be carefully collected—the hardest crust may satisfy the cravings of a starving wretch—the superfluities that are frequently wasted in families would rescue many from the extremities of wretchedness: and there are other fragments which would be very acceptable to poor people: a present of odd bits to mend their clothes would be a treasure to many.

An hospitable custom prevails in this country of dispensing gifts, and making contributions for the parish poor in severe weather; and they are of the utmost benefit to many deserving objects, but are often obtained by persons who do not need them, and who make them subservient to their vices. These donations would be more efficacious, and answer the intention of the benevolent donors much better, if distributed from house to house by some person who could inspect into the real distress which exists in each family; for distresses are various, and require variety of relief; besides, the poor often stand in need of advice how to lay out their money.

MRS. TRIMMER.

ON WASTE OF TIME.

TRUTHS that the learn'd pursue with eager thought
Are not important always as dear-bought,
Proving at last, though told in pompous strains,
A childish waste of philosophic pains;
But truths, on which depends our main concern,
That 'tis our shame and mis'ry not to learn,
Shine by the side of ev'ry path we tread,
With such a lustre he that runs may read.
'Tis true that, if to trifle life away
Down to the sun-set of their latest day,
Then perish on futurity's wide shore,
Like fleeting exhalations, found no more,
Were all that Heav'n requir'd of human kind,
And all the plan their destiny design'd,
What none could rev'rence all might justly blame,
And man would breathe but for his Maker's shame.

But

But reason heard, and nature well perus'd,
At once the dreaming mind is disabus'd.
If all we find possessing earth, sea, air,
Reflect his attributes who plac'd them there,
Fulfil the purpose, and appear design'd
Proofs of the wisdom of th' All-seeing mind.

COWPER.

INDOLENCE AND WANT OF THOUGHT.

There are two sorts of understandings; one of which hinders a man from ever being considerable, and the other commonly makes him ridiculous; I mean the lazy mind, and the trifling frivolous mind. Yours I hope is neither. The lazy mind will not take the trouble of going to the bottom of any thing; but, discouraged by the first difficulties, (and every thing worth knowing or having is attended with some) stops short, contents itself with easy, and consequently superficial, knowledge, and prefers a great degree of ignorance to a small degree of trouble. These people either think or represent most things as impossible; whereas few things are so to industry and activity. But difficulties seem to them impossibilities, or at least they pretend to think them so, by way of excuse for their laziness. An hour's attention to the same object is too laborious for them; they take every thing in the light in which it at first presents itself, never considering it in all its different views; and, in short, never think thoroughly. The consequence of this is that, when they come to speak upon these subjects before people who have considered them with attention, they only discover their own ignorance and laziness, and lay themselves open to answers that put them in confusion.

The trifling and frivolous mind is always busied, but to little purpose; it takes little objects for great ones, and throws away upon trifles that time and attention which only important things deserve. Knick-knacks, butterflies, shells, insects, &c. are the objects of their most serious researches. They contemplate the dress, not the characters, of the company they keep. They attend more to the decorations of a play than to the sense of it, and to the ceremonies of a court more than to its politics. Such an employment of time is an absolute loss of it.

CHESTERFIELD.

THE BAD EFFECTS OF INDOLENCE.

No other disposition or turn of mind so totally unfits a man for all the social offices of life as indolence. An idle man is a mere blank in the creation; he seems made for no end, and lives to no purpose. He cannot engage himself in any employment or profession, because he will never have diligence enough to follow it: he can succeed in no undertaking, for he will never pursue it; he must be a bad husband, father, and relation, for he will not take the least pains to preserve his wife, children, and family from starving; and he must be a worthless friend, for he would not draw his hand from his bosom, though to prevent the destruction of the universe. If he is born poor he will remain so all his life, which he will probably end in a ditch, or at the gallows. If he embarks in trade he will become a bankrupt; and if he is a person of fortune his stewards will acquire immense estates, and he himself perhaps will die in the Fleet.

It should be considered that nature did not bring us into the world in a state of perfection, but has left us in a capacity of improvement; which should seem to intimate that we should labour to render ourselves excellent. Very few are such absolute idiots as not to be able to become at least decent, if not eminent, in their several stations, by unwearied and keen application: nor are there any possessed of such transcendent genius and abilities as to render all pains and diligence unnecessary. Perseverance will overcome difficulties which at first appear insuperable; and it is amazing to consider how great and numerous obstacles may be removed by a continual attention to any particular point. I will not mention here the trite example of Demosthenes, who got over the greatest natural impediments to oratory, but content myself with a more modern and familiar instance. Being at Sadler's Wells a few nights ago, I could not but admire the surprising feats of activity there exhibited, and at the same time reflected what incredible pains and labour it must have cost the performers to arrive at the art of writhing their bodies into such various and unnatural contorsions. But I was most taken with an ingenious artist, who, after fixing two bells to each foot, the same number to each hand, and, with great propriety, a cap and bells on his head, played several tunes, and went through as regular treble peals and bob-majors as the boys of Christ-church Hospital; all which he effected by the due jerking of his arms and legs, and nodding his head backward and forward. If this artist had taken equal pains to employ his head in another way, he might perhaps have been as deep a proficient in numbers as Jedediah Buxton, or at least a tolerable modern rhymer, of which he is not a bad emblem; and if our ladies would use equal diligence they might fashion their minds as successfully as Madam Catherina distorts her body.

There is not in the world a more useless, idle animal than he who contents himself with being merely a gentleman. He has an estate, therefore he will not endeavour to acquire knowledge; he is not to labour in any vocation, therefore he will do nothing. But the misfortune is that there is no such thing in nature as negative virtue, and that absolute idleness is impracticable. He who does no good will certainly do mischief; and the mind, if it is not stored with useful knowledge, will necessarily become a magazine of nonsense and trifles: wherefore a gentleman, although he is not obliged to rise to open his shop, or work at his trade, should always find some ways of employing his time to advantage. If he makes no advances in wisdom he will become more and more a slave to folly; and he who does nothing because he has nothing to do will become vicious and abandoned, or at least ridiculous and contemptible.

I do not know a more melancholy object than a man of an honest heart and fine natural abilities whose good qualities are thus destroyed by indolence. Such a person is a constant plague to all his friends and acquaintance, with all the means in his power of adding to their happiness; and suffers himself to take rank among the lowest characters, when he might render himself conspicuous among the highest. Nobody is more universally avoided than my friend Careless. He is a humane man, who never did a beneficent action, and a man of unshaken integrity, on whom it is impossible to depend. With the best head, and the best heart, he regulates his conduct in the most absurd manner, and frequently injures his friends; for whoever neglects to do justice to himself must inevitably wrong those with whom he is connected; and it is by no means a true maxim that an idle man hurts no body but himself.

Virtue, then, is not to be considered in the light of mere innocence, or abstaining from harm, but as the exertion of our faculties in doing good: as Titus, when he had let a day slip undistinguished by some act of virtue, cried out ' I have lost a day.' If we regard our time in this light how many days shall we look back upon as irretrievably lost! and to how narrow a compass would such a method of calculation frequently reduce the longest life! If we were to number our days according as we have applied to virtue, it would occasion strange revolutions in the manner of reckoning the ages of men. We should see some few arrived to a good old age in the prime of their youth, and meet several young fellows of fourscore.

Agreeable to this way of thinking I remember to have met with the epitaph of an aged man four years old, dating his existence from the time of his reformation from evil courses. The inscriptions on many tomb-stones commemorate no acts of virtue performed by the persons who lie under them, but only record that they were born one day and died another. But I would fain have those people whose lives have been useless rendered of some service after their deaths, by affording lessons of instruction and morality to those they leave behind them. Wherefore I could wish, that in every parish several acres were marked out for a new and spacious burying-ground, in which every person whose remains are there deposited should have a stone laid over them, reckoning their age according to the manner in which they have improved or abused the time allotted them in their lives. In such circumstances the plate on a coffin might be the highest panegyric which the deceased could receive; and a little square stone, inscribed with Ob. Ann. Æta. 80, would be a nobler eulogium than all the lapidary adulation of modern epitaphs.

CONNOISSEUR.

ON THE GOVERNMENT OF THE TEMPER.

The smallest disappointment in pleasure, or difficulty in the most trifling employment, will put wilful young people out of temper; and their very amusements frequently become sources of vexation and peevishness. How often have I seen a girl, preparing for a ball, or for some other public appearance, unable to satisfy her own vanity, fret over every ornament she put on, quarrel with her maid, with her clothes, her hair; and, growing still more unlovely as she grew more cross, be ready to fight with her looking-glass for not making her as handsome as she wished to be. She did not consider that the traces of this ill-humour on her countenance would be a greater disadvantage to her appearance than any defect in her dress, or even than the plainest features enlivened by joy and good-humour. There is a degree of resignation necessary even to the enjoyment of pleasure; we must be ready and willing to give up some part of what we wish for before we can enjoy that which is indulged to us. I have no doubt that she who frets all the while she is dressing for an assembly will suffer still greater uneasiness when she is there. The same craving restless vanity will there

there endure a thousand mortifications which in the midst of seeming pleasure will secretly corrode her heart, whilst the meek and humble generally find more gratification than they expected, and return home pleased and enlivened from every scene of amusement, though they could have staid away from it with perfect ease and contentment.

Mrs. Chapone.

A soft answer turneth away wrath: but grievous words stir up anger. The tongue of the wise useth knowledge aright: but the mouth of fools poureth out foolishness. He that is void of wisdom despiseth his neighbour: but a man of understanding holdeth his peace.

Proverbs.

ON OBEDIENCE.

Hear, ye children, the instruction of a father, and attend to know understanding; for I give you good doctrine: forsake ye not my law.

For I was my father's son, tender, and only beloved in the sight of my mother. He taught me also, and said unto me, Let thine heart retain my words: keep my commandments, and live.

Get wisdom, get understanding, forget it not; neither decline from the words of my mouth. Forsake her not, and she shall preserve thee; love her, and she shall keep thee. Wisdom is the principal thing; therefore get wisdom; and with all thy getting get understanding: exalt her, and she shall promote thee; she shall bring thee to honour when thou dost embrace her; she shall give to thine head an ornament of grace; a crown of glory shall she deliver to thee. Hear, O my son, and receive my sayings; and the years of thy life shall be many. I have taught thee in the way of wisdom; I have led thee in the right paths. When thou goest thy steps shall not be straitened; and when thou runnest thou shalt not stumble. Take fast hold of instruction: let her not go: keep her, for she is thy life.

Enter not into the path of the wicked, and go not in the way of evil men; avoid it, pass not by it, turn from it, and pass away. For they sleep not except they have done mischief; and their sleep is taken away unless they cause some to fall; for they eat the bread of wickedness, and drink the wine of violence: but the path of the just is as the shining light, that shineth more and more unto the perfect day. The way of the wicked is as darkness, they know not at what they stumble.

My son, attend to my words, incline thine ear unto my sayings: let them not depart from thine eyes: keep them in the midst in thine heart. For they are life unto those that find them, and health to all their flesh.

Keep thy heart with all diligence; for out of it are the issues of life. Put away from thee a froward mouth, and perverse lips put far from thee. Let thine eyes look right on, and let thine eyelids look straight before thee. Ponder the path of thy feet, and let all thy ways be established. Turn not to the right hand nor to the left: remove thy foot from evil.

PROVERBS.

HUMILITY.

HUMILITY.

And he came to Capernaum, and, being in the house, he asked them, What was it that ye disputed among yourselves by the way? But they held their peace. For by the way they had disputed among themselves who should be the greatest. And he sat down and called the twelve, and saith unto them, If any man desire to be first, the same shall be last of all, and servant of all. And he took a child, and set him in the midst of them: and when he had taken him in his arms, he said unto them, Whosoever shall receive one of such children in my name, receiveth me: and whosoever receiveth me receiveth not me, but him that sent me.

S. Mark.

And seeing the multitudes he went up into a mountain: and when he was set his disciples came unto him: and he opened his mouth, and taught them, saying,

Blessed are the poor in spirit: for their's is the kingdom of heaven. Blessed are they that mourn: for they shall be comforted. Blessed are they that hunger and thirst after righteousness: for they shall be filled. Blessed are the meek: for they shall inherit the earth. Blessed are the merciful: for they shall obtain mercy. Blessed are the pure in heart: for they shall see God. Blessed are the peace-makers: for they shall be called the children of God.

S. Matthew.

ON POLITENESS.

Politeness is the just medium between form and rudeness. It is the consequence of a benevolent nature, which shews itself to general acquaintance in an obliging unconstrained civility, as it does to more particular ones in distinguished acts of kindness. This good nature must be directed by a justness of sense, and a quickness of discernment, that knows how to use every opportunity of exercising it, and to proportion the instances of it to every character and situation. It is a restraint laid by reason and benevolence upon every irregularity of the temper, which, in obedience to them, is forced to accommodate itself even to the fantastic cares which custom and fashion have established, if by that means it can procure in any degree the satisfaction or good opinion of any part of mankind; thus paying an obliging deference to their judgment, so far as it is not inconsistent with the higher obligations of virtue and religion.

This must be accompanied with an elegance of taste, and a delicacy observant of the least trifles which tend to please or to oblige; and, though its foundation must be rooted in the heart, it can scarce be perfect without a complete knowledge of the world. In society it is the medium that blends all different tempers into the most pleasing harmony, while it imposes silence on the loquacious, and inclines the most reserved to furnish their share of the conversation. It represses the desire of shining alone, and increases the desire of being mutually agreeable. It takes off the edge of raillery, and gives delicacy to wit. It preserves a proper subordination amongst all ranks of people, and can reconcile a perfect ease with the most exact propriety.

To superiors it appears in a respectful freedom; no greatness can awe it into servility, and no intimacy can sink it into a regardless familiarity.

To inferiors it shews itself in an unassuming good-nature. Its aim is to raise them to you, not to let you down to them. It at once maintains the dignity of your station, and expresses the goodness of your heart. To equals it is every thing that is charming; it studies their inclinations, prevents their desires, attends to every little exactness of behaviour, and all the time appears perfectly disengaged and careless.

Such and so amiable is true politeness: by people of wrong heads and unworthy hearts disgraced in its two extremes; and by the generality of mankind confined within the narrow bounds of mere good breeding, which, in truth, is only one instance of it.

There is a kind of character which does not in the least deserve to be reckoned polite, though it is exact in every punctilio of behaviour; such as would not, for the world, omit paying you the civility of a bow, or fail in the least circumstance of decorum. But then these people do this merely for their own sake, that, whether you are pleased or embarrassed with it, is little of their care. They have performed their own parts, and are satisfied. One there is who says more civil things than half mankind besides, and yet is 'so obliging that he never obliged.' For while he is paying the highest court to some one person of the company, he must, of course, neglect the rest, which is ill made up by a forced recollection at last, and some lame civility; which, however it may be worded, does, in effect,

effect, express only this: 'I protest I had quite forgot
'you; but, as insignificant as you are, I must not, for my
'own sake, let you go home out of humour.' Thus
every one in his turn finding his civility to be just as
variable as his interest, no one thinks himself obliged to
him for it.

This then is a proof that true politeness, whose great
end is giving real pleasure, can have its source only in a
virtuous and benevolent heart. Yet this is not all; it
must observe propriety too. There is a character of perfect good-nature, that loves to have every thing about it
happy and merry. This is a character greatly to be loved,
but has little claim to the title of politeness. Such persons have no notion of freedom without noise and tumult: and, by taking off every proper restraint, and
sinking themselves to the level of their companions, even
lessen the pleasure these would have in the company of
their superiors.

Miss Talbot.

FALSE SENSIBILITY.

THERE is nothing in which self-deception is more notorious than in what regards sentiment and feeling. Let
a vain young woman be told that tenderness and softness
is the peculiar charm of the sex—that even their weakness
is lovely, and their fears becoming—and you will presently observe her grow so tender as to be ready to weep
for a fly; so fearful, that she starts at a feather; and so
weak-hearted, that the smallest accident quite overpowers
her. Her fondness and affectation become ridiculous; her
compassion

compassion grows contemptible weakness; and her apprehensiveness the most abject cowardice: for, when once she quits the direction of nature, she knows not where to stop, and continually exposes herself by the most absurd extremes.

Nothing so effectually defeats its own ends as this kind of affectation; for though warm affections, and tender feelings, are beyond measure amiable and charming, when perfectly natural, and kept under the due controul of reason and principle; yet nothing is so truly disgusting as the affectation of them, or even the unbridled indulgence of such as are real.

Remember that our feelings were not given us for our ornament, but to spur us on to right actions. Compassion, for instance, was not impressed upon the human heart only to adorn the fair face with tears, and to give an agreeable languor to the eyes; it was designed to excite our utmost endeavours to relieve the sufferer. Yet, how often have I heard that selfish weakness which flies from the sight of distress dignified with the name of tenderness!—' My friend is I hear in the deepest afflic-
' tion and misery;—I have not seen her—for, indeed,
' I cannot bear such scenes—they affect me too much!—
' Those who have less sensibility are fitter for this world;
' —but, for my part, I own I am not able to support
' such things.—I shall not attempt to visit her till I hear
' she has recovered her spirits.'—This have I heard said with an air of complacence; and the poor selfish creature has persuaded herself that she had finer feelings than those generous friends who are sitting patiently in the house of mourning; watching, in silence, the proper moment to pour in the balm of comfort; who suppressed their own sensations, and only attended to those of the afflicted person;

fon; and those tears flowed in secret, whilst their eyes and voices were taught to enliven the sinking heart with the appearance of cheerfulness.

That sort of tenderness which makes us useless may indeed be pitied and excused, if owing to natural imbecility; but if it pretends to loveliness and excellence it becomes truly contemptible.

Mrs. CHAPONE.

FALSE NOTIONS OF SENTIMENT.

In the enthusiasm of sentiment there is much the same danger as in the enthusiasm of religion, of substituting certain impulses and feelings of what may be called a visionary kind in the place of real practical duties, which, in morals as in theology, we might not improperly denominate good works. In morals as in religion there are not wanting instances of refined sentimentalists, who are contented with talking of virtues which they never practise, who pay in words what they owe in actions; or, perhaps, what is fully as dangerous, who open their minds to impressions which never have any effect upon their conduct, but are considered as something foreign to, and distinct from, it. This separation of conscience from feeling is a depravity of the most pernicious sort; it eludes the strongest obligation to rectitude, it blunts the strongest incitement to virtue; when the ties of the first bind the sentiment and not the will; and the rewards of the latter crown not the heart but the imagination.

LOUNGER.

A FABLE.

BOOK II.   DIDACTIC AND MORAL PIECES.

A FABLE.

THE POET, THE OYSTER, AND SENSITIVE PLANT.

An oyster cast upon the shore
Was heard, though never heard before,
Complaining in a speech well worded,
And worthy thus to be recorded:
  Ah, hapless wretch! condemn'd to dwell
For ever in my native shell;
Ordain'd to move when others please,
Not for my own content or ease;
But toss'd and buffeted about,
Now in the water, and now out.
'Twere better to be born a stone
Of ruder shape, and feeling none,
Than with a tenderness like mine
And sensibilities so fine;
I envy that unfeeling shrub
Fast rooted against ev'ry rub.
  The plant he meant grew not far off,
And felt the sneer with scorn enough;
Was hurt, disgusted, mortify'd,
And with asperity reply'd:
  When (cry botanists, and stare)
Did plants call'd sensitive grow there?
No matter when.——A poet's muse is
To make them grow just where she chuses.
You shapeless nothing in a dish,
You that are but almost a fish,

I scorn

I scorn your coarse insinuation,
And have most plentiful occasion
To wish myself the rock I view,
Or such another dolt as you:
For many a grave and learned clerk,
And many a gay unletter'd spark,
With curious touch examines me,
If I can feel as well as he;
And when I bend, retire, and shrink,
Says, Well, 'tis more than one would think.—
Thus life is spent, oh, fie upon't!
In being touch'd, and crying, Don't.

   A poet in his evening walk
O'erheard and check'd this idle talk.
And your fine sense, he said, and your's,
Whatever evil it endures,
Deserves not, if so soon offended,
Much to be pitied or commended.
Disputes, though short, are far too long
Where both alike are in the wrong;
Your feelings in their full amount
Are all upon your own account.

   You, in your grotto-work enclos'd,
Complain of being thus expos'd;
Yet nothing feel in that rough coat,
Save when the knife is at your throat;
Wherever driv'n by wind or tide,
Exempt from ev'ry ill beside.

   And as for you, my Lady Squeamish,
Who reckon ev'ry touch a blemish,
If all the plants that can be found
Embellishing the scene around

Should

Should droop and wither where they grow,
You would not feel at all, not you.
The noblest minds their virtue prove
By pity, sympathy, and love:
These, these are feelings truly fine,
And prove their owner half divine.

His censure reach'd them as he dealt it,
And each by shrinking shew'd he felt it.

COWPER.

VANITY AND AFFECTATION.

I MUST with more than ordinary earnestness give you caution against vanity, it being the fault to which your sex seems to be the most inclined: and, since affectation for the most part attends it, I do not know how to divide them. I will not call them twins; because more properly vanity is the mother, and affectation is the darling daughter; vanity is the sin, and affectation the punishment; the first may be called the root of self-love, the other the fruit. Vanity is never at its full growth till it spreads into affectation, and then it is complete.

Not to dwell any longer upon the definition of them, I will pass to the means and motives to avoid them. In order to it you are to consider that the world challenges the right of distributing esteem and applause; so that where any assume by their single authority to be their own carvers it grows angry, and never fails to seek revenge. And, if we may measure a fault by the greatness of the penalty, there are few of a higher size than
vanity,

vanity, as there is scarce a punishment which can be heavier than that of being laughed at.

Vanity makes a woman tainted with it so top-full of herself that she spills it upon the company. And, because her own thoughts are entirely employed in self-contemplation, she endeavours, by a cruel mistake, to confine her acquaintance to the same narrow circle of that which only concerns her ladyship, forgetting that she is not of half that importance to the world that she is to herself; so mistaken is she in her value, by being her own appraiser. She will fetch such a compass in discourse to bring in her beloved self, and, rather than fail, her fine petticoat, that there can hardly be a better scene than such a trial of ridiculous ingenuity. It is a pleasure to see her angle for commendation, and rise so dissatisfied with the ill-bred company if they will not bite. To observe her throwing her eyes about to fetch in prisoners, and go about cruising like a privateer, and so out of countenance if she returns without booty, is no ill piece of comedy. She is so eager to draw respect that she always misses it, yet thinks it so much her due, that when she fails she grows waspish, not considering that it is impossible to commit a rape upon the will; that it must be fairly gained, and will not be taken by storm; and that in this case the tax ever rises highest by a benevolence. If the world, instead of admiring her imaginary excellencies, takes the liberty to laugh at them, she appeals for it to herself; for whom she gives sentence, and proclaims it in all companies. On the other side, if encouraged by a civil word she is so obliging that she will give thanks for being laughed at in good language. She takes a compliment for a demonstration, and sets it up as an evidence even

against

against her looking-glass. But the good lady being all this while in a most profound ignorance of herself forgets that men would not let her talk upon them, and throw so many senseless words at their heads, if they did not intend to put her person to fine and ransom for her impertinence. Good words of any other lady are so many stones thrown at her, she can by no means bear them; they make her so uneasy that she cannot keep her seat, but up she rises and goes home half burst with anger and strait lacing. If by great chance she saith any thing that hath sense in it she expects such an excessive rate of commendations that, to her thinking, the company ever rises in her debt. She looks upon rules as things made for the common people, and not for persons of her rank; and this opinion sometimes tempts her to extend her prerogative to the dispensing with the commandment. If, by great fortune she happens, in spite of her vanity, to be honest, she is so troublesome with it that, as far as in her lies, she makes a scurvy thing of it. Her bragging of her virtue looks as if it cost her so much pains to get the better of herself that the inferences are very ridiculous. Her good humour is generally applied to the laughing at good sense. It would do one good to see how heartily she despises any thing that is fit for her to do. The greatest part of her fancy is laid out in chusing her gown, as her discretion is chiefly employed in not paying for it. She is faithful to the fashion, to which not only her opinion but her senses are wholly resigned; so obsequious is she to it, that she would be ready to be reconciled even to virtue, with all its fault, if she had her dancing-master's word that it was practised at court.

To a woman so composed, when affectation comes in to improve her character, it is then raised to the highest perfection.

perfection. She first sets up for a fine thing, and for that reason will distinguish herself, right or wrong, in every thing she doth. She would have it thought that she is made of so much the finer clay, and so much more sifted than ordinary, that she hath no common earth about her. To this end she must neither move nor speak like other women, because it would be vulgar; and therefore must have a language of her own, since ordinary English is too coarse for her. The looking-glass in the morning dictates to her all the motions of the day, which, by how much the more studied, are are so much the more mistaken. She comes into a room as if her limbs were set on with ill made screws, which makes the company fear the pretty thing would leave some of its artificial person upon the floor. She doth not like herself as God Almighty made her, but will have some of her own workmanship; which is so far from making her a better thing than a woman that it turns her into a worse creature than a monkey. When she hath a mind to be soft and languishing there is something so unnatural in that affected easiness that her frowns could not be by many degrees so forbidding. When she would appear unreasonably humble, one may see she is so excessively proud that there is no enduring it. There is such an impertinent smile, such a satisfied simper, when she faintly disowns some fulsome commendation a man happens to bestow upon her against his conscience, that her thanks for it are more visible under such a thin disguise than they could be if she should print them. If a handsomer woman takes any liberty of dressing out of the ordinary rules, the mistaken lady follows, without distinguishing the unequal pattern, and makes herself uglier

by

by an example misplaced; either forgetting the privilege of good looks in another, or presuming, without sufficient reason, upon her own. Her discourse is a senseless chime of empty words, a heap of compliments so equally applied to differing persons, that they are neither valued nor believed. Her eyes keep pace with her tongue, and are therefore always in motion. One may discern that they generally incline to the compassionate side, and that, notwithstanding her pretences to virtue, she is gentle to distressed lovers and ladies that are merciful. She will repeat the tender part of a play so feelingly that the company may guess without injustice she was not altogether a disinterested spectator. She thinks that paint and sin are concealed by railing at them. Upon the latter she is less hard; and, being divided between the two opposite prides of her beauty and her virtue, she is often tempted to give broad hints that somebody is dying for her; and of the two she is less unwilling to let the world think she may be sometimes profaned than that she is never worshipped.

Very great beauty may perhaps so dazzle for a time that men may not so clearly see the deformity of these affectations; but when the brightness goes off, and the lover's eyes are by that means set at liberty to see things as they are, he will naturally return to his senses, and recover the mistake into which the lady's good looks had at first engaged him; and, being once undeceived, ceases to worship that as a goddess which he sees only as an artificial shrine, moved by wheels and springs to delude him. Such women please only like the first opening of a scene that hath nothing to recommend it but the being new. They may be compared to flies that have pretty
shining

shining wings for two or three hot months, but the first cold weather makes an end of them; so the latter season of these fluttering creatures is dismal: from their nearest friends they receive a very faint respect, from the rest of the world the utmost degree of contempt.

Let this picture supply the place of any other rules which might be given to prevent your resemblance to it. The deformity of it, well considered, is instructions enough; from the same reason that the sight of a drunkard is a better sermon against that vice than the best that was ever preached upon that subject.

Lord HALIFAX.

DISSIMULATION.

It is necessary to recommend to you sincerity and truth. This is the basis of every virtue. That darkness of character where we can see no heart, those foldings of art through which no native affection is able to penetrate, present an object unamiable in every season of life, but particularly odious in youth. If, at an age when the heart is warm, when the emotions are strong, and when nature is expected to shew herself free and open, you can already smile and deceive, what are we to look for when you shall be longer hacknied in the ways of men, when interest shall have completed the obduration of your heart, and experience shall have improved you in all the arts of guile? Dissimulation in youth is the forerunner of perfidy in old age. Its first appearance is the fatal omen of growing depravity and future shame. It degrades parts and learning, obscures the lustre of every accomplishment, and sinks you into contempt with God and man. As you value, therefore, the approbation of heaven, or the esteem of the world, cultivate the love of truth; in all your proceedings be direct and consistent. Ingenuity and candour possess the most powerful charm; they bespeak universal favour, and carry an apology for almost every failing. The path of truth is a plain and a safe way, that of falsehood is a perplexing maze. After the first departure from sincerity, it is not in your power to stop; one artifice unavoidably leads on to another, till, as the intricacy of the labyrinth increases, you are left entangled in your own snare. Deceit discovers a little mind, which stops at temporary expedients, without rising to comprehensive views of conduct. It betrays, at the same time, a dastardly spirit; it is the resource of one who wants courage to avow his designs or to rest upon himself. Whereas openness of character displays that generous boldness which ought to distinguish youth. To set out in the world with no other principle than a crafty attention to interest, betokens one who is destined for creeping through the inferior walks of life; but to give an early preference to honour above gain, when they stand in competition, to despise every advantage which cannot be attained without dishonest arts, to brook no meanness, and to stoop to no dissimulation, are the indications of a great mind, the presages of future eminence and distinction in life. At the same time this virtuous sincerity is perfectly consistent with the most prudent vigilance and caution. It is opposed to cunning, not to true wisdom. It is not the simplicity of a weak and improvident, but the candour of an enlarged and noble

F

mind;

mind; of one who scorns deceit, because he accounts it both base and unprofitable; and who seeks no disguise, because he needs none, to hide him.

BLAIR.

THE NATURAL BEAUTY.

WHETHER Stella's eyes are found
Fix'd on earth, or glancing round,
If her face with pleasure glow,
If she sigh at others' woe,
If her easy air express
Conscious worth or soft distress,
Stella's eyes, and air, and face,
Charm with undiminish'd grace.
 If on her we see display'd
Pendant gems and rich brocade,
If her chintz with less expense
Flows in easy negligence,
Still she lights the conscious flame,
Still her charms appear the same;
If she strikes the vocal strings,
If she's silent, speaks, or sings,
If she sit, or if she move,
Still we love, and still approve.
 Vain the casual transient glance,
Which alone can please by chance,
Beauty which depends on art,
Changing with the changing art,
Which demands the toilet's aid,
Pendant gems, and rich brocade.

I those charms alone can prize,
Which from constant nature rise,
Which nor circumstance, nor dress,
E'er can make or more or less.

Dr. Johnson.

A DEFINITION OF TASTE.

It has been often observed that a good taste and a good heart commonly go together: but that sort of taste which is constantly prying into blemishes and deformity can have no good effect either on the temper or the heart. The mind naturally takes a taint from those objects and pursuits in which it is usually employed; disgust, often recurring, spoils the temper; and a habit of nicely discriminating, when carried into real life, contracts the heart; and, by holding up to view the faults and weaknesses inseparable from every character, not only checks all the benevolent and generous affections, but stifles all the pleasing emotions of love and admiration.

The habit of dwelling too much on what is ridiculous in subjects of taste, when transferred into life, has likewise a bad effect upon the character, if not softened by a large portion of humanity and good-humour, as it confers only a sullen and gloomy pleasure, by feeding the worst and most painful feelings of the human heart, envy and malignity: but an intimate acquaintance with the works of nature and genius in their most beautiful and amiable forms humanizes and sweetens the temper, opens and extends the imagination, and disposes to the most pleasing views of mankind and providence. By considering

sidering nature in this favourable point of view, the heart is dilated, and filled with the most benevolent sentiments; and then indeed the secret sympathy and connexion between the feelings of natural and moral beauty, the connexion between a good taste and a good heart, appears with the greatest lustre.

GREGORY.

TRUE ELEGANCE.

It has been observed that the mind has always a taste for truth, for gratitude, for generosity and greatness of soul; these, which are peculiarly called *sentiments*, stamp upon the human spirit a dignity and worth not to be found in any other animated being. However great and surprising the most glorious objects in nature be; the heaving ocean, the moon that guides it, and casts a soft lustre over the night; the starry firmament, or the sun itself; yet their beauty and grandeur instantly appear of an inferior kind, beyond all comparison, to this of the soul of man. These sentiments are united under the general name of virtue; and such are the embellishments they diffuse over the mind, that Plato, a very polite philosopher, says finely, 'If virtue was to appear in a visible 'shape, all men would be enamoured of her.'

Virtue and truth are inseparable, and take their flight together. A mind devoid of truth is a frightful wreck; it is like a great city in ruins, whose mouldering towers just bring to the imagination the mirth and life that once were there, and is now no more. Truth is the genius of taste, and enters into the essence of simple beauty, in wit, in writing, and throughout the fine arts.

Generosity

Generosity covers almost all other defects, and raises a blaze around them in which they disappear and are lost: like sovereign beauty it makes a short cut to our affections, it wins our hearts without resistance or delay, and unites all the world to favour and support its designs.

Grandeur of soul, fortitude and resolution, that haughtily struggles with despair, and will neither yield to, nor make terms with, misfortunes, which, through every situation, reposes a noble confidence in itself, and has an immovable view to future glory and honour, astonishes the world with admiration and delight. We, as it were, lean forward with surprise; and, trembling, joy to behold the human soul collecting its strength, and asserting a right to superior fates. When you leave man out of your account, and view the whole visible creation beside, you indeed see several traces of grandeur and unspeakable power, and the intermixture of a rich scenery of beauty; yet still the whole appears to be but a solemn absurdity, and to have a littleness and insignificancy; but when you restore man to the prospect, and put him at the head of it, endued with genius and an immortal soul; when you give him a a passion for truth, boundless views that spread along through eternity, and a fortitude that struggles with fate, and yields not to misfortunes; then the skies, the ocean, and the earth, take the stamp of worth and dignity from the noble inhabitant whose purposes they serve.

A mind fraught with the virtues is the natural soil of elegance. Unaffected truth, generosity, and grandeur of soul, for ever please and charm; even when they break from the common forms, and appear wild and unmethodized by education, they are still beautiful. On the contrary, as soon as we discover that outward elegance, which is formed by the mode, to want truth, generosity, or grandeur of soul, it instantly sinks in our esteem like counterfeit coin.

CLIO.

RIDICULE.

PEOPLE are rendered totally incapable of elegance by the want of good-nature and the other gentle passions; by the want of modesty and sensibility; and by a want of that noble pride which arises from a consciousness of lofty and generous sentiments. The absence of these native charms is generally supplied by a brisk stupidity, an impudence unconscious of defect, a cast of malice, and an uncommon tendency to ridicule; as if nature had given these her step-children an instinctive intelligence that they can rise out of contempt only by the depression of others. For the same reason it is that persons of true and finished taste seldom affect ridicule, because they are conscious of their own superior merit. Pride is the cause of ridicule in the one, as it is of candour in the other; but the effects differ, as the studied parade of poverty does from the negligent grandeur of riches. You will see nothing more common in the world than for people, who by stupidity and insensibility are incapable of the graces, to commence wits on the strength of the *petite* talents of mimicry, and the brisk tartness that ill-nature never fails to supply.

CLIO.

MUSIC.

MUSIC.

Music is the science of sounds so far as they affect the mind. Nature, independent of custom, has connected certain sounds or tones with certain feelings of the mind. Measure and proportion in sounds have likewise their foundation in nature. Thus certain tones are naturally adapted to solemn, plaintive, and mournful subjects, and the movement is slow; others are expressive of the joyous and elevating, and the movement is quick. Sounds likewise affect the mind as they are loud or soft, rough or smooth, distinct from the consideration of their gravity or acuteness. Thus in the Æolian harp the tones are pleasant and soothing, though there is no succession of notes varying in acuteness, but only in loudness. The effect of the common drum in rousing and elevating the mind is very strong, yet it has no variety of notes, though the effect indeed here depends much on the proportion and measure of the notes.

Melody consists in the agreeable succession of single sounds.—The melody that pleases in one country does not equally please in another, though there are certain general principles which universally regulate it, the scale of music being the same in all countries.—Harmony consists in the agreeable effects of sounds differing in acuteness produced together; the general principles of it are likewise fixed.

One end of music is merely to communicate pleasure by giving a slight and transient gratification to the ear; but the far nobler and more important is to command the passions and move the heart. In the first view it is an innocent amusement, well fitted to give an agreeable relaxation to the mind from the fatigue of study or business; in the other it is one of the most useful arts in life.

GREGORY.

AN ASSOCIATION OF IDEAS PRODUCED BY RURAL SOUNDS.

THERE is in souls a sympathy with sounds;
And as the mind is pitch'd the ear is pleas'd
With melting airs, or martial, brisk or grave:
Some chord in unison with what we hear
Is touch'd within us, and the heart replies.
How soft the music of those village bells
Falling at intervals upon the ear
In cadence sweet! Now dying all away,
Now pealing loud again, and louder still,
Clear and sonorous, as the gale comes on;
With easy force it opens all the cells
Where mem'ry slept. Wherever I have heard
A kindred melody the scene recurs,
And with it all its pleasures and its pains.
Such comprehensive views the spirit takes,
That in a few short moments I retrace
(As in a map the voyager his course)
The windings of my way through many years.
Short as in retrospect the journey seems,
It seem'd not always short; the rugged path,
And prospect oft so dreary and forlorn,
Mov'd many a sigh at its disheartening length:
Yet, feeling present evils, while the past

Faintly

Faintly impress the mind, or not at all,
How readily we wish time spent revok'd,
That we might try the ground again, where once
(Through inexperience, as we now perceive)
We miss'd that happiness we might have found!
Some friend is gone, perhaps his son's best friend,
A father, whose authority, in show
When most severe, and must'ring all its force,
Was but the graver countenance of love;
Whose favour, like the clouds of spring, might low'r,
And utter now and then an awful voice,
But had a blessing in its darkest frown,
Threat'ning at once and nourishing the plant.
We lov'd, but not enough, the gentle hand
That rear'd us. At a thoughtless age, allur'd
By every gilded folly, we renounc'd
His shelt'ring side, and wilfully forewent
That converse which we now in vain regret.
How gladly would the man recall to life
The boy's neglected sire! A mother too,
That softer friend, perhaps more gladly still,
Might he demand them at the gates of death.
Sorrow has, since they went, subdu'd and tam'd
The playful humour; he could now endure
(Himself grown sober in the vale of tears),
And feel a parent's presence no restraint.
But not to understand a treasure's worth
Till time has stol'n away the slighted good,
Is cause of half the poverty we feel,
And makes the world the wilderness it is.

         COWPER.

ESSAY ON TALKATIVENESS.

—— 'Empty bodies yield the greatest sound.'
ANON.

Some writer (whose name I cannot just now recollect) has observed that 'There is a wide difference between a man's saying nothing when in a mixed company, and having nothing to say.' This observation contains much truth; and it has been frequently verified, both to the reputation and disgrace of the respective characters.

Persons, whose tongues are in perpetual motion from 'morn to dewy eve,' are always disappointed, and sometimes disgusted, when they fall in company with one of your silent men. Being themselves strangers to thought and reflection, and accustomed, like parrots, to repeat by rote what they hear from others, they measure the extent of a man's understanding by the number of words he utters when in their company. That silence, which is at once the strongest and most delicate satire on the insignificancy and nothingness of common small-talk, is by such attributed to a deficiency in sense and abilities for conversation. Your unwearied chatterers value themselves highly on account of their volubility. They think every man beneath them, and unworthy of their favours, who cannot be as noisy and incoherent as themselves.

These geniuses may not unaptly be compared to those little bells the Chinese hang round their public temples, which are under no direction but that of the wind, but which every breeze puts in motion, and causes to give forth inarticulate and unmeaning sounds. As talking is the principal employment of their waking hours, and furnishes the greatest part of their happiness, silence is consequently their aversion. But, notwithstanding their loquacity, they seldom take any care to regulate their conversation so as to render it either entertaining, rational, or useful. It is sufficient for them that they can hear themselves, and are heard by others. No matter whether what they say means any thing; sound supplies the place of sense; and, by being indulged in their unmeaning verbocity, they are happy. If a man happens to be silent in their company they soon conclude he has nothing to say, and take great pains to be heard themselves, although what they are saying amounts to nothing. The same scanty portion of sense, which estimates the crude ebullitions of folly and inanity to be marks of wisdom, will always suppose silence to indicate a barren fancy and a weak understanding.

I was lately a witness of the effects which silence, in a gentleman who had much to say, produced in a company of voluble empty-headed prattlers, who took great delight in saying nothing to the purpose. The scene was in a stage-coach; a mode of travelling to me not disagreeable, as it frequently throws new characters in my way, which I generally contemplate with the taciturnity of a dumb spectator. I survey a new character with the same pleasing avidity that an astronomer would a new star, or an antiquarian a newly-discovered coin or relic of antiquity. But to return to the coach—We entered, six in number, about two hours before day-light. The company consisted of a waiting abigail to Lady Chatter, a rosy butler to Lord Bluster; the hostess of an inn, who, having lately lost her husband, was in weeds, and had all the care and weight of the business on her own hands; a perfumed milliner;

a gentleman of great sensibility and of a studious turn of mind, and myself. From the free use the major part of the *dramatis personæ* made of their tongues while the horses were putting to, I formed but an indifferent opinion of my company, except the gentleman above-mentioned, of whom I had some knowledge. Had not it been for the hope of receiving some rational entertainment from him, I should have put myself in a sleeping posture, at least till day-light enabled me to reconnoitre the enemy; but I was soon convinced this would have been in vain. I might as well have attempted to sleep in the workshop of a trunk-maker, or among the gossips at a country christening.

I presently found the butler and the three ladies (for so custom now obliges us to term all females who rank above the scourers of brass and pewter) were disposed to give each other the clearest demonstration of their respective abilities in the science of talking. Each of them, like a bottle of new small beer, seemed impatient to get vent; and so fond were they of exercising their vocal powers in the discovery of trite common-place knowledge, that there seemed little left for the rest to know. Law, politics, trade, fashions, good-breeding, were hauled into the dispute; but in such a manner did they handle and mangle every subject that it was soon evident they had no coherent ideas about any thing. In short, their conversation was a mere chaos of senseless jargon, which tired the ear without conveying any pleasure or instruction to the mind.

In the course of the debate, which was carried on with much vehemence of sound, they would frequently appeal to the gentleman for his assent to the justness of their remarks and the wisdom of their conclusions; but, as he generally answered them in monosyllables only, it was

easy

easy to perceive they soon formed a very contemptible idea of his understanding. This was for a while expressed by smiles, winks, nods, and half sentences; afterwards by more pointed proofs of disapprobation.

The waiting woman observed, with a toss of her head, that ' Every body isn't fit for company, as my lady says;
' that to be sure some was born to speak, and others to
' hear and larn; and that when a person have nothing to
' say why he must e'en hold his tongue, and hear them
' as can convarse porlitely.'

The butler, rising into dignity as he spoke, remarked that he had found by experience the office he *filled* (here his chest swelled) had greatly improved him; for that good liquors raised people's *genuses*, and gave free vent to discourse; that every one, as they might see, was'nt *collified* for *porlite* conversation; but that *them that was* should make use of their tongues for the benefit of them that cou'dn't speak for themselves.

' Aye, aye, Mr. Fasset,' said the landlady, ' I has
' no notion of your dull souls that can sit by the hour
' together like Methodists, and say nothing but yes
' or no like children. My tongue,' (here she bridled up)
' have brought a great deal of the best company to
' my house; and, between you and I,' (here she lowered her voice) ' they often tells me I am *never* at a loss
' what to say.' The word *never* being pronounced with a strong emphasis, she adjusted her handkerchief, and looked round on the company for a confirmation of what she had asserted. This she soon received in a volley of compliments as aukward as they were insincere. The milliner joined in the praises of conversation, and said she would as soon be a nun as to be so uncivil as to sit moping

with her finger in her mouth in such monstrous good company. 'Why, ladies, it is so intolerably impertinent, you
'know, to be so stupid—One can't bear one's self—I should
'die of the vapours presently if I did'nt talk—And then
''tis always expected, you know, of ladies in my way—
'Pray, Ma'am, isn't this new blond a perdidgus pretty
'pattern—And this ribbun—I assure you, Ma'am, 'tis
'just imported from Paris—Oh, how charming!'

At length I counterfeited sleep to avoid their impertinence, and for an hour or two sustained, without a moment's intermission,

'The shock of nonsense ringing in my ears.'

About nine we stopped to breakfast; and soon after we quitted the coach I overheard our female orators in the adjoining room treating us with the greatest ridicule and contempt for our silence, which the waiting woman said she was sure in such good company was intolerable, and could only proceed from our vast stupidity and monstrous ignorance of the world.

My friend, as well as myself, being heartily tired of their conversation, we discharged the coach, and took a chaise the remaining part of our journey. As we proceeded I could not help congratulating myself on being thus freed from the impertinence of my late companions, especially when my friend made the following observations on the folly of estimating a man's character by the number of words he utters in a public or mixed company.

'I have frequently wondered, Sir,' said he, 'that
'people, who do not appear destitute of common sense,
'should deem occasional silence an indication of weak in-
'tellects, and measure a man's understanding merely by
'the number of his words.

'Were

'Were this allowed to be a just criterion, we might
'readily admit our late companions among the class who
'possess the greatest abilities. But these incessant talkers
'seem ignorant that, while they burden others with their
'impertinence, they are laying a tax on themselves too
'heavy for human beings to sustain. Sense and wisdom
'are articles so scarce in the commerce of the tongue,
'that no individual possesses a stock sufficient to distribute
'them in every company, and on all occasions. Men of
'real abilities and knowledge are so diffident of them-
'selves, so conscious of the difficulty there is in talking
'sensibly and wisely on any subject long together, that in
'general their words are fewer than those of others. All
'conversation that has not a tendency to entertain the
'imagination, inform the understanding and the judgment,
'or to improve the mind, is, to all sensible persons, unpro-
'fitable, tedious, and disgusting.

'The passion for talking immoderately arises either
'from self-conceit or inconsideration; a high opinion of
'themselves, and a mean one of those they converse with.
'These are all indications of a little mind, in which pride
'occupies the place of modesty and good sense. Did they
'but give themselves the time and trouble of thinking
'before they speak, they would not utter so much folly.
'Could they but see the motley figure their conversation
'would make on paper, I think they must receive such
'full conviction of its absurdity as would check their
'ardour, and teach them to be less ridiculous in future.
'They would, on a retrospection, be convinced of their
'own insignificance, and learn to practise that silence
'which the vanity of their own hearts has led them
'to despise in others.

'In

'In the course of my observation I have remarked that persons who possess most sense and knowledge are the most cautious of discovering it in common company. They seek not to shine out of their proper sphere; and are generally sparing of their discourse in public. Such display not their knowledge through ostentation, 'to 'make the unlearned stare,' but reserve it for those who are qualified to receive it with advantage and pleasure, and repay it with interest. They have no pleasure in the common insignificant chit-chat of the vulgar, where mere common-place sounds are reverberated from one solid head to another without exciting ideas or increasing knowledge; but when they cannot retreat from this penance are content to suffer in silence. By these means they preserve their sentiments till occasions offer wherein they may be communicated with advantage and pleasure both to themselves and others.

'The mind, like the body, must concoct and digest what it receives before it can be really benefited or benefit others by it. There is more advantage gained in silence and reflection than little minds can comprehend. Sentiments and ideas which are received without thought, and bolted out on every occasion, unmatured by reflection and judgment, are like 'the crackling of thorns under 'a pot;' they are noisy, and may flash for a moment, without animating, and then sink and expire in smoke and darkness.

'The mind that is collected within itself, and feeds on its own stock, will neither thirst after nor relish that vulgar vapid aliment which floats on the impertinent tongues of the common throng.

'It

'It is a kind of food which reason cannot partake of, nor sense approve. But those superficial minds, who have no entertainment within themselves, who are indebted to the news of the day, or the puerile conversation of every one they meet; for subsistence, are truly in a very pitiable situation. They verify the words of the Oriental moralist: "A fool is full of words, but the heart proclaimeth foolishness, while a prudent man concealeth knowledge."'

RACK.

ON TELLING OF SECRETS.

THERE is, besides, a very general inclination amongst us to hear a secret, to whomsoever it relates, known or unknown to us, of whatever import, serious or trifling, so it be but a secret: the delight of telling it and of hearing it are nearly proportionate and equal. The possessor of the valuable treasure appears, indeed, rather to have the advantage; and he seems to claim his superiority. I have discovered at once in a large company, by an air and deportment that is assumed upon such occasions, who it is that is conscious of this happy charge: he appears restless and full of doubt for a considerable time, has frequent consultations with himself, like a bee undetermined where to settle in a variety of sweets; till at last one happy ear attracts him more forcibly than the rest, and there he fixes, 'stealing and giving odours.'

In a little time it becomes a matter of great amazement that the whole town is as well acquainted with the story as the two who were so busily engaged; and the consternation is greater as each reporter is confident that he only

only communicated it to one person. 'A report,' says Strada, 'thus transmitted from one to one, is like a drop 'of water at the top of a house; it descends but from tile 'to tile, yet at last makes its way to the gutter, and then 'is involved in the general stream.' And, if I may add to the comparison, the drop of water, after its progress through all the channels of the street, is not more contaminated with filth and dirt, than a simple story after it has passed through the mouths of a few modern talebearers.

ADVENTURER.

Out of the same mouth proceedeth blessing and cursing. My brethren, these things ought not so to be. Doth a fountain send forth at the same place sweet water and bitter? Can the fig-tree, my brethren, bear olive-berries? either a vine figs? So can no fountain both yield salt water and fresh. Who is a wise man, and endued with knowledge amongst you? let him shew out of a good conversation his works with meekness of wisdom. But if ye have bitter envying and strife in your hearts, glory not, and lie not against the truth. This wisdom descendeth not from above, but is earthly, sensual, devilish. For where envying and strife is there is confusion, and every evil work. But the wisdom that is from above is first pure, then peaceable, gentle, and easy to be entreated, full of mercy and good fruits, without partiality, and without hypocrisy. And the fruit of righteousness is sown in peace of them that make peace.

JAMES.

JUSTICE DEFINED.

Mankind in general are not sufficiently acquainted with the import of the word justice: it is commonly believed to consist only in a performance of those duties to which the laws of society can oblige us. This I allow is sometimes the import of the word, and in this sense justice is distinguished from equity; but there is a justice still more extensive, and which can be shewn to embrace all the virtues united.

Justice may be defined—that virtue which impels us to give to every person what is his due. In this extended sense of the word it comprehends the practice of every virtue which reason prescribes or society should expect. Our duty to our Maker, to each other, and to ourselves, are fully answered if we give them what we owe them. Thus justice, properly speaking, is the only virtue; and all the rest have their origin in it.

The qualities of candour, fortitude, charity, and generosity, for instance, are not in their natures virtues; and if ever they deserve the title it is owing only to justice, which impels and directs them. Without such a moderator, candour might become indiscretion, fortitude obstinacy, charity imprudence, and generosity mistaken profusion.

A disinterested action, if it be not conducted by justice, is, at best, indifferent in its nature, and not unfrequently even turns to vice. The expenses of society, of presents, of entertainments, and the other helps to cheerfulness, are actions merely indifferent, when not repugnant to a

better

better method of disposing of our superfluities; but they become vicious when they obstruct or exhaust our abilities from a more virtuous disposition of our circumstances. True generosity is a duty as indispensably necessary as those imposed on us by law. It is a rule imposed on us by reason, which should be the sovereign law of a rational being. But this generosity does not consist in obeying every impulse of humanity, in following blind passion for our guide, and impairing our circumstances by present benefactions, so as to render us incapable of future ones.

GOLDSMITH.

ON COVETOUSNESS.

And he spake a parable unto them, saying, The ground of a certain rich man brought forth plentifully. And he thought within himself, saying, What shall I do, because I have no room where to bestow my fruits? And he said, This will I do: I will pull down my barns and build greater; and there will I bestow all my fruits and my goods. And I will say to my soul, Soul, thou hast much goods laid up for many years: take thine ease, eat, drink, and be merry. But God said unto him, Thou fool, this night thy soul shall be required of thee: then whose shall those things be which thou hast provided? So is he that layeth up treasure for himself, and is not rich towards God.

And he said unto his disciples, Therefore I say unto you, take no thought for your life what ye shall eat; neither for the body what ye shall put on. The life is more than meat, and the body is more than raiment. Consider the ravens: for they neither sow nor reap; which
neither

neither have storehouse nor barn; and God feedeth them: how much more are ye better than the fowls? And which of you with taking thought can add to his stature one cubit? If ye then be not able to do that thing which is least, why take ye thought for the rest? Consider the lilies, how they grow: they toil not, they spin not; and yet I say unto you, that Solomon in all his glory was not arrayed like one of these. If then God so clothe the grass, which is to-day in the field and to-morrow is cast into the oven, how much more will he clothe you, O ye of little faith? And seek not ye what ye shall eat or what ye shall drink, neither be ye of doubtful mind; for all these things do the nations of the world seek after: and your Father knoweth that ye have need of these things.

But rather seek ye the kingdom of God; and all these things shall be added unto you. S. LUKE.

TRUE PLEASURE DEFINED.

WE are affected with delightful sensations when we see the inanimate parts of the creation, the meadows, flowers, and trees, in a flourishing state. There must be some rooted melancholy at the heart, when all nature appears smiling about us, to hinder us from corresponding with the rest of the creation, and joining in the universal chorus of joy. But if meadows and trees in their bloom, and all the vegetable parts of the creation in their most advantageous dress, can inspire gladness into the heart, and drive away all sadness but despair, to see the rational creation happy and flourishing ought to give us a pleasure as much

superior

superior as the latter is to the former in the scale of beings. But the pleasure is still heightened if we ourselves have been instrumental in contributing to the happiness of our fellow-creatures, if we have helped to raise an heart drooping beneath the weight of grief, and revived that barren and dry land where no water was with refreshing showers of love and kindness.

SEED.

TRUE END OF LIFE.

Reflect that life and death, affecting sounds,
Are only varied modes of endless being:
Reflect that life, like every other blessing,
Derives its value from its use alone:
Not for itself, but for a nobler end
Th' Eternal gave it, and that end is virtue.
When inconsistent with a greater good,
Reason commands to cast the less away;
Thus life with loss of wealth is well preserv'd,
And virtue cheaply sav'd with loss of life.

JOHNSON.

A LETTER ON LETTER-WRITING.

I thank you for you letter, because there are manifest signs in it of your endeavouring to excel yourself, and by consequence to please me. You have succeeded in both respects; and will always succeed, if you think it worth your while to consider what you write, and to whom, and let nothing, though of a trifling nature, pass through your pen negligently; get but the way of writing correctly and justly, time and use will teach you to write readily afterwards; not but that too much care may give a stiffness to your style, which ought in letters, by all means, to be avoided. The turn of them should be always natural and easy, for they are an image of private and familiar conversation. I mention this with respect to the four or five first lines of yours, which have an air of poetry, and do therefore naturally resolve themselves into blank verses. I send you your letter again, that yourself may now make the same observation. But you took the hint of that thought from a poem, and it is no wonder, therefore, that you heightened the phrase a little when you were expressing it. The rest is as it should be; and particularly there is an air of duty and sincerity, which, if it comes from your heart, is the most acceptable present you can make me. With these good qualities an incorrect letter would please me, and without them the finest thoughts and language would make no lasting impression on me. The Great Being says, you know, *My son, give me thy heart*; implying, that without it all other gifts signify nothing. Let me conjure you, therefore, never to say any thing, either in a letter or common conversation, that you do not think, but always to let your mind and your words go together on the most trivial occasions. Shelter not the least degree of insincerity under the notion of a compliment; which, as far as it deserves to be practised by a man of probity, is only the most civil and obliging way of saying what you really mean; and whoever employs it otherwise throws away truth for breeding: I need not tell you how little his character gets by such an exchange.

I say

I say not this as if I suspected that in any part of your letter you intended to write what was proper, without any regard to what was true; for I am resolved to believe that you were in earnest from the beginning to the end of it, as much as I am, when I tell you that I am,

Your loving father, &c.

Bp. ATTERBURY.

THE ADVANTAGES ARISING FROM READING.

To read with profit and advantage we should read with attention and deliberation, and endeavour to improve the truths we read by remembrance. Without attention in in reading it is impossible to remember, and without remembering it is time and labour lost to read or learn.

Bishop Sanderson having acquired a large fund of useful knowledge was once asked how he attained it; the inquirer supposing he must have read a great number of books. The Bishop answered that he had read but very few, but that those authors he had read were well chosen: that he had made them his study, and had never let a single sentence pass without thoroughly making himself master of the author's meaning.

'There are some persons,' says Dr. Watts, 'who never
' arrive at any deep, solid, or valuable knowledge in any
' science or business of life, because they are perpetually
' fluttering over the surface of things in endless search of
' variety; ever inquiring after something that is new, with-
' out taking any pains to lay up and preserve the ideas they
' have gained. Their minds may be compared to a look-
' ing-glass, which receives a variety of impressions without
' retaining any.'

BOOK III.

ALLEGORIES AND PATHETIC PIECES,

A VISION.

I was yesterday comparing the industry of man with that of other creatures; in which I could not but observe that, notwithstanding we are obliged by duty to keep ourselves in constant employ, after the same manner as inferior animals are prompted to it by instinct, we fall very short of them in this particular. We are here the more inexcusable, because there is a greater variety of business to which we may apply ourselves. Reason opens to us a large field of affairs which other creatures are not capable of. Beasts of prey, and I believe all other kinds, in their natural state of being, divide their time between action and rest; they are always at work or asleep: in short, their waking hours are wholly taken up in seeking after their food, or in consuming it. The human species only, to the great reproach of our natures, are filled with complaints—that the day hangs heavy on them, that they do not know what to do with themselves, that they are at a loss how to pass away their time, with many of the like shameful murmurs, which we often find in the mouths of those who are styled reasonable beings. How monstrous are such expressions among creatures who have the labours of the mind, as well as those of the body, to furnish them with proper employments; who, besides the business of their callings and professions, can apply themselves to the duties of religion, to meditation, to the reading of useful books, to discourse; in a word, who may exercise themselves in the unbounded pursuits of knowledge and virtue, and every hour of their lives make themselves wiser or better than they were before.

After having been taken up for some time in this course of thought, I diverted myself with a book, according to my usual custom, in order to unbend my mind before I went to sleep. The book I made use of on this occasion was Lucian, where I amused my thoughts for about an hour among the dialogues of the dead, which in all probability produced the following dream:

I was conveyed methought into the entrance of the infernal regions, where I saw Rhadamanthus, one of the judges of the dead, seated on his tribunal. On his left hand stood the keeper of Erebus, on his right the keeper of Elysium; I was told he sat upon women that day, there being several of the sex lately arrived who had not as yet their mansions assigned them. I was surprised to hear him ask every one of them the same question, namely, *What they had been doing?* Upon this question being proposed to the whole assembly, they stared one upon another as not knowing what to answer; he then interrogated each of them separately: Madam, says he to the first of them, you have been upon the earth about fifty years, what have you been doing there all this while? Doing, says she, really

really I don't know what I have been doing; I desire I may have time given me to recollect. After about half an hour's pause she told him that she had been playing at crimp; upon which Rhadamanthus beckoned to the keeper on his left hand to take her into custody. And you, Madam, says the Judge, that look with such a soft and languishing air; I think you set out for this place in your nine-and-twentieth year; what have you been doing all this while? I had a great deal of business on my hand, says she, being taken up the first twelve years of my life in dressing a jointed baby, and all the remaining part of it in reading plays and romances. Very well, says he, you have employed your time to good purpose.—Away with her. The next was a plain country woman: Well, Mistress, says Rhadamanthus, and what have you been doing? An't please your Worship, says she, I did not live quite forty years; and in that time brought my husband seven daughters, made him nine thousand cheeses, and left my eldest girl with him, to look after his house in my absence; and who, I may venture to say, is as pretty a housewife as any in the country. Rhadamanthus smiled at the simplicity of the good woman, and ordered the keeper of Elysium to take her into his care. And you, fair lady, says he, what have you been doing these five-and-thirty years? I have been doing no hurt, I assure you, Sir, said she. That is well, says he, but what good have you been doing? The lady was in great confusion at this question, and not knowing what to answer, the two keepers leaped out to seize her at the same time; the one took her by the hand to convey her to Elysium, the other caught hold of her to carry her to Erebus; but Rhadamanthus observing an ingenuous modesty in her countenance and behaviour, bid them both let her loose, and set her aside for a re-examination when he was more at leisure. An old woman of a proud and sour look presented herself next at the bar, and being asked what she had been doing? Truly, says she, I lived threescore and ten years in a very wicked world; and was so angry at the behaviour of a parcel of young flirts, that I past almost all my last years in condemning the follies of the times; I was every day blaming the silly conduct of people about me, in order to deter those I conversed with from falling into the like errors and miscarriages. Very well, says Rhadamanthus, but did you keep the same watchful eye over your own actions? Why, truly, says she, I was so taken up with publishing the faults of others, that I had no time to consider my own. Madam, says Rhadamanthus, be pleased to file off to the left, and make room for the venerable matron that stands behind you. Old gentlewoman, says he, I think you are fourscore? you have heard the question, what have you been doing so long in the world? Ah, Sir, says she, I have been doing what I should not have done; but I had made a firm resolution to have changed my life, if I had not been snatched off by an untimely end. Madam, says he, you will please to follow your leader; and, spying another of the same age, interrogated her in the same form. To which the matron replied, I have been the wife of a husband who was as dear to me in his old age as in his youth. I have been a mother, and very happy in my children, whom I endeavoured to bring up in every thing that is good; my eldest son is blest by the poor, and beloved by every one that knows him: I lived within my income, and left my family much more wealthy than I found it. Rhadamanthus,

manthus, who knew the value of the old lady, smiled upon her in such a manner, that the keeper of Elysium, who knew his office, reached out his hand to her; he no sooner touched her but her wrinkles vanished, her eyes sparkled, her cheeks glowed with blushes, and she appeared in full bloom and beauty. A young woman, observing that this officer who conducted the happy to Elysium was so great a beautifier, longed to be in his hands; so that, pressing thro' the crowd, she was the next who appeared at the bar, and being asked what she had been doing the five-and-twenty years that she had passed in the world; I have endeavoured, says she, ever since I came to years of discretion, to make myself lovely and to gain admirers: in order to it I passed my time in bottling up May-dew, inventing white washes, mixing colours, cutting out patches, consulting my glass, suiting my complexion, tearing off my tucker, sinking my stays. Rhadamanthus, without hearing her out, gave the sign to take her off. Upon the approach of the keeper of Erebus her colour faded, her face puckered up with wrinkles, and her whole person was lost in deformity.

I was then surprised with a distant sound of a whole troop of females that came forward laughing, singing, and dancing: I was very desirous to know the reception they would meet with, and withal was very apprehensive that Rhadamanthus would spoil their mirth; but at their nearer approach the noise grew so very great that it awaked me.

GUARDIAN.

CARAZAN: A VISION.

ON SOCIAL LOVE.

CARAZAN, the merchant of Bagdat, was eminent throughout all the East for his avarice and his wealth: his origin was obscure as that of the spark which, by the collision of steel and adamant, is struck out of darkness; and the patient labour of persevering diligence alone had made him rich. It was remembered that when he was indigent he was thought to be generous, and he was still acknowledged to be inexorably just. But whether in his dealings with men he discovered a perfidy which tempted him to put his trust in gold; or whether in proportion as he accumulated wealth he discovered his own importance to increase; Carazan prized it more as he used it less: he gradually lost the inclination to do good as he acquired the power; and as the hand of time scattered snow upon his head the freezing influence extended to his bosom.

But, though the door of Carazan was never opened by hospitality, nor his hand by compassion, yet fear led him constantly to the mosque at the stated hours of prayer; he performed all the rites of devotion with the most scrupulous punctuality, and had thrice paid his vows at the temple of the prophet. That devotion which rises from the love of God, and necessarily includes the love of man, as it connects gratitude with beneficence, and exalts that which was mortal to divine, confers new dignity upon goodness, and is the object not only of affection but reverence. On the contrary, the devotion of the selfish,

whether

whether it be thought to avert the punishment which every one wishes to be inflicted, or to ensure it by the complication of hypocrisy with guilt, never fails to excite indignation and abhorrence. Carazan, therefore, when he had locked his door, and, turning round with a look of circumspective suspicion, proceeded to the mosque, was followed by every eye with silent malignity; the poor suspended their supplications when he passed by; and though he was known by every man yet no man saluted him.

Such had long been the life of Carazan, and such was the character which he had acquired, when notice was given by proclamation that he was removed to a magnificent building in the centre of the city; that his table should be spread for the public, and that the stranger should be welcome to his bed. The multitude soon rushed like a torrent to his door, where they beheld him distributing bread to the hungry, and apparel to the naked; his eye softened with compassion, and his cheek glowing with delight. Every one gazed with astonishment at the prodigy; and the murmur of innumerable voices increasing like the sound of approaching thunder, Carazan beckoned with his hand; attention suspended the tumult in a moment, and he thus gratified the curiosity which had procured him audience.

To him who touches the mountains and they smoke, the Almighty and the most merciful, be everlasting honour! He has ordained sleep to be the minister of instruction, and his visions have reproved me in the night. As I was sitting alone in my Haram, with my lamp burning before me, computing the product of my merchandise, and exulting in the increase of my wealth, I fell into a deep sleep, and the hand of him who dwells in the third heaven was upon me. I beheld the angel of death coming forward like a whirlwind, and he smote me before I could deprecate the blow; at the same moment I felt myself lifted from the ground, and transported with astonishing rapidity through the regions of the air: the earth was contracted to an atom beneath, and the stars glowed round me with a lustre that obscured the sun: the gate of Paradise was now in sight; and I was intercepted by a sudden brightness which no human eye could behold: the irrevocable sentence was now to be pronounced; my day of probation was past; and from the evil of my life nothing could be taken away, nor could any thing be added to the good. When I reflected that my lot for eternity was cast, which not all the powers of nature could reverse, my confidence totally forsook me; and, while I stood trembling and silent, covered with confusion and chilled with horror, I was thus addressed by the radiance that flamed before me.

' Carazan, thy worship has not been accepted, be-
' cause it was not prompted by the love of God; neither
' can thy righteousness be rewarded, because it was not
' produced by the love of man; for thy own sake only hast
' thou rendered to every man his due; and thou hast ap-
' proached the Almighty only for thyself. Thou hast not
' looked up with gratitude, nor round thee with kindness.
' Around thee thou hast indeed beheld vice and folly, but if
' vice and folly could justify thy parsimony, would they not
' condemn the bounty of heaven? If not upon the foolish and
' the vicious, where shall the sun diffuse his light, or the
' clouds distil their dew? Where shall the lips of the spring
' breathe fragrance, or the hand of autumn diffuse plenty?
' Remember, Carazan, that thou hast shut compassion from
' thine heart, and grasped thy treasures with a hand of iron:
' thou

'thou hast lived for thyself; and, therefore, henceforth for
'ever thou shalt subsist alone. From the light of heaven,
'and from the society of all beings, shalt thou be driven;
'solitude shall protract the lingering hours of eternity, and
'darkness aggravate the horrors of despair.'

At this moment I was driven by some secret and irresistible power through the glowing system of creation, and passed innumerable worlds in a moment; as I approached the verge of nature I perceived the shadows of total and boundless vacuity deepen before me, a dreadful region of eternal silence, solitude and darkness! unutterable horror seized me at the prospect, and this exclamation burst from me with all the vehemence of desire: *Oh! that I had been doomed for ever to the common receptacle of impenitence and guilt: there society would have alleviated the torment of despair, and the rage of fire could not have excluded the comfort of light: or, if I had been condemned to reside in a comet, that would return but once in a thousand years to the regions of light and life; the hope of these periods, however distant, would cheer men in the dreary interval of cold and darkness, and the vicissitude would divide eternity into time.* While this thought passed over my mind I lost sight of the remotest star, and the last glimmering of light was quenched in utter darkness. The agonies of despair increased every moment, as every moment augmented my distance from the last habitable world; I recollected with intolerable anguish that, when ten thousand thousand years had carried me beyond the reach of all but that power who fills infinitude, I should still look forward into an immense abyss of darkness, through which I should still drive without succour and without society, farther and farther still, for ever and for ever. I then stretched out my hand towards the regions of existence, with an emotion that awaked me. Thus have I been taught to estimate society, like every other blessing, by its loss; my heart is warmed to liberality, and I am zealous to communicate the happiness which I feel to those from whom it is derived; for the society of one wretch whom, in the pride of prosperity, I would have spurned from my door, would, in the dreadful solitude to which I was condemned, have been more highly prized than the gold of Afric or the gems of Golconda.

At this reflexion upon his dream Carazan became suddenly silent, and looked upwards in an ecstasy of gratitude and devotion. The multitude was struck at once with the precept and example; and the caliph, to whom the event was related, that he might be liberal beyond the power of gold, commanded it to be recorded for the benefit of posterity.

ADVENTURER.

VERSES;

Supposed to be written by ALEXANDER SELKIRK, during his solitary abode in the island of JUAN FERNANDEZ.

I AM monarch of all I survey,
  My right there is none to dispute,
From the centre all round to the sea,
  I am lord of the fowl and the brute.
Oh Solitude! where are the charms
  That sages have seen in thy face?
Better dwell in the midst of alarms
  Than reign in this horrible place.

II.

I am out of Humanity's reach,
   I must finish my journey alone,
Never hear the sweet music of speech,
   I start at the sound of my own.
The beasts that roam over the plain
   My form with indifference see,
They are so unacquainted with man
   Their tameness is shocking to me.

III.

Society, friendship, and love,
   Divinely bestow'd upon man,
Oh had I the wings of a dove
   How soon would I taste you again!
My sorrows I then might assuage
   In the ways of religion and truth,
Might learn from the wisdom of age,
   And be cheer'd by the sallies of youth.

IV.

Religion! what treasure untold
   Resides in that heavenly word!
More precious than silver and gold,
   Or all that this world can afford.
But the sound of the church-going bell
   These vallies and rocks never heard,
Ne'er sigh'd at the sound of a knell,
   Or smil'd when a sabbath appear'd.

V.

Ye winds, that have made me your sport,
  Convey to this desolate shore
Some cordial endearing report
  Of the land I shall visit no more.
My friends, do they now and then send
  A wish or a thought after me?
O! tell me I yet have a friend,
  Though a friend I am never to see.

VI.

How fleet is a glance of the mind!
  Compar'd with the speed of its flight,
The tempest itself lags behind,
  And the swift winged arrows of light.
When I think of my own native land
  In a moment I seem to be there;
But alas! recollection at hand
  Soon hurries me back to despair.

VII.

But the sea-fowl is gone to her nest,
  The beast is laid down in his lair;
Ev'n here is a season of rest,
  And I to my cabin repair.
There is mercy in every place,
  And mercy, encouraging thought!
Gives even affliction a grace,
  And reconciles man to his lot.

COWPER.

AN ALLEGORY.

'Life,' says Seneca, ' is a voyage, in the progress of
' which we are perpetually changing our scenes: we first
' leave childhood behind us, then youth, then the years
' of ripened manhood, then the better or more pleasing
' part of old age.' The perusal of this passage having in-
cited in me a train of reflections on the state of man, the
incessant fluctuation of his wishes, the gradual change of
his disposition to all external objects, and the thoughtless-
ness with which he floats along the stream of time, I sunk
into a slumber amidst my meditations, and, on a sudden,
found my ears filled with the tumult of labour, the shouts
of alacrity, the shrieks of alarm, the whistle of winds, and
the dash of waters.

My astonishment for a time repressed my curiosity; but,
soon recovering myself so far as to inquire whither we
were going, and what was the cause of such clamour and
confusion, I was told that they were launching out into
the ocean of life; that we had already passed the Streights
of Infancy, in which multitudes had perished, some by the
weakness and fragility of their vessels, and more by the
folly, perverseness, or negligence of those who undertook
to steer them; and that we were now on the main sea,
abandoned to the winds and billows, without any other
means of security than the care of the pilot, whom it was
always in our power to chuse, among great numbers that
offered their direction and assistance.

I then looked round with anxious eagerness; and first
turning my eyes behind me saw a stream flowing through
flowery islands, which every one that sailed along seemed

to behold with pleasure; but no sooner touched than the current, which, though not noisy or turbulent, was yet irresistible, bore him away. Beyond these islands all was darkness; nor could any of the passengers describe the shore at which he first embarked.

Before me, and each other side, was an expanse of waters violently agitated, and covered with so thick a mist, that the most perspicuous eyes could see but a little way. It appeared to be full of rocks and whirlpools, for many sunk unexpectedly while they were courting the gale with full sails, and insulting those whom they had left behind. So numerous indeed were the dangers, and so thick the darkness, that no caution could confer security. Yet there were many, who, by false intelligence, betrayed their followers into whirlpools, or by violence pushed those whom they found in their way against the rocks.

The current was invariable and insurmountable; but, though it was impossible to sail against it, or to return to the place that was once passed, yet it was not so violent as to allow no opportunities for dexterity or courage; since, though none could retreat back from danger, yet they might often avoid it by oblique direction.

It was however not very common to steer with much care or prudence; for, by some universal infatuation, every man appeared to think himself safe, though he saw his consorts every moment sinking round him; and no sooner had the waves closed over them than their fate and their misconduct were forgotten; the voyage was pursued with the same jocund confidence; every man congratulated himself upon the soundness of his vessel, and believed himself able to stem the whirlpool in which his friend was swallowed, or glide over the rocks on which he was dashed; nor was it

often

often observed that the sight of a wreck made any man change his course; if he turned aside for a moment he soon forgot the rudder, and left himself again to the disposal of chance.

This negligence did not proceed from indifference, or from weariness of their present condition; for not one of those who thus rushed upon destruction failed, when he was sinking, to call loudly upon his associates for that help which could not now be given him: and many spent their last moments in cautioning others against the folly by which they were intercepted in the midst of their course. Their benevolence was sometimes praised, but their admonitions were unregarded.

The vessels in which we had embarked, being confessedly unequal to the turbulence of the stream of life, were visibly impaired in the course of the voyage, so that every passenger was certain that, how long soever he might by favourable accidents, or by incessant vigilance, be preserved, he must sink at last.

This necessity of perishing might have been expected to sadden the gay and intimidate the daring, at least to keep the melancholy and timorous in perpetual torments, and hinder them from any enjoyment of the varieties and gratifications which nature offered them as the solace of their labours; yet in effect none seemed less to expect destruction than those to whom it was most dreadful; they had all the art of concealing their danger from themselves; and those, who knew their inability to bear the sight of the terrors that embarrassed their way, took care never to look forward, but found some amusement for the present moment, and generally entertained themselves by playing with Hope, who was the constant associate of the voyage of life.

Yet

Yet all that Hope ventured to promise, even to those whom she favoured most, was, not that they should escape, but that they should sink last; and with this promise every one was satisfied, though he laughed at the rest for seeming to believe it. Hope, indeed, apparently mocked the credulity of her companions; for, in proportion as their vessels grew leaky, she redoubled her assurances of safety; and none were more busy in making provisions for a long voyage, than they whom all but themselves saw likely to perish soon by irreparable decay.

In the midst of the current of Life was the gulf of Intemperance, a dreadful whirlpool, interspersed with rocks, of which the pointed crags were concealed under water, and the tops covered with herbage, on which Ease spread couches of repose, and with shades, where Pleasure warbled the song of invitation: within sight of these rocks, all who sailed on the ocean of Life must necessarily pass. Reason indeed was always at hand to steer passengers through a narrow outlet, by which they might escape, but very few could, by her entreaties or remonstrances, be induced to put the rudder into her hand, without stipulating that she should approach so near unto the rocks of Pleasure, that they might solace themselves with a short enjoyment of that delicious region, after which they always determined to pursue their course without any other deviation.

Reason was too often prevailed upon so far by these promises, as to venture her charge within the eddy of the gulf of Intemperance, where, indeed, the circumvolution was weak, but yet interrupted the course of the vessel, and drew it, by insensible rotations, towards the centre. She then repented her temerity, and with all her force endeavoured

deavoured to retreat, but the draught of the gulf was generally too strong to be overcome; and the passenger, having danced in circles with a pleasing and giddy velocity, was at last overwhelmed and lost. Those few, whom reason was able to extricate, generally suffered so many shocks upon the points which shot out from the rocks of Pleasure, that they were unable to continue their course with the same strength and facility as before, but floated along timorously and feebly, endangered by every breeze, and shattered by every ruffle of the water, till they sunk, by slow degrees, after long struggles and innumerable expedients, always repining at their own folly, and warning others against the first approach of the gulf of Intemperance.

There were artists who professed to repair the breaches and stop the leaks of the vessels which had been shattered on the rocks of Pleasure. Many appeared to have great confidence in their skill; and some, indeed, were preserved by it from sinking, who had received only a single blow; but I remarked that few vessels lasted long which had been much repaired, nor was it found that the artists themselves continued afloat longer than those who had least of their assistance.

The only advantage, which in the voyage of Life the cautious had above the negligent, was, that they sunk later, and more suddenly; for they passed forward till they had sometimes seen all those, in whose company they had issued from the streights of Infancy, perish in the way, and at last were overset by a cross breeze, without the toil of resistance or the anguish of expectation. But such as had often fallen against the rocks of Pleasure commonly subsided by sensible degrees, contended long with
the

the encroaching waters, and harassed themselves by labours that scarcely Hope herself could flatter with success.

As I was looking upon the various fate of the multitude about me, I was suddenly alarmed with an admonition from some unknown power, 'Gaze not idly upon others 'when thou thyself art sinking. Whence is this thought-'less tranquillity, when thou and they are equally endan-'gered?' I looked, and, seeing the gulf of Intemperance before me, started and awaked.

RAMBLER.

PITY: AN ALLEGORY.

In the happy period of the Golden Age, when all the celestial inhabitants descended to the earth and conversed familiarly with mortals, among the most cherished of the heavenly powers were twins, the offspring of Jupiter, Love and Joy. Where they appeared the flowers sprung up beneath their feet, the sun shone with a brighter radiance, and all nature seemed embellished by their presence. They were inseparable companions, and their growing attachment was favoured by Jupiter, who had decreed that a lasting union should be solemnized between them as soon they arrived at maturer years. But, in the mean time, the sons of men deviated from their native innocence, vice and ruin overran the earth with giant strides, and Astrea, with her train of celestial visitants, forsook their polluted abodes. Love alone remained, having been stolen away by Hope, who was his nurse, and conveyed by her to the forests of Arcadia, where he was brought up among the shepherds. But Jupiter assigned him a different

rent partner, and commanded him to espouse Sorrow, the daughter of Até. He complied with reluctance; for her features were harsh and disagreeable, her eyes sunk, her forehead contracted into perpetual wrinkles, and her temples were covered with a wreath of cypress and wormwood. From this union sprung a virgin in whom might be traced a strong resemblance to both her parents, but the sullen and unamiable features of her mother were so mixed and blended with the sweetness of her father that her countenance, though mournful, was highly pleasing. The maids and shepherds of the neighbouring plains gathered round and called her Pity. A redbreast was observed to build in the cabin where she was born; and, while she was an infant, a dove, pursued by a hawk, flew into her bosom. This nymph had a dejected appearance, but so soft and gentle a mien that she was beloved to a degree of enthusiasm. Her voice was low and plaintive, but inexpressively sweet; and she loved to lie for hours together on the banks of some wild and melancholy stream singing to her lute. She taught men to weep, for she took strange delight in tears; and often, when the virgins of the hamlet were assembled at their evening sports, she would steal in amongst them, and captivate their hearts by her tales full of a charming sadness. She wore on her head a garland, composed of her father's myrtles, twisted with her mother's cypress.

One day, as she sat musing by the waters of Helicon, her tears by chance fell into the fountain; and ever since the Muses' spring has retained a strong taste of the infusion. Pity was commanded by Jupiter to follow the steps of her mother through the world, dropping balm into the wounds she made, and binding up the hearts she had broken.

ken. She follows with her hair loose, her bosom bare and throbbing, her garments torn by the briers, and her feet bleeding with the roughness of the path. The nymph is mortal, for her mother is so; and when she has fulfilled her destined course upon the earth, they shall both expire together, and Love be again united to Joy, his immortal and long-betrothed bride.

AIKIN'S MISCELL.

ESTHER's INTERVIEW WITH THE KING.

AND upon the third day, when she had ended her prayer, she laid away her mourning garments, and put on her glorious apparel. And being gloriously adorned, after she had called upon God, who is the beholder and saviour of all things, she took two maids with her. And upon the one she leaned, as carrying herself daintily; and the other followed, bearing up her train: and she was ruddy through the perfection of her beauty, and her countenance was cheerful, and very amiable: but her heart was in anguish for fear.

Then, having passed through all the doors, she stood before the king, who sat upon his royal throne, and was clothed with all his robes of majesty, all glittering with gold and precious stones; and he was very dreadful.

Then, lifting up his countenance that shone with majesty, he looked very fiercely upon her; and the queen fell down, and was pale, and fainted, and bowed herself upon the head of the maid that went before her.

Then God changed the spirit of the king into mildness, who in a fear leaped from his throne, and took her in his arms, till she came to herself again, and comforted her with loving words, and said unto her, Esther, what is the matter? I am thy brother, be of good cheer. Thou shalt not die, though our commandment be general: come near. And so he held up his golden sceptre, and laid it on her neck; and embraced her, and said, Speak unto me. Then she said unto him, I saw thee, my lord, as an angel of God, and my heart was troubled for fear of thy majesty. For wonderful art thou, lord, and thy countenance is full of grace. And as she was speaking she fell down for faintness. Then the king was troubled, and all his servants comforted her.

ESTHER.

ST. PAUL TAKING LEAVE OF HIS FRIENDS.

AND from Miletus he sent to Ephesus and called the elders of the church. And when they were come to him he said unto them, Ye know from the first day that I came into Asia after what manner I have been with you at all seasons, serving the Lord with all humility of mind, and with many tears and temptations, which befell me by the lying in wait of the Jews: and how I kept back nothing that was profitable unto you, but have shewed you, and have taught you publicly, and from house to house, testifying both to the Jews, and also to the Greeks, repentance toward God, and faith toward our Lord Jesus Christ. And now behold I go bound in the spirit unto Jerusalem, not knowing the things that shall befall me there; save that the Holy Ghost witnesseth in every city, saying, That bonds and afflictions abide me. But none of these things
move

move me, neither count I my life dear unto myself, so that I might finish my course with joy, and the ministry which I have received of the Lord Jesus, to testify the gospel of the grace of God. And now behold I know that ye all, among whom I have gone preaching the kingdom of God, shall see my face no more. Wherefore I take you to record this day that I am pure from the blood of all men. For I have not shunned to declare unto you all the counsel of God.

Take heed therefore unto yourselves, and to all the flock over the which the Holy Ghost hath made you overseers, to feed the church of God, which he hath purchased with his own blood. For I know this, that after my departing shall grievous wolves enter in among you, not sparing the flock. Also of your ownselves shall men arise, speaking perverse things, to draw away disciples after them. Therefore watch, and remember that by the space of three years I ceased not to warn every one night and day with tears.

And now, brethren, I commend you to God, and to the word of his grace, which is able to build you up, and to give you an inheritance among all them which are sanctified. I have coveted no man's silver, or gold, or apparel. Yea, ye yourselves know that these hands have ministered unto my necessities, and to them that were with me. I have shewed you all things, how that so labouring ye ought to support the weak, and to remember the words of the Lord Jesus, how he said, It is more blessed to give than to receive.

And when he had thus spoken, he kneeled down and prayed with them all. And they all wept sore, and fell on Paul's neck, and kissed him; sorrowing most of all for
the

the words which he spake, that they should see his face no more. And they accompanied him unto the ship.

And the next day we that were of Paul's company departed and came unto Cesarea, and we entered into the house of Philip the evangelist (which was one of the seven) and abode with him. And, the same man had four daughters, virgins, which did prophesy. And, as we tarried there many days, there came down from Judea a certain prophet named Agabus. And when he was come unto us he took Paul's girdle, and bound his own hands and feet, and said, Thus saith the Holy Ghost. So shall the Jews at Jerusalem bind the man that owneth this girdle, and shall deliver him into the hands of the Gentiles. And when we heard these things both we and they of that place besought him not to go up to Jerusalem. Then Paul answered, What mean ye to weep and to break mine heart? for I am ready, not to be bound only, but also to die at Jerusalem for the name of the Lord Jesus. And when he would not be persuaded, we ceased, saying, The will of the Lord be done. THE ACTS.

LAZARUS RAISED FROM THE DEAD.

Now a certain man was sick named Lazarus of Bethany, the town of Mary and her sister Martha. (It was that Mary which anointed the Lord with ointment, and wiped his feet with her hair, whose brother Lazarus was sick.) Therefore his sister sent unto him, saying, Lord, behold, he whom thou lovest is sick. When Jesus heard that, he said, This sickness is not unto death, but for the glory of God, that the Son of God might be glorified thereby.

Now Jesus loved Martha, and her sister, and Lazarus. When he had heard therefore that he was sick, he abode two days still in the same place where he was. Then after that saith he to his disciples, Let us go into Judea again. His disciples say unto him, Master, the Jews of late sought to stone thee; and goest thou thither again? Jesus answered, Are there not twelve hours in the day? If any man walk in the day, he stumbleth not, because he seeth the light of this world: but if a man walk in the night, he stumbleth, because there is no light in him.

These things said he, and after that he saith unto them, Our friend Lazarus sleepeth; but I go, that I may awake him out of sleep. Then said his disciples, Lord, if he sleep he shall do well. Howbeit Jesus spake of his death: but they thought that he had spoken of taking of rest in sleep. Then said Jesus unto them plainly, Lazarus is dead: and I am glad for your sakes that I was not there, to the intent ye may believe; nevertheless, let us go unto him. Then said Thomas, which is called Didymus, unto his fellow disciples, Let us also go, that we may die with him. Then when Jesus came he found that he had lain in the grave four days already. (Now Bethany was nigh unto Jerusalem, about fifteen furlongs off.) And many of the Jews came to Martha and Mary to comfort them concerning their brother. Then Martha, as soon as she heard that Jesus was coming, went and met him: but Mary sat still in the house. Then said Martha unto Jesus, Lord, if thou hadst been here, my brother had not died. But I know that, even now, whatsoever thou wilt ask of God, God will give it thee. Jesus saith unto her, Thy brother shall rise again. Martha saith unto him, I know that he shall rise again in the resurrection at the last day. Jesus said unto her,

her, I am the resurrection and the life: he that believeth in me, though he were dead, yet shall he live. And whosoever liveth and believeth in me shall never die. Believest thou this? She saith unto him, Yea, Lord; I believe that thou art the Christ the Son of God, which should come into the world.

And when she had so said she went her way, and called Mary her sister secretly, saying, The Master is come, and calleth for thee. As soon as she heard that, she arose quickly, and came unto him.

Now Jesus was not yet come into the town, but was in that place where Martha met him. The Jews then which were with her in the house, and comforted her, when they saw Mary that she rose up hastily, and went out, followed her, saying, She goeth unto the grave, to weep there.

Then when Mary was come where Jesus was, and saw him, she fell down at his feet, saying unto him, Lord, if thou hadst been here my brother had not died. When Jesus therefore saw her weeping, and the Jews also weeping which came with her, he groaned in the spirit, and was troubled, and said, Where have ye laid him? They said unto him, Lord, come and see. Jesus wept.

Then said the Jews, Behold how he loved him! And some of them said, Could not this man, which opened the eyes of the blind, have caused that even this man should not have died? Jesus therefore again groaning in himself cometh to the grave. It was a cave, and a stone lay upon it. Jesus said, Take ye away the stone. Martha, the sister of him that was dead, saith unto him, Lord, by this time he stinketh, for he hath been dead four days. Jesus saith unto her, Said I not unto thee, that, if thou wouldest believe, thou shouldest see the glory of God?

Then they took away the stone from the place where the dead was laid. And Jesus lift up his eyes, and said, Father, I thank thee that thou hast heard me. And I knew that thou hearest me always: but because of the people which stand by I said it, that they may believe that thou hast sent me.

And when he had thus spoken, he cried with a loud voice, Lazarus, come forth. And he that was dead came forth, bound hand and foot with grave clothes; and his face was bound about with a napkin. Jesus saith unto them, Loose him, and let him go.

Then many of the Jews which came to Mary, and had seen the things which Jesus did, believed on him. But some of them went their ways to the Pharisees, and told them what things Jesus had done.

S. JOHN.

THE WIDOW'S SON RAISED FROM THE DEAD.

And it came to pass the day after, that he went into a city called Nain; and many of his disciples went with him, and much people. Now when he came nigh to the gate of the city, behold, there was a dead man carried out, the only son of his mother, and she was a widow; and much people of the city was with her. And when the Lord saw her he had compassion on her, and said unto her, Weep not. And he came and touched the bier; and they that bare him stood still. And he said, Young man, I say unto thee, Arise. And he that was dead sat up, and began to speak. And he delivered him to his mother. And there came a fear on all: and they glorified God, saying, That

a great

a great prophet is risen up among us; and, That God hath visited his people. And this rumour of him went forth throughout all Judea, and throughout all the region round about.

S. LUKE.

CHRIST'S AGONY.—PETER'S DENIAL OF CHRIST.

Now, when the even was come, he sat down with the twelve. And as they did eat he said, Verily I say unto you, that one of you shall betray me. And they were exceeding sorrowful, and began every one of them to say unto him, Lord, is it I? And he answered and said, He that dippeth his hand with me in the dish, the same shall betray me. The Son of man goeth, as it is written of him; but woe unto that man by whom the Son of man is betrayed! it had been good for that man if he had not been born. Then Judas, which betrayed him, answered and said, Master, is it I? He said unto him, Thou hast said. And as they were eating Jesus took bread, and blessed it, and brake it, and gave it to the disciples, and said, Take, eat; this is my body. And he took the cup and gave thanks, and gave it to them, saying, Drink ye all of it; for this is my blood of the new testament which is shed for many for the remission of sins. But I say unto you, I will not drink henceforth of this fruit of the vine until that day when I drink it new with you in my Father's kingdom. And when they had sung an hymn they went out into the mount of Olives. Then said Jesus unto them, All ye shall be offended because of me this night: for it is written, I will smite the shepherd, and the sheep of the flock shall be scattered abroad.

abroad. But after I am risen again I will go before you into Galilee. Peter answered and said unto him, Though all men shall be offended because of thee, yet will I never be offended. Jesus said unto him, Verily I say unto thee, that this night before the cock crow thou shalt deny me thrice. Peter said unto him, Though I should die with thee, yet will I not deny thee. Likewise also said all the disciples.

Then cometh Jesus with them unto a place called Gethsamene, and saith unto the disciples, Sit ye here while I go and pray yonder. And he took with him Peter and the two sons of Zebedee, and began to be sorrowful and very heavy. Then saith he unto them, My soul is exceeding sorrowful, even unto death: tarry ye here, and watch with me. And he went a little farther, and fell on his face, and prayed, saying, O my Father, if it be possible, let this cup pass from me: nevertheless, not as I will, but as thou wilt. And, being in an agony, he prayed more earnestly; and his sweat was as it were great drops of blood falling down to the ground. And he cometh unto the disciples, and findeth them asleep, and saith unto Peter, What, could ye not watch with me one hour? Watch and pray, that ye enter not into temptation. The spirit indeed is willing, but the flesh is weak. He went away again the second time, and prayed, saying, O my Father, if this cup may not pass away from me, except I drink it, thy will be done. And he came and found them asleep again: for their eyes were heavy. And he left them, and went away again, and prayed the third time, saying the same words. Then cometh he to his disciples, and saith unto them, Sleep on now, and take your rest: behold, the hour is at hand, and the Son of man is betrayed into the hands of sinners. Rise, let us be going: behold, he is at hand that doth betray me.

And

And while he yet spake, lo, Judas, one of the twelve, came, and with him a great multitude with swords and staves from the chief priests and elders of the people. Now he that betrayed him gave them a sign, saying, Whomsoever I shall kiss, that same is he; hold him fast. And forthwith he came to Jesus, and said, Hail, master; and kissed him. And Jesus said unto him, Friend, wherefore art thou come? Then came they and laid hands on Jesus, and took him. And behold, one of them which were with Jesus stretched out his hand, and drew his sword, and struck a servant of the high priest, and smote off his ear. Then said Jesus unto him, Put up again thy sword into its place; for all they that take the sword shall perish with the sword. Thinkest thou that I cannot now pray to my Father, and he shall presently give me more than twelve legions of angels? but how then shall the scriptures be fulfilled, That thus it must be? In that same hour said Jesus to the multitudes, Are ye come out as against a thief with swords and with staves for to take me? I sat daily with you teaching in the temple, and ye laid no hold on me. But all this was done that the scriptures of the prophets might be fulfilled. Then all the disciples forsook him and fled. And they that had laid hold on Jesus led him away to Caiaphas the high priest, where the scribes and the elders were assembled. But Peter followed him afar off unto the high priest's palace, and went in, and sat with the servants, to see the end. Now the chief priests and elders, and all the council, sought false witness against Jesus to put him to death; but found none; yea, though many false witnesses came, yet found they none. At the last came two false witnesses, and said, This fellow said, I am able to destroy the temple of God, and to build it in three days.

days. And the high priest arose, and said unto him, Answerest thou nothing? What is it which these witness against thee? But Jesus held his peace, and the high priest answered, and said unto him, I adjure thee by the living God, that thou tell us whether thou be the Christ the Son of God. Jesus saith unto him, Thou hast said. Nevertheless, I say unto you, Hereafter shall ye see the Son of man sitting on the right hand of Power, and coming in the clouds of heaven. Then the high priest rent his clothes, saying, He hath spoken blasphemy: what further need have we of witnesses? Behold, now ye have heard his blasphemy, what think ye? They answered and said, He is guilty of death. Then did they spit in his face, and buffeted him; and others smote him with the palms of their hands, saying, Prophesy unto us, thou Christ, Who is he that smote thee? Now Peter sat without in the palace: and a damsel came unto him, saying, Thou also wast with Jesus of Galilee. But he denied before them all, saying, I know not what thou sayest. And when he was gone out into the porch another maid saw him, and said unto them that were there, This fellow was also with Jesus of Nazareth. And again he denied with an oath, I do not know the man. And after a while came unto him they that stood by, and said to Peter, Surely thou also art one of them; for thy speech betrayeth thee. And Peter said, Man, I know not what thou sayest. And while he yet spake the cock crew. And the Lord turned, and looked upon Peter. And Peter remembered the words of Jesus, how he had said unto him, Before the cock crow thou shalt deny me thrice. And he went out, and wept bitterly. S. MATTHEW.

THE DEATH OF CHRIST, AND THE PENITENT THIEF.

Soldiers mocked him, saying, If thou be the King of the Jews, save thyself. And a superscription also was written over him in letters of Greek, and Latin, and Hebrew, THIS IS THE KING OF THE JEWS. And one of the malefactors which were hanged railed on him, saying, If thou be Christ, save thyself and us. But the other, answering, rebuked him, saying, Dost not thou fear God, seeing thou art in the same condemnation? and we indeed justly; for we receive the due reward of our deeds; but this man hath done nothing amiss. And he said unto Jesus, Lord, remember me when thou comest into thy kingdom. And Jesus said unto him, Verily I say unto thee, To-day shalt thou be with me in Paradise. Now there stood by the cross of Jesus his mother, and his mother's sister, Mary the wife of Cleophas, and Mary Magdalene. When Jesus therefore saw his mother and the disciple standing by whom he loved, he saith unto his mother, Woman, behold thy son! Then saith he to the disciple, Behold thy mother! And from that hour that disciple took her unto his home. And it was about the sixth hour, and there was darkness over all the earth until the ninth hour. And the sun was darkened, and the vail of the temple was rent in the midst. And when Jesus had cried with a loud voice, he said, Father, into thy hands I commend my spirit. And, having said thus, he gave up the ghost. Now when the centurion saw what was done, he glorified God, saying, Certainly this was a righteous man. And all the people that came together

gether to that sight, beholding the things which were done, smote their breasts, and returned. And all his acquaintance, and the women that followed him from Galilee, stood afar off beholding these things.

S. LUKE.

And there followed him a great multitude of people, and of women, which also bewailed and lamented him. But Jesus, turning unto them, said, Daughters of Jerusalem, weep not for me, but weep for yourselves, and for your children. For, behold, the days are coming in the which they shall say, Blessed are the barren, and the wombs that never bare, and the paps which never gave suck. Then shall they begin to say to the Mountains, Fall on us; and to the hills, Cover us.

S. MATTHEW.

A CHARACTER OF CHRIST.

Behold my servant, whom I uphold; mine elect, in whom my soul delighteth; I have put my spirit upon him: he shall bring forth judgment to the Gentiles! he shall not cry, nor lift up, nor cause his voice to be heard in the street. A bruised reed shall he not break, and the smoking flax shall he not quench: he shall bring forth judgment unto truth. He shall not fail, nor be discouraged, till he have set judgment in the earth; and the isles shall wait for his law.

Thus saith God the Lord, he that created the heavens, and stretched them out; he that spread forth the earth, and that which cometh out of it; he that giveth breath unto the people upon it, and spirit to them that walk therein. I the
Lord

Lord have called thee in righteousness, and will hold thine hand, and will keep thee, and give thee for a covenant of the people, for a light of the Gentiles; to open the blind eyes, to bring out the prisoners from the prison, and them that sit in darkness out of the prison-house.

ISAIAH.

THE IGNORANCE AND WEAKNESS OF MAN.

Then the Lord answered Job out of the whirlwind, and said,

Who is this that darkeneth council by words without knowledge?

Gird up now thy loins like a man; for I will demand of thee, and answer thou me.

Where wast thou when I laid the foundations of the earth? declare, if thou hast understanding.

Who hath laid the measures thereof, if thou knowest? or who hath stretched the line upon it?

Whereupon are the foundations thereof fastened? or who laid the corner stone thereof?

When the morning stars sang together, and all the sons of God shouted for joy.

Or who shut up the sea with doors, when it brake forth as if it had issued out of the womb?

When I made the cloud the garment thereof, and thick darkness a swaddling band for it.

And brake up for it my decreed place, and set bars and doors,

And said, Hitherto shalt thou come, but no further; and here shall thy proud waves be stayed?

Haſt thou commanded the morning ſince thy days? and cauſed the day-ſpring to know his place,

That it might take hold of the ends of the earth, that the wicked might be ſhaken out of it?

It is turned as clay to the ſeal, and they ſtand as a garment.

And from the wicked their light is withholden, and the high arm ſhall be broken.

Haſt thou entered into the ſprings of the ſea? or haſt thou walked in the ſearch of the depth?

Have the gates of death been opened unto thee? or haſt thou ſeen the doors of the ſhadow of death?

Haſt thou perceived the breadth of the earth? Declare, if thou knoweſt it all.

Where is the way where light dwelleth; and, as for darkneſs, where is the place thereof?

That thou ſhouldeſt take it to the bound thereof, and that thou ſhouldeſt know the paths to the houſe thereof.

Knoweſt thou it, becauſe thou waſt then born? or becauſe the number of thy days is great?

Haſt thou entered into the treaſures of the ſnow? or haſt thou ſeen the treaſures of the hail,

Which I have reſerved againſt the time of trouble, againſt the day of battle and war?

By what way is the light parted which ſcattereth the eaſt wind upon the earth?

Who hath divided a water courſe for the overflowing of waters, or a way for the lightning of thunder;

To cauſe it to rain on the earth, where no man is; on the wilderneſs, wherein there is no man?

To ſatisfy the deſolate and waſte ground, and to cauſe the bud of the tender herb to ſpring forth?

Hath

Hath the rain a father? or who hath begotten the drops of dew?

Out of whose womb came the ice? and the hoary frost of heaven, who hath gendered it?

The waters are hid as with a stone, and the face of the deep is frozen.

Canst thou bind the sweet influences of Pleiades? or loose the bands of Orion?

Canst thou bring forth Mazzaroth in his season? or canst thou guide Arcturus with his sons?

Knowest thou the ordinances of heaven? canst thou set the dominion thereof in the heart?

Canst thou lift up thy voice to the clouds, that abundance of waters may cover thee?

Canst thou send lightnings, that they may go, and say unto thee, Here we are?

Who hath put wisdom in the inward parts? or who hath given understanding to the heart?

Who can number the clouds in wisdom; or who can stay the bottles of heaven,

When the dust groweth into hardness, and the clods cleave fast together?

Wilt thou hunt the prey for the lion; or fill the appetite of the young lions,

When they couch in their dens, and abide in the covert to lie in wait?

Who provideth for the raven his food? when his young ones cry unto God, they wander for lack of meat.

Job.

THE IGNORANCE OF MAN.

Behold yon new-born infant, griev'd
  With hunger, thirst, and pain,
That asks to have the wants reliev'd
  It knows not to explain.

Aloud the speechless suppliant cries,
  And utters, as it can,
The woes that in its bosom rise,
  And speak its nature—man.

That infant, whose advancing hour
  Life's various sorrows try;
(Sad proof of sin's transmissive pow'r)
  That infant, Lord, am I!

A childhood yet my thoughts confess,
  Though long in years mature;
Unknowing whence I feel distress,
  And where, or what, its cure.

Author of Good! to Thee I turn:
  Thy ever wakeful eye
Alone can all my wants discern,
  Thy hand alone supply.

O let thy fear within me dwell,
  Thy love my footsteps guide;
That love shall vainer loves expel,
  That fear all fear beside.

And oh! by error's force subdu'd,
   Since oft my stubborn will,
Prepost'rous, shuns the latent good,
   And grasps the specious ill;

Not to my wish, but to my want,
   Do thou Thy gifts apply:
Unask'd, what good thou knowest, grant;
   What ill, though ask'd, deny.

MERRICK.

A GRATEFUL EFFUSION.

O LORD, thou art my God; I will exalt thee, I will praise thy name, for thou hast done wonderful things: thy counsels of old are faithfulness and truth. For thou hast made of a city an heap, of a defenced city a ruin: a palace of strangers to be no city; it shall never be built. Therefore shall the strong people glorify thee; the city of the terrible nations shall fear thee: for thou hast been a strength to the poor, a strength to the needy in his distress, a refuge from the storm, a shadow from the heat, when the blast of the terrible ones is as a storm against the wall. Thou shalt bring down the noise of strangers as the heat in a dry place; even the heat with the shadow of a cloud; the branch of the terrible ones shall be brought low.

And in this mountain shall the Lord of Hosts make unto all people a feast of fat things, a feast of wines on the lees; of fat things full of marrow; of wines on the lees well refined. And he will destroy in this mountain the face of the covering cast over all people, and the vail that is

spread

spread over all nations. He will swallow up death in victory: and the Lord God will wipe away tears from all faces; and the rebuke of his people shall he take away from off all the earth: for the Lord hath spoken it.

And it shall be said in that day, Lo, this is our God; we have waited for him, and he will save us: this is the Lord; we have waited for him; we will be glad and rejoice in his salvation. For in this mountain shall the hand of the Lord rest, and Moab shall be trodden down under him, even as straw is trodden down for the dunghill. And he shall spread forth his hands in the midst of them, as he that swimmeth spreadeth forth his hands to swim: and he shall bring down their pride, together with the spoils of their hands. And the fortress of the high fort of thy wall shall he bring down, lay low, and bring to the ground, even to the dust.

In that day shall this song be sung in the land of Judah; we have a strong city; salvation will God appoint for walls and bulwarks. Open ye the gates, that the righteous nation which keepeth the truth may enter in. Thou wilt keep him in perfect peace whose mind is stayed on thee, because he trusteth in thee. Trust ye in the Lord for ever, for in the Lord Jehovah is everlasting strength. For he bringeth down them that dwell on high: the lofty city he layeth it low: he layeth it low, even to the ground, he bringeth it even to the dust. The foot shall tread it down, even the feet of the poor, and the steps of the needy. The way of the just is uprightness; thou, most upright, dost weigh the path of the just. Yea, in the way of thy judgments, O Lord, have we waited for thee: the desire of our soul is to thy name, and to the remembrance of thee. With my soul have I desired thee in the

night;

night; yea, with my spirit within me will I seek thee early: for when thy judgments are in the earth the inhabitants of the world will learn righteousness. Let favour be shewed to the wicked, yet will he not learn righteousness: in the land of uprightness will he deal unjustly, and will not behold the majesty of the Lord. Lord, when thy hand is lifted up they will not see: but they shall see and be ashamed for their envy at the people; yea, the fire of thine enemies shall devour them. Lord, thou wilt ordain peace for us; for thou also hast wrought all our works in us.

ISAIAH.

PETER'S WANT OF FAITH.

AND straightway Jesus constrained his disciples to get into a ship, and to go before him unto the other side, while he sent the multitudes away. And when he had sent the multitudes away he went up into a mountain apart to pray: and when the evening was come he was there alone. But the ship was now in the midst of the sea tossed with waves: for the wind was contrary. And in the fourth watch of the night Jesus went unto them walking on the sea. And when the disciples saw him walking on the sea they were troubled, saying, It is a spirit. And they cried out for fear. But straightway Jesus spake unto them, saying, Be of good cheer; it is I; be not afraid. And Peter answered him, and said, Lord, if it be thou, bid me come unto thee on the water. And he said, Come. And when Peter was come down out of the ship he walked on the water to go to Jesus. But when he saw the wind boisterous he was afraid; and, beginning to sink, he cried, saying,

ing, Lord, save me. And immediately Jesus stretched forth his stand, and caught him, and said unto him, O thou of little faith, wherefore didst thou doubt? And when they were come into the ship the wind ceased. Then they that were in the ship came, and worshipped him, saying, Of a truth thou art the Son of God.

MATTHEW.

A PARAPHRASE ON THE LATTER PART OF THE SIXTH CHAPTER OF SAINT MATTHEW.

WHEN my breast labours with oppressive care,
And o'er my cheek descends the falling tear;
While all my warring passions are at strife,
O, let me listen to the words of life!
Raptures deep-felt his doctrine did impart,
And thus he rais'd from earth the drooping heart.
  Think not, when all your scanty stores afford
Is spread at once upon the sparing board;
Think not, when worn the homely robe appears,
While on the roof the howling tempest bears;
What farther shall this feeble life sustain,
And what shall clothe these shiv'ring limbs again.
Say, does not life its nourishment exceed,
And the fair body its investing weed?
Behold! and look away your low despair—
See the light tenants of the barren air:
To them nor stores nor granaries belong,
Nought but the woodland, and the pleasing song;
Yet your kind heav'nly Father bends his eye
On the least wing that flits along the sky.

To him they sing when spring renews the plain;
To him they cry in winter's pinching reign:
Nor is their music nor their plaint in vain:
He hears the gay and the distressful call,
And with unsparing bounty fills them all.

Observe the rising lily's snowy grace,
Observe the various vegetable race;
They neither toil nor spin, but careless grow,
Yet see how warm they blush! how bright they glow!
What regal vestments can with them compare!
What king so shining, or what queen so fair!

If ceaseless thus the fowls of heaven he feeds,
If o'er the fields such lucid robes he spreads;
Will he not care for you, ye faithless?—say,
Is he unwise? or are ye less than than they?

THOMSON.

THE PEACE OF GOD.

HEARKEN unto me, O Jacob, and Israel, my called; I am the first; I also am the last. Mine hand also hath laid the foundation of the earth, and my right hand hath spanned the heavens: when I call unto them, they stand up together. All ye, assemble yourselves, and hear: which among them hath declared these things? The Lord hath loved him: he will do his pleasure on Babylon, and his arm shall be on the Chaldeans. I, even I, have spoken; yea, I have called him: I have brought him, and he shall make his way prosperous. Come ye near unto me, hear ye this, I have not spoken in secret from the beginning: from the time that it was there am I: and now the Lord God and his spirit hath sent me. Thus saith the Lord thy Redeemer, the Holy one of Israel; I am the Lord thy God, which teacheth thee to profit, which leadeth thee by the way that thou shouldest go. O that thou hadst hearkened to my commandments! then had thy peace been as a river, and thy righteousness as the waves of the sea: thy seed also had been as the sand, and the offspring of thy bowels like the gravel thereof; his name should not have been cut off, nor destroyed from before me. Go ye forth of Babylon, flee ye from the Chaldeans, with a voice of singing declare ye, tell this, utter it even to the end of the earth; say ye, The Lord hath redeemed his servant Jacob. And they thirsted not when he led them through the deserts: he caused the waters to flow out of the rock for them: he clave the rock also, and the waters gushed out. There is no peace, saith the Lord, unto the wicked.

ISAIAH.

DYING FRIENDS.

Our dying friends come o'er us like a cloud,
To damp our brainless ardours, and abate
That glare of life which often blinds the wise.
Our dying friends are pioneers, to smooth
Our rugged pass to death; to break those bars
Of terror and abhorrence Nature throws
Cross our obstructed way; and thus to make
Welcome as safe our port from ev'ry storm.
Each friend by fate snatch'd from us is a plume
Pluckt from the wing of human vanity,
Which makes us stoop from our aerial heights;
And, dampt with omen of our own disease,

On

On drooping pinions of ambition low'r'd,
Just skim earth's surface, ere we break it up,
O'er putrid earth to scratch a little dust,
And save the world a nuisance. Smitten friends
Are angels sent on errands full of love;
For us they languish, and for us they die:
And shall they languish, shall they die, in vain?
Ungrateful, shall we grieve their hov'ring shades,
Which wait the revolution in our hearts?
Shall we disdain their silent, soft address;
Their posthumous and pious pray'r?
Senseless as herds that graze their hallow'd graves,
Tread under foot their agonies and groans,
Frustrate their anguish, and destroy their deaths?
Lorenzo! no; the thought of death indulge;
Give it its wholesome empire! let it reign,
That kind chastiser of thy soul enjoy!
Its reign will spread thy glorious conquests far,
And still the tumults of thy ruffled breast:
Auspicious era! golden days, begin!
The thought of death shall, like a god, inspire.

YOUNG.

HYMN ON DEATH.

CHILD of mortality, whence comest thou? why is thy countenance sad, and why are thine eyes red with weeping?

I have seen the rose in its beauty; it spread its leaves to the morning sun. I returned; it was dying upon its stalk; the grace of the form of it was gone; its loveliness was vanished away: the leaves thereof were scattered on the ground, and no one gathered them again.

A stately

A stately tree grew on the plain; its branches were covered with verdure; its boughs spread wide, and made a goodly shadow; the trunk was like a strong pillar; the roots were like crooked fangs. I returned; the verdure was nipt by the east wind; the branches were lopt away by the axe; the worm had made its way into the trunk, and the heart thereof was decayed; it mouldered away, and fell to the ground.

I have seen the insects sporting in the sun-shine, and darting along the stream; their wings glittered with gold and purple; their bodies shone like the green emerald: they were more numerous than I could count; their motions were quicker than my eye could glance. I returned; they were brushed into the pool; they were perishing with the evening breeze; the swallow had devoured them; the pike had seized them: there were none found of so great a multitude.

I have seen man in the pride of his strength; his cheeks glowing with beauty; his limbs were full of activity; he leaped; he walked; he ran; he rejoiced in that he was more excellent than those. I returned; he lay stiff and cold on the bare ground; his feet could no longer move, nor his hands stretch themselves out; his life was departed from him, and the breath out of his nostrils: therefore do I weep, because death is in the world; the spoiler is among the works of God: all that is made must be destroyed; all that is born must die: let me alone, for I will weep yet longer.

Mrs. Barbauld.

ON THE RESURRECTION.

I have seen the flower withering on the stalk, and its bright leaves spread on the ground. I looked again, and it sprung forth afresh; the stem was crowned with new buds, and the sweetness thereof filled the air.

I have seen the sun set in the west, and the shades of night shut in the wide horizon: there was no colour, nor shape, nor beauty, nor music; gloom and darkness brooded around. I looked; the sun broke forth again from the east, and gilded the mountain tops; the lark rose to meet him from her low nest, and the shades of darkness fled away.

I have seen the insect, being come to its full size, languish, and refuse to eat: it spun itself a tomb, and was shrouded in the silken cone; it lay without feet, or shape, or power to move. I looked again; it had burst its tomb; it was full of life, and sailed on coloured wings through the soft air; it rejoiced in its new being.

Thus shall it be with thee, O man! and so shall thy life be renewed.

Beauty shall spring up out of ashes, and life out of the dust.

A little while shalt thou lie on the ground, as the seed lieth in the bosom of the earth: but thou shalt be raised again; and, if thou art good, thou shalt never die any more.

Who is he that cometh to burst open the prison doors of the tomb; to bid the dead awake, and to gather his redeemed from the four winds of heaven?

He

He descendeth on a fiery cloud; the sound of a trumpet goeth before him; thousands of angels are on his right hand. It is Jesus, the Son of God; the saviour of men; the friend of the good! He cometh in the glory of his Father; he hath received power from on high! Mourn not, therefore, child of immortality! for the spoiler, the cruel spoiler that laid waste the works of God, is subdued; Jesus hath conquered death. Child of immortality, mourn no longer!*

Mrs. Barbauld.

THE LAST JUDGMENT.

When the Son of man shall come in his glory, and all the holy angels with him, then shall he sit upon the throne of his glory: and before him shall be gathered all nations; and he shall separate them one from another, as a shepherd divideth his sheep from the goats: and he shall set the sheep on his right-hand, but the goats on the left. Then shall the King say unto them on his right hand, Come, ye blessed of my Father, inherit the kingdom prepared for you from the foundation of the world: for I was an-hungred, and ye gave me meat; I was thirsty, and ye gave me drink; I was a stranger, and ye took me in; naked, and ye clothed me; I was sick, and ye visited me; I was in prison, and ye came unto me. Then shall the righteous answer him, saying, Lord, when saw we thee an-hungred,

---

* These poetical little pieces were written for children, who overlook their beauties. Two are here selected to gratify those readers who wish to cultivate a simple taste, and unite them in the young mind with sentiments of religion.

and fed thee? or thirsty, and gave thee drink? when saw we thee a stranger, and took thee in? or naked, and clothed thee? Or when saw we thee sick or in prison and came unto thee? And the King shall answer and say unto them, Verily I say unto you, inasmuch as ye have done it unto one of the least of these my brethren, ye have done it unto me. Then shall he say also unto them on the left hand, Depart from me, ye cursed, into everlasting fire, prepared for the devil and his angels: for I was an-hungred, and ye gave me no meat: I was thirsty, and ye gave me no drink; I was a stranger, and ye took me not in; naked, and ye clothed me not; sick, and in prison, and ye visited me not. Then shall they also answer him, saying, Lord, when saw we thee an-hungred, or a-thirst, or a stranger, or naked, or sick, or in prison, and did not minister unto thee? Then shall he answer them, saying, Verily I say unto you, Inasmuch as ye did it not to one of the least of these, ye did it not to me. And these shall go away into everlasting punishment, but the righteous into life eternal.

S. MATTHEW.

AND the stars of heaven fell unto the earth, even as a fig-tree casteth her untimely figs when she is shaken of a mighty wind. And the heaven departed as a scroll when it is rolled together, and every mountain and island were moved out of their places. And the kings of the earth and the great men, and the rich men, and the chief captains, and the mighty men, and every bondman, and every freeman, hid themselves in the dens, and in the rocks of the mountains; and said to the mountains and rocks, Fall on us, and hide us from the face of him that sitteth on the Throne, and from the wrath of the Lamb: for the great day of his wrath is come, and who shall be able to stand?

And

And I heard a great voice out of heaven, saying, Behold, the Tabernacle of God is with men, and he will dwell with them, and they shall be his people, and God himself shall be with them, and be their God. And God shall wipe away all tears from their eyes: and there shall be no more death; neither sorrow, nor crying; neither shall there be any more pain: for the former things are passed away.

And he that sat upon the throne said, Behold, I make all things new. And he said unto me, Write: for these words are true and faithful. And he said unto me, It is done: I am Alpha and Omega, the beginning and the end: I will give unto him that is a-thirst of the fountain of the water of life freely. He that overcometh shall inherit all things, and I will be his God, and he shall be my son.

After this I beheld, and lo a great multitude, which no man could number, of all nations, and kindreds, and people, and tongues, stood before the Throne, and before the Lamb, clothed with white robes, and palms in their hands: and cried with a loud voice, saying, Salvation to our God, which sitteth upon the Throne, and unto the Lamb! And all the angels stood round about the Throne, and about the elders, and the four beasts, and fell before the Throne on their faces, and worshipped God, saying, Amen: Blessing, and glory, and wisdom, and thanksgiving, and honour, and power, and might, be unto our God for ever and ever. Amen.

And one of the elders answered, saying unto me, What are these which are arrayed in white robes, and whence came they? And I said unto him, Sir, thou knowest. And he said to me, These are they which came out of great tribulation, and have washed their robes, and made them white, in the blood of the Lamb. Therefore are they be-

fore the Throne of God, and ferve him day and night in his Temple: and he that fitteth on the Throne fhall dwell among them. They fhall hunger no more, neither thirft any more, neither fhall the fun light on them, nor any heat. For the Lamb which is in the midft of the Throne fhall feed them, and fhall lead them unto living fountains of water: and God fhall wipe away all tears from their eyes.
REVELATION.

THE JUDGMENTS OF GOD.

THE burden of Damafcus. Behold, Damafcus is taken away from being a city, and it fhall be a ruinous heap. The cities of Aroer are forfaken: they fhall be for flocks, which fhall lie down, and none fhall make them afraid. The fortrefs alfo fhall ceafe from Ephraim, and the kingdom from Damafcus, and the remnant of Syria: they fhall be as the glory of the children of Ifrael, faith the Lord of Hofts. And in that day it fhall come to pafs that the glory of Jacob fhall be made thin, and the fatnefs of his flefh fhall wax lean. And it fhall be as when the harveft-man gathereth the corn, and reapeth the ears with his arm: and it fhall be as he that gathereth ears in the valley of Rephaim.

Yet gleaning-grapes fhall be left in it, as the fhaking of an olive-tree, two or three berries on the top of the uppermoft bough, four or five in the outmoft fruitful branches thereof, faith the Lord God of Ifrael. At that day fhall a man look to his Maker, and his eyes fhall have refpect to the Holy One of Ifrael. And he fhall not look to the altars, the work of his hands, neither fhall refpect that which his fingers have made, either the groves or the images.

In that day shall his strong cities be as a forsaken bough, and an uppermost branch, which they left because of the children of Israel; and there shall be desolation. Because thou hast forgotten the God of thy salvation, and hast not been mindful of the Rock of thy strength, therefore shalt thou plant pleasant plants, and shalt set it with strange slips: in the day shalt thou make thy plant to grow, and in the morning shalt thou make thy seed to flourish: but the harvest shall be a heap in the day of grief and of desperate sorrow. Wo to the multitude of many people, which make a noise like the noise of the seas; and to the rushing of nations, that make a rushing like the rushing of mighty waters; the nations shall rush like the rushing of many waters: but God shall rebuke them, and they shall flee far off, and shall be chased as the chaff of the mountains before the wind, and like a rolling thing before the whirlwind. And behold at evening-tide trouble; and before the morning he is not. This is the portion of them that spoil us, and the lot of them that rob us.

ISAIAH.

Howl, ye shepherds, and cry, and wallow yourselves in the ashes, ye principal of the flock; for the days of your slaughter and of your dispersions are accomplished, and ye shall fall like a pleasant vessel. And the shepherds shall have no way to flee, nor the principal of the flock to escape. A voice of the cry of the shepherds, and an howling of the principal of the flock, shall be heard: for the Lord hath spoiled their pasture. And the peaceable habitations are cut down, because of the fierce anger of the Lord. He hath forsaken his covert, as the lion: for their land is desolate, because of the fierceness of the oppressor, and because of his fierce anger. Therefore the wild beasts of of the desert, with the wild beasts of the islands, shall dwell there, and the owls shall dwell therein: and it shall be no more inhabited for ever: neither shall it be dwelt in from generation to generation.

JEREMIAH.

THE LAMENTATIONS OF THE JEWS IN CAPTIVITY.

By the rivers of Babylon, there we sat down, yea we wept, when we remembered Zion.

We hanged our harps upon the willows in the midst thereof.

For there they that carried us away captive required of us a song; and they that wasted us required of us mirth, saying, Sing us one of the songs of Zion.

How shall we sing the Lord's song in a strange land?

If I forget thee, O Jerusalem, let my right hand forget her cunning.

If I do not remember thee, let my tongue cleave to the roof of my mouth: if I prefer not Jerusalem above my chief joy.

PSALMS.

Negro woman, who sittest pining in captivity, and weepest over thy sick child: though no one seeth thee, God seeth thee; though no one pitieth thee, God pitieth thee; raise thy voice, forlorn and abandoned one; call upon him from amidst thy bonds, for assuredly he will hear thee.

MRS. BARBAULD.

A PROPHETIC DESCRIPTION OF THE DESTRUCTION OF BABYLON.

Babylon, the glory of kingdoms, the beauty of the Chaldees' excellency, shall be as when God overthrew Sodom and Gomorrah. It shall never be inhabited, neither shall it be dwelt in from generation to generation: neither shall the Arabian pitch tent there; neither shall the shepherds make their folds there; but wild beasts of the desert shall lie there: and their houses shall be full of doleful creatures, and owls shall dwell there, and satyrs shall dance there. And the wild beasts of the islands shall cry in their desolate houses, and dragons in their pleasant palaces. And her time is near to come, and her days shall not be prolonged.

Isaiah.

And the merchants of the earth shall weep and mourn over her, for no man buyeth their merchandise any more. The merchandise of gold, and silver, and precious stones, and of pearls, and fine linen, and purple, and silk, and scarlet, and all thyine wood, and all manner of vessels of ivory, and all manner of vessels of most precious wood, and of brass, and iron, and marble, and cinnamon, and odours, and ointment, and frankincense, and wine, and oil, and fine flour, and wheat, and beasts, and sheep, and horses, and chariots, and slaves, and souls of men. And the fruits that thy soul lusted after are departed from thee; and all things which were dainty and goodly are departed from thee, and thou shalt find them no more at all.

The merchants of these things, which were made rich by her, shall stand afar off for the fear of her torment, weeping and wailing, and saying, Alas, alas, that great city that was clothed in fine linen, and purple, and scarlet, and decked with gold, and precious stones, and pearls: for in one hour so great riches is come to nought. And every ship-master, and all the company in ships, and sailors, and as many as trade by sea, stood afar off, and cried when they saw the smoke of her burning, saying, What city is like unto this great city? And they cast dust on their heads, and cried, weeping and wailing, saying, Alas, alas, that great city wherein were made rich all that had ships in the sea, by reason of her costliness, for in one hour is she made desolate. Rejoice over her, thou heaven, and ye holy apostles and prophets, for God hath avenged you on her. And a mighty angel took up a stone like a great milstone, and cast it into the sea, saying, Thus with violence shall that great city Babylon be thrown down, and shall be found no more at all. And the voice of harpers, and musicians, and of pipers, and trumpeters, shall be heard no more at all in thee: and no craftsman, of whatsoever craft he be, shall be found any more in thee: and the sound of a milstone shall be heard no more at all in thee: and the light of a candle shall shine no more at all in thee: and the voice of the bridegroom, and of the bride, shall be heard no more at all in thee: for thy merchants were the great men of the earth: for by thy sorceries were all nations deceived.

REVELATION.

THE PUNISHMENT OF THE WICKED FORETOLD.

We have heard of the pride of Moab (he is very proud), even of his haughtiness, and his pride, and his wrath: but his lies shall not be so. Therefore shall Moab howl: for the foundations of Kir-hareseth shall ye mourn, surely they are stricken. For the fields of Heshbon languish, and the vine of Sibmah, the lords of the heathen have broken down the principal plants thereof; they are come even unto Jazar, they wandered through the wilderness: her branches are stretched out, they are gone over the sea. Therefore I will bewail, with the weeping of Jazar, the vine of Sibmah: I will water thee with my tears, O Heshbon, and Elealeh: for the shouting for thy summer-fruits, and for thy harvest, is fallen. And gladness is taken away, and joy out of the plentiful field; and in the vineyards there shall be no singing, neither shall there be shouting: the treaders shall tread out no wine in their presses; I have made their vintage-shouting to cease.

Isaiah.

DIVINE MERCY.

Sing, O heavens; and be joyful, O earth; and break forth into singing, O mountains: for the Lord hath comforted his people, and will have mercy upon his afflicted. But Zion said, The Lord hath forsaken me, and my Lord hath forgotten me. Can a woman forget her sucking child,

child, that she should not have compassion on the son of her womb? Yea, she may forget, yet will I not forget thee.
ISAIAH.

And when he was come near he beheld the city, and wept over it, saying, If thou hadst known, even thou, at least in this thy day, the things which belong unto thy peace! but now they are hid from thine eyes. For the days shall come upon thee, that thine enemies shall cast a trench about thee, and compass thee round, and keep thee in on every side, and shall lay thee even with the ground, and thy children within thee; and they shall not leave in thee one stone upon another, because thou knewest not the time of thy visitation.
S. LUKE.

O Jerusalem, Jerusalem, thou that killest the prophets and stonedst them which are sent unto thee, how often would I have gathered thy children together, even as a hen gathereth her chickens under her wings, and ye would not! Behold your house is left unto you desolate.
S. MATTHEW.

ESAU DEPRIVED OF HIS FATHER's BLESSING.

And it came to pass that when Isaac was old, and his eyes were dim so that he could not see, he called Esau his eldest son, and said unto him, My son? and he said unto him, Behold, here am I. And he said, Behold now, I am old, I know not the day of my death: now therefore take, I pray thee, thy weapons, thy quiver and thy bow, and go out to the field and take me some venison, and make me favoury meat, such as I love, and bring it to me that I may eat, that my soul may bless thee before I die. And Rebekah heard when Isaac spake to Esau his son: and Esau went to the field to hunt for venison, and to bring it.

And Rebekah spake unto Jacob her son, saying, Behold, I heard thy father speak unto Esau thy brother, saying, Bring me venison, and make me favoury meat, that I may eat, and bless thee before the Lord before my death. Now therefore, my son, obey my voice, according to that which I command thee. Go now to the flock and fetch me from thence two good kids of the goats, and I will make them favoury meat for thy father, such as he loveth: and thou shalt bring it to thy father that he may eat, and that he may bless thee before his death. And Jacob said to Rebekah his mother, Behold, Esau my brother is a hairy man, and I am a smooth man: my father peradventure will feel me, and I shall seem to him as a deceiver; and I shall bring a curse upon me and not a blessing. And his mother said unto him, Upon me be thy curse, my son: only obey my voice, and go fetch me them. And he went and fetched and brought them to his mother: and his mother made favoury meat, such as his father loved. And Rebekah took goodly raiment of her eldest son Esau, which were with her in the house, and put them upon Jacob her younger son. And she put the skins of the kids of the goats upon his hands and upon the smooth of his neck. And she gave the favoury meat and the bread which she had prepared into the hand of her son Jacob. And he came unto his father and said, My father! and he said, Here am I; who art thou, my son? And Jacob said unto his father, I am Esau thy firstborn; I have done according as thou badest me: arise, I pray thee, sit

and

and eat of my venison, that thy soul may bless me. And Isaac said unto his son, How is it that thou hast found it so quickly, my son? And he said, Because the Lord thy God brought it to me. And Isaac said unto Jacob, Come near, I pray thee, that I may feel thee, my son, whether thou be my very son Esau or not. And Jacob went near unto Isaac his father; and he felt him, and said, The voice is Jacob's voice, but the hands are the hands of Esau. And he discerned him not, because his hands were hairy as his brother Esau's hands: so he blessed him. And he said, Art thou my very son Esau? And he said, I am. And he said, Bring it near to me, and I will eat of my son's venison, that my soul may bless thee: and he brought it near to him and he did eat: and he brought him wine and he drank. And his father Isaac said unto him, Come near now and kiss me, my son. And he came near and kissed him: and he smelled the smell of his raiment, and blessed him, and said, See, the smell of my son is as the smell of a field which the Lord hath blessed; therefore God give thee of the dew of heaven, and the fatness of the earth, and plenty of corn and wine: let people serve thee, and nations bow down to thee; be lord over thy brethren, and let thy mother's sons bow down to thee: cursed be every one that curseth thee, and blessed be he that blesseth thee.

And it came to pass as soon as Isaac had made an end of blessing Jacob, and Jacob was yet scarce gone out from the presence of Isaac his father, that Esau his brother came in from his hunting. And he also had made savoury meat and brought it unto his father, and said unto his father, Let my father arise and eat of his son's venison, that thy soul may bless me. And Isaac his father said unto him, Who art thou? And he said, I am thy son, thy firstborn, Esau. And Isaac trembled very exceedingly, and said, Who! where is he that hath taken venison and brought it me, and I have eaten of all before thou camest, and have blessed him? yea, and he shall be blessed. And when Esau heard the words of his father, he cried with a great and exceeding bitter cry, and said unto his father, Bless me, even me also, O my father. And he said, Thy brother came with subtilty and hath taken away thy blessing. And he said, Is not he rightly named Jacob? for he hath supplanted me these two times: he took away my birthright; and behold now he hath taken away my blessing: and he said, Hast thou not reserved a blessing for me? And Isaac answered and said unto Esau, Behold, I have made him thy lord, and all his brethren have I given to him for servants; and with corn and wine have I sustained him: and what shall I do now unto thee, my son? And Esau said unto his father, Hast thou but one blessing, my father? Bless me, even me also, O my father. And Esau lifted up his voice and wept. And Isaac his father answered and said unto him, Behold, thy dwelling shall be the fatness of the earth, and of the dew of heaven from above; and by thy sword shalt thou live, and shalt serve thy brother: and it shall come to pass, when thou shalt have the dominion, that thou shalt break his yoke from off thy neck. GENESIS.

DAVID's LAMENTATION FOR THE DEATH OF HIS SON.

AND David sat between the two gates: and the watchman went up to the roof over the gate unto the wall, and lifted

lifted up his eyes and looked, and behold a man running alone. And the watchman cried and told the king. And the king said, If he be alone there is tidings in his mouth. And he came apace and drew near. And the watchman saw another man running, and the watchman called unto the porter and said, Behold another man running alone. And the king said, He also bringeth tidings. And the watchman said, Methinketh the running of the foremost is like the running of Ahimaaz the son of Zadok. And the king said, He is a good man, and cometh with good tidings. And Ahimaaz called and said unto the king, All is well. And he fell down to the earth upon his face before the king, and said, Blessed be the Lord thy God, which hath delivered up the men that lift up their hand against my lord the king. And the king said, Is the young man Absalom safe? And Ahimaaz answered, When Joab sent the king's servant, and me thy servant, I saw a great tumult, but I knew not what it was. And the king said unto him, Turn aside and stand here. And he turned aside and stood still. And behold Cushi came, and Cushi said, Tidings, my lord the king; for the Lord hath avenged thee this day of all them that rose up against thee. And the king said unto Cushi, Is the young man Absalom safe? And Cushi answered, The enemies of my lord the king, and all that rise against thee to do thee hurt, be as that young man is.

And the king was much moved, and went up to the chamber over the gate and wept; and as he went thus he said, O my son Absalom, my son, my son Absalom! would God I had died for thee, O Absalom, my son, my son!

And it was told Joab, Behold the king weepeth and mourneth for Absalom. And the victory that day was

turned

turned into mourning unto all the people: for the people heard say that day how the king was grieved for his son. And the people gat them by stealth that day into the city; as people being ashamed steal away when they flee in battle. But the king covered his face, and the king cried with a loud voice, O my son Absalom, O Absalom, my son, my son!

SAMUEL.

GLOSTER, EDGAR, AND OLD MAN.

Old Man. O my good lord, I have been your tenant
And your father's tenant these fourscore years!

Glo. Away, get thee away: good friend, be gone:
Thy comforts can do me no good at all,
Thee they may hurt.

O. Man. You cannot see your way.

Glo. I have no way, and therefore want no eyes:
I stumbled when I saw. Full oft 'tis seen
Meanness secures us, and our mere defects
Prove our commodities. O, dear son Edgar,
The food of thy abused father's wrath;
Might I but live to see thee in my touch,
I'd say I had eyes again!

O. Man. How now? Who's there?

Edgar. O Gods! who is't can say I'm at the worst?
I am worse than e'er I was.

O. Man. 'Tis poor mad Tom.

Edg. And worse I may be yet: the worst is not
So long as we can say this is the worst.

O. Man. Fellow, where goest?

Glo.

Glo. Is it a beggar-man?

O. Man. Madman and beggar too.

Glo. He has some reason, else he could not beg.
I'th' last night's storm I such a fellow saw,
Which made me think a man a worm. My son
Came then into my mind, and yet my mind
Was then scarce friends with him. I've heard more since.
As flies to wanton boys are we to th' Gods;
They kill us for their sport.

Edg. How should this be?
Bad is the trade must play the fool to sorrow,
Anguishing 'tself and others.—Bless thee, master!

Glo. Is that the naked fellow?

O. Man. Ay, my lord.

Glo. Get thee away: if for my sake
Thou wilt o'ertake us hence a mile or twain
I'th' way tow'rd Dover, do it for ancient love;
And bring some covering for this naked soul,
Whom I'll entreat to lead me.

O. Man. Alack, Sir, he is mad.

Glo. 'Tis the time's plague when madmen lead the
   blind.
Do as I bid, or rather do thy pleasure:
Above the rest, be gone.

O. Man. I'll bring him the best 'parel that I have
Come on't what will.

Glo. Sirrah, you naked fellow.

Edg. Poor Tom's a-cold! I cannot daily further.
(*Aside.*

Glo. Come hither, fellow.

Edg. And yet I must:—
Bless thy sweet eyes, they bleed.

Glo.

Glo. Know'st thou the way to Dover?

Edg. Both stile and gate, horseway and footpath: poor Tom hath been scar'd out of his good wits. Bless thee, good man, from the foul fiend. Five fiends have been in poor Tom at once; of lust as Obidicut, Hobbididen prince of dumbness, Mahu of stealing, Mohu of murdering, Flibbertigibbet of mopping and mowing, who since possesses chambermaids and waiting-women.

Glo. Here, take this purse, thou whom the heavens' plagues
Have humbled to all strokes. That I am wretched
Makes thee the happier: heavens deal so still!
Let the superfluous and lust-dieted man
That braves your ordinance, that will not see
Because he does not feel, feel your power quickly:
So distribution should undo excess,
And each man have enough. Dost thou know Dover?

Edg. Ay, master.

Glo. There is a cliff whose high and bending head
Looks fearfully on the confined deep:
Bring me but to the very brim of it,
And I'll repair the misery thou dost bear
With something rich about me: from that place
I shall no leading need.

Edg. Give me thy arm;
Poor Tom shall lead thee.

SHAKSPEARE.

GLOSTER AND EDGAR.

Glo. WHEN shall I come to th' top of that same hill?

Edg. You do climb up it now. Look how we labour.

Glo.

Glo. Methinks the ground is even.

Edg. Horrible steep.
Hark, do you hear the sea?

Glo. No, truly, not.

Edg. Why then your other senses grow imperfect
By your eyes' anguish.

Glo. So, may it be indeed.
Methinks thy voice is alter'd, and thou speak'st
In better phrase and matter than thou didst.

Edg. You're much deceiv'd: in nothing am I chang'd
But in my garments.

Glo. Sure you're better spoken.

Edg. Come on, Sir, here's the place;—stand still.
How fearful
And dizzy 'tis to cast one's eyes so low!
The crows and choughs that wing the midway air
Shew scarce so gross as beetles. Half-way down
Hangs one that gathers samphire; dreadful trade!
Methinks he seems no bigger than his head.
The fishermen that walk upon the beach
Appear like mice, and yon tall anchoring bark
Diminish'd to her cock, her cock a buoy
Almost too small for sight. The murmuring surge
That on th' unnumber'd idle pebbles chafes
Cannot be heard so high. I'll look no more
Lest my brain turn, and the deficient sight
Topple down headlong.

Glo. Set me where you stand.

Edg. Give me your hand: you're now within a foot
Of the extreme verge: for all below the moon
Would I not leap outright.

Glo. Let go my hand:
Here friend's another purse, in it a jewel

Well

Well worth a poor man's taking. Fairies and gods
Prosper it with thee! Go thou further off,
Bid me farewell, and let me hear thee going.

   Edg. Now fare ye well, good Sir!   [*Seems to go.*

   Glo. With all my heart.

   Edg. Why do I trifle thus with his despair?—
'Tis done to cure it.

   Glo. O you mighty gods!
This world I do renounce, and in your sights
Shake patiently my great affliction off:
If I could bear it longer and not fall,
To quarrel with your great opposeless wills,
My snuff and lothed part of nature should
Burn itself out. If Edgar live, O bless him!
Now, fellow, fare thee well!   [*He leaps and falls along.*

   Edg. Good Sir, farewell!
And yet I know not how conceit may rob
The treasury of life when life itself
Yields to the theft. Had he been where he thought,
By this had thought been past.——Alive or dead?
Hoa, you, Sir! friend! hear you, Sir? Speak!
Thus might he pass indeed.—Yet he revives.
What are you, Sir?

   Glo. Away, and let me die.

   Edg. Hadst thou been ought but gossomer, feathers, air,
So many fathom down precipitating
Thou'dst shiver'd like an egg: but thou dost breathe,
Hast heavy substance, bleed'st not; speak, art sound?
Ten masts attach'd make not the altitude
Which thou hast perpendicularly fall'n.
Thy life's a miracle. Speak yet again.

   Glo. But have I fall'n or no?

                                            Edg.

Edg. From the dread summit of this chalky bourne!
Look up a height; the shrill-gorg'd lark so far
Cannot be seen or heard: do but look up.

Glo. Alack, I have no eyes!
Is wretchedness depriv'd that benefit
To end itself by death? 'Twas yet some comfort,
When misery could beguile the tyrant's rage
And frustrate his proud will.

Edg. Give me your arm.
Up! so—How is't? Feel you your legs? You stand.

Glo. Too well, too well.

Edg. This is above all strangeness.
Upon the crown of the cliff what thing was that
Which parted from you?

Glo. A poor unfortunate beggar.

Edg. As I stood here below, methought his eyes
Were two full moons; he had a thousand noses,
Horns welk'd and wav'd like the enridged sea:—
It was some fiend. Therefore, thou happy father,
Think that the clearest Gods, who make them honours
Of men's impossibilities, have preserv'd thee.

Glo. I do remember now: henceforth I'll bear
Affliction till it do cry out itself
Enough, enough, and die. That thing you speak of,
I took it for a man; often 'twould say
The fiend, the fiend.—He led me to that place.

Edg. Bear free and patient thoughts.

SHAKSPEARE.

KENT AND GENTLEMAN.

Kent. Did your letters pierce the queen to any demonstration of grief?

Gent. Ay, Sir, she took 'em, read 'em in my presence,
And now and then an ample tear trill'd down
Her delicate cheek. It seems she was a queen
Over her passion, which, most rebel-like,
Sought to be king o'er her.

Kent. O, then it mov'd her.

Gent. But not to rage. Patience and sorrow strove
Which should express her goodliest; you have seen
Sunshine and rain at once. Those happy smiles
That play'd on her ripe lip seem'd not to know
What guests were in her eyes, which parted thence
As perils from diamonds dropt; in brief,
Sorrow would be a rarity most belov'd
If all could so become it.

Kent. Made she no verbal guests?

Gent. Yes; once or twice she heav'd the name of father
Pantingly forth, as if it press'd her heart.
Cry'd, Sisters! sisters! what! I'th' storm of night!
Let pity ne'er believe it! There she shook
The holy water from her heavenly eyes,
And then retir'd to deal with grief alone.

Kent. The stars above us govern our conditions:
Else one self mate and mate could not beget
Such different issues. Spoke you with her since?

Gent. No.

Kent.

Kent. Was this before the king return'd?
Gent. No, since.
Kent. The poor distressed Lear's in town,
Who sometimes in his better time remembers
What we are come about, and by no means
Will yield to see his daughter.
Gent. Why, good Sir?
Kent. A sov'reign shame so bows him: his unkindness
That stript her from his benediction, turn'd her
To foreign casualties, gave her dear rights
To his dog-hearted daughters; these things sting him
So venomously, that burning shame detains him
From his Cordelia.
Gent. Alack, poor gentleman.
Kent. Of Albany's and Cornwall's powers you heard not?
Gent. 'Tis so they are a-foot.
Kent. Well, Sir, I'll bring you to our master Lear,
And leave you to attend him. Some dear cause
Will in concealment wrap me up awhile:
When I am known aright you shall not grieve
Lending me this acquaintance. Pray, along with me.

Enter CORDELIA, PHYSICIAN, *and* SOLDIERS.

Cor. Alack, 'tis he! why he was met even now
As mad as the vext sea, singing aloud,
Crown'd with rank fumitory and furrow-weeds,
With burdock, hemlock, nettles, cuckoo-flowers,
Darnel, and all the idle weeds that grow
On our sustaining corn. Send forth a sentry,
Search every acre in the the high-grown field,
And bring him to our eye. What can man's wisdom

In the restoring his bereaved sense?
He that helps him take all my outward worth.

 Phys. There are means, Madam:
Our foster nurse of nature is repose,
The which he lacks; that to provoke in him
Are many simples operative, whose power
Will close the eye of anguish.

 Cor. All blest secrets,
All you unpublish'd virtues of the earth,
Spring with my tears; be aidant and remediate
In the good man's distress! Seek, seek for him,
Lest his ungovern'd rage dissolve the life
That wants the means to lead it.

    Enter a Messenger.

 Mess. News, Madam:
The British powers are marching hitherward.

 Cor. 'Tis known before. Our preparation stands
In expectation of them. O dear father,
It is thy business that I go about;
Therefore great France my important tears have pitied.
No blown ambition doth our arms incite,
But love, dear love, our aged father's right:
So may I hear and see him!
       SHAKSPEARE.

CORDELIA, KENT, AND PHYSICIAN.

 Cor. O THOU good Kent, how shall I live and work
To match thy goodness! Life will be too short,
And ev'ry measure fail me.
       Kent.

Kent. To be acknowledg'd, Madam, is o'erpaid;
All my reports go with the modest truth:
Nor more, nor clipt, but so.

Cor. Be better suited;
These weeds are memories of those worser hours:
I pray thee put them off.

Kent. Pardon, dear madam,
Yet to be known shortens my made intent;
My boon I make it that you know me not
Till time and I think meet.

Cor. Then be it so,
My lord.—How does the king?   [*To the Physician.*

Phys. Madam, sleeps still.

Cor. O you kind Gods!
Cure this great breach in his abused nature,
Th' untun'd and jarring senses O wind up
Of this child-charged father!

Phys. Please your majesty
That we may wake the king?—he hath slept long.

Cor. Be govern'd by your knowledge and proceed
I'th' sway of your own will: is he array'd?

Enter LEAR *in a Chair carried by Servants.*

Phys. Ay, madam; in the heaviness of sleep
We put fresh garments on him.
Be by, good madam, when we do awake him:
I doubt not of his temperance.

Cor. O my dear father! restoration hang
Her medicine on my lips, and let this kiss
Repair those violent harms that my two sisters
Have in thy reverence made.

Phys. Kind and dear princess!

Cor.

Cor. Had you not been their father, these white flakes
Did challenge pity of them. Was this face
To be expos'd against the warring winds?
Mine enemy's dog, though he had bit me, should
Have stood that night against my fire: and wast
Thou fain, poor father, to hovel thee with swine
And rogues forlorn, in short and musty straw!
Alack, 'tis wonder that thy life and wits
At once had not concluded all. He wakes!—
Speak to him.

   Phys. Madam, do you speak, 'tis fittest.

   Cor. How does my royal lord? How fares your
      majesty?

   Lear. You do me wrong to take me out o'th' grave;
Thou art a soul in bliss, but I am bound
Upon a wheel of fire, that mine own tears
Do scald like molten lead.

   Cor. Sir, do you know me?

   Lear. You are a spirit, I know, when did you die?

   Cor. Still, still far wide.———

   Phys. He's scarce awake, let him alone awhile.

   Lear. Fair day-light, where have I been?
Where am I?———
I'm much abus'd. I should ev'n die with pity
To see another thus. I know not what;
I will not swear these are my hands: let's see,
I feel this pin prick: would I were assur'd
Of my condition.

   Cor. O look on me, Sir,
And hold your hand in benediction o'er me.—
No, Sir, you must not kneel.

   Lear. Pray do not mock me;
I am a very foolish fond old man,

Fourscore

Fourscore and upward; and, to deal plainly with you,
I fear I am not in my perfect mind.
Methinks I should know you, and know this man,
Yet I am doubtful: for I'm mainly ignorant
What place this is, and all the skill I have
Remembers not these garments; nay, I know not
Where I did lodge last night. Do not laugh at me,
For, as I am a man, I think this lady
To be my child Cordelia.

 Cor. And so I am, I am!

 Lear. Be your tears wet? Yes, 'faith; I pray you
   weep not.
If you have poison for me I will drink it;
I know you do not love me; for your sisters
Have, as I do remember, done me wrong.
You have some cause, they have none.

 Cor. No cause, no cause!

 Lear. Am I in France?

 Kent. In your own kingdom, Sir.

 Lear. Do not abuse me.

 Phys. Be comforted, good madam; the great rage
You see is cur'd: desire him to go in,
And trouble him no more till further settling.

 Cor. Will't please your highness walk?

 Lear. You must bear with me;
Pray you now forget and forgive;
I am old and foolish.

Enter BASTARD, *and* LEAR *and* CORDELIA *as prisoners.*

 Bast. Some officers take them away, good guard,
Until their greater pleasures first be known
That are to censure them.

           Cor.

Cor. We're not the first
Who with best meaning have incurr'd the worst:
For thee, oppressed king, I am cast down,
Myself could else out-frown false fortune's frown.
Shall we not see these daughters and these sisters?

Lear. No, no, no, no; come, let's away to prison;
We two alone will sing like birds i'th' cage:
When thou dost ask me blessing, I'll kneel down
And ask of thee forgiveness: so we'll live,
And pray, and sing, and tell old tales, and laugh
As gilded butterflies; and hear poor rogues
Talk of court-news, and we'll talk with them too,
Who loses, and who wins; who's in, who's out;
And take upon's the mystery of things
As if we were God's spies. And we'll wear out
In a wall'd prison packs and sects of great ones,
That ebb and flow by th' moon.

Bast. Take them away—

Lear. Upon such sacrifices, my Cordelia,
The gods themselves throw incense. Have I caught thee?
He that parts us shall bring a brand from heav'n,
And fire us hence like foxes; wipe thine eye,
The gougers shall devour them flesh and fell,
Ere they shall make us weep; we'll see e'm starv'd first.
Come.
                                        SHAKSPEARE.

HUBERT AND EXECUTIONERS.

Hub. Heat me these irons hot; and look you stand
Within the arras; when I strike my foot

Upon the bosom of the ground, rush forth,
And bind the boy which you shall find with me
Fast to the chair; be heedful; hence, and watch!

Exe. I hope your warrant will bear out the deed.

Hub. Uncleanly scruples! Fear not you; look to't.—
Young lad, come forth; I have to say with you.

Enter ARTHUR.

Arth. Good morrow, Hubert.

Hub. Morrow, little prince.

Arth. As little prince (having so great a title
To be more prince) as may be. You are sad.

Hub. Indeed I have been merrier.

Arth. Mercy on me!
Methinks nobody should be sad but I.
Yet I remember when I was in France
Young gentlemen would be as sad as night
Only for wantonness. By my Christendom,
So I were out of prison and kept sheep
I should be merry as the day is long;
And so I would be here, but that I doubt
My uncle practises more harm to me.
He is afraid of me, and I of him.
Is it my fault that I was Geffrey's son?
Indeed it is not; and I would to heav'n
I were your son, so you would love me, Hubert.

Hub. If I talk to him, with his innocent prate
He will awake my mercy, which lies dead;
Therefore I will be sudden, and dispatch. [*Aside.*

Arth. Are you sick, Hubert? You look pale to-day;
In sooth, I would you were a little sick,
That I might sit all night and watch with you.
Alas, I love you more than you do me!

Hub. His words do take possession of my bosom!
Read here, young Arthur— [*Shewing a paper.*
How now, foolish rheum, [*Aside.*
Turning despiteous Nature out of door!
I must be brief, lest resolution drop
Out at mine eyes in tender womanish tears.—
Can you not read it? Is it not fair writ?

Arth. Too fairly, Hubert, for so foul effect.
Must you with irons burn out both mine eyes?

Hub. Young boy, I must.

Arth. And will you?

Hub. And I will.

Arth. Have you the heart? when your head did but ache
I knit my handkerchief about your brows,
(The best I had, a princess wrought it me!)
And I did never ask it you again;
And with my hand at midnight held your head;
And, like the watchful minutes to the hour,
Still and anon cheer'd up the heavy time,
Saying, what lack you? and where lies your grief?
Or what good love may I perform for you?
Many a poor man's son would have lain still,
And ne'er have spoke a loving word to you;
But you at your sick service had a prince.
Nay, you may think my love was crafty love,
And call it cunning. Do, and if you will;
If Heav'n be pleas'd that you must use me ill,
Why then you must.—Will you put out mine eyes?
These eyes that never did, and never shall,
So much as frown on you?

Hub. I've sworn to do it;
And with hot irons must I burn them out.

Arth.

Arth. Oh! if an angel should have come to me,
And told me Hubert should put out mine eyes,
I would not have believ'd a tongue but Hubert's.
        [*Stamps, and then men enter.*

Hub. Come forth!—Do as I bid you.

Arth. O, save me, Hubert, save me! my eyes are out,
E'en with the fierce looks of these bloody men.

Hub. Give me the iron, I say, and bind him here.

Arth. Alas, what need you be so boist'rous rough?
I will not struggle, I will stand stone-still.
For heav'n's sake, Hubert, let me not be bound.
Nay, hear me, Hubert—Drive these men away,
And I will sit as quiet as a lamb.
I will not stir, nor wince, nor speak a word,
Nor look upon the iron angrily:
Thrust but these men away, and I'll forgive you,
Whatever torment you do put me to.

Hub. Go, stand within; let me alone with him.

Exe. I am best pleas'd to be from such a deed.
        [*Exeunt.*

Arth. Alas, I then have chid away my friend;
He hath a stern look, but a gentle heart;
Let him come back, that his compassion may
Give life to your's.

Hub. Come, boy, prepare yourself.

Arth. Is there no remedy?

Hub. None, but to lose your eyes.

Arth. O heav'n! that there were but a moth in your's,
A grain, a dust, a gnat, or wandering hair,
Any annoyance in that precious sense;
Then, feeling what small things are boist'rous there,
Your vile intent must needs seem horrible.

Hub. Is this your promise? Go to, hold your tongue.

Arth. Let me not hold my tongue; let me not, Hubert!
Or, Hubert, if you will cut out my tongue,
So I may keep mine eyes—O spare mine eyes!
Though to no use, but still to look on you.
Lo, by my troth, the instrument is cold,
And would not harm me!

Hub. I can heat it, boy.

Arth. No, in good sooth, the fire is dead with grief,
Being create for comfort, to be us'd
In undeserv'd extremes; see else yourself;
There is no malice in this burning coal;
The breath of heav'n hath blown its spirit out,
And strew'd repentant ashes on its head.

Hub. But with my breath I can revive it, boy.

Arth. All things that you should use to do me wrong
Deny their office; only you do lack
That mercy which fierce fire and iron extend,—
Creatures of note for mercy-lacking uses.

Hub. Well, see to live; I will not touch thine eye
For all the treasures that thine uncle owns:
Yet I am sworn, and I did purpose, boy,
With this same very iron to burn them out.

Arth. O now you look like Hubert. All this while
You were disguised.

Hub. Peace; no more, adieu!
Your uncle must not know but you are dead.
I'll fill these dogged spies with false reports:
And, pretty child, sleep doubtless and secure,
That Hubert, for the wealth of all the world,
Will not offend thee.

Arth. O heaven! I thank you, Hubert.

Hub.

Hub. Silence, no more; go closely in with me.
Much danger do I undergo for thee.
SHAKSPEARE.

Enter ARTHUR *on the walls, disguised.*

Arth. The wall is high, and yet will I leap down.
Good ground, be pitiful and hurt me not!
There's few or none do know me: if they did,
This ship-boy's semblance hath disguis'd me quite.
I am afraid, and yet I'll venture it.
If I get down, and do not break my limbs,
I'll find a thousand shifts to get away;
As good to die and go as die and stay.   [*Leaps down.*
Oh me! my uncle's spirit is in these stones:
Heav'n take my soul and England keep my bones!   [*Dies.*

Enter PEMBROKE, SALISBURY *and* BIGOT.

Sal. Lords, I will meet him at St. Edmondsbury;
It is our safety, and we must embrace
This gentle offer of the perilous time.

Pemb. Who brought that letter from the Cardinal?

Sal. The Count Melun, a noble lord of France,
Whose private with me of the Dauphin's love
Is much more than these gen'ral lines import.

Big. To-morrow morning let us meet him then.

Sal. Or rather then set forward, for 'twill be
Two long days journey, Lords, or e'er we meet.

Enter BASTARD.

Bast. Once more to-day well met, distemper'd Lords!
The King by me requests your presence strait.

Sal. The King hath dispossest himself of us;
We will not line his thin bestained cloak

With our pure honours, nor attend the foot
That leaves the print of blood where'er it walks.
Return, and tell him so: we know the worst.

Baſt. Whate'er you think, good words I think were beſt.

Sal. Our griefs, and not our manners, reaſon now.

Baſt. But there is little reaſon in your grief,
Therefore 'twere reaſon you had manners now.

Pemb. Sir, Sir, impatience hath its privilege.

Baſt. 'Tis true, to hurt its maſter, no man elſe.

Sal. This is the priſon: what is he lies here?

[*Seeing Arthur.*

Pemb. O death, made proud by pure and princely beauty!
The earth hath not a hole to hide this deed.

Sal. Murder, as hating what himſelf hath done,
Doth lay it open to urge on revenge.

Bigot. Or when he doom'd this beauty to the glave,
Found it too precious princely for a grave.

Sal. Sir Richard, what think you? have you beheld,
Or have you read or heard, or could you think,
Or do you almoſt think, although you ſee,
That do you ſee? Could thought, without this object,
Form ſuch another? 'tis the very top,
The height, the creſt, or creſt unto the creſt,
Of Murder's arm; this is the bloodieſt ſhame,
The wildeſt ſavag'ry, the vileſt ſtroke,
That ever wall-eye'd wrath, or ſtarting rage,
Preſented to the tears of ſoft remorſe.

Pemb. All murders paſt do ſtand excus'd in this;
And this ſo ſole, and ſo unmatchable,
Shall give a holineſs, a purity,
To the yet unbegotten ſins of time;
And prove a deadly blood-ſhed but a jeſt,
Exampled by this heinous ſpectacle.

Baſt.

Bast. It is a damn'd and bloody work;
The graceless action of a heavy hand,
If that it be the work of any hand.

Sal. If that it be the work of any hand?
We had a kind of light what would ensue.
It is the shameful work of Hubert's hand;
The practice and the purpose of the king;
From whose obedience I forbid my soul,
Kneeling before this ruin of sweet life,
And breathing to this breathless excellence
The incense of a vow, a holy vow!
Never to taste the pleasures of the world,
Never to be infected with delight,
Nor conversant with ease and idleness,
'Till I have set a glory to this hand,
By giving it the worship of revenge.

Pemb. Big. Our souls religiously confirm thy word.

SHAKSPEARE.

KING PHILIP, CONSTANCE, AND PANDULPHO.

Philip. Look, who comes here? a grave unto a soul;
Holding th' eternal spirit 'gainst her will
In the vile prison of afflicted breath;
I pr'ythee, lady, go away with me.

Const. Lo now, now see the issue of your peace!

K. Philip. Patience, good lady; comfort, gentle
Constance.

Const. No, I defy all council, all redress,
But that which ends all council, true redress,
Death!—Death, O amiable, lovely death,

Arise forth from thy couch of lasting night,
Thou hate and terror to posterity,
And I will kiss thy bones detestable,
And put my eye-balls in thy vaulty brows,
And ring these fingers with thy household worms,
And stop this gap of breath with fulsome dust,
And be a carrion monster like thyself!
Come, grin on me, and I will think thou smil'st,
And kiss thee as thy wife! thou love of mis'ry,
O come to me!

 K. Philip.   O fair affliction, peace!

 Const.   No, no, I will not, having breath to cry;
O that my tongue were in the thunder's mouth,
Then with a passion I would shake the world,
And rouse from sleep that fell anatomy
Which cannot hear a lady's feeble voice,
And scorns a modern invocation.

 Pand.   Lady, you utter madness, and not sorrow.

 Const.   Thou art not holy to belie me so:
I am not mad; this hair I tear is mine;
My name is Constance, I was Geffrey's wife—
Young Arthur is my son, and he is lost!
I am not mad, I would to heav'n I were;
For then 'tis like I should forget myself.
O, if I could, what grief should I forget!
I am not mad; too well, too well I feel
The different plagues of each calamity.
Oh, father Cardinal, I have heard you say
That we shall see and know our friends in heav'n;
If that be, I shall see my boy again.
For since the birth of Cain, the first male-child,
To him that did but yesterday suspire,

There

There was not such a gracious creature born.
But now will canker sorrow eat my bud,
And chase the native beauty from his cheek,
And he will look as hollow as a ghost,
As dim and meagre as an ague's fit,
And so he'll die; and, rising so again,
When I shall meet him in the court of heav'n
I shall not know him; therefore never, never
Must I behold my pretty Arthur more.

 Pand. You hold too heinous a respect of grief!

 Const. He talks to me who never had a son!

 K. Philip. You are as fond of grief as of your child!

 Const. Grief fills the room up of my absent child:
Lies in his bed, walks up and down with me;
Puts on his pretty looks, repeats his words,
Remembers me of all his gracious parts;
Stuffs out his vacant garments with his form;
Then have I reason to be fond of grief.
Fare you well!—Had you such a loss as I,
I could give better comfort than you do.
I will not keep this form upon my head,
      [*Tearing off her head-clothes.*
When there is so much disorder in my wit.
O Lord, my boy, my Arthur, my fair son!
My life, my joy, my food, my all the world,
My widow's comfort, and my sorrow's cure!   [*Exit.*

 K. Philip. I fear some outrage, and I'll follow her.
        SHAKSPEARE.

LADY MACBETH.

Lady. That which hath made them drunk hath made me bold:
What hath quench'd them hath giv'n me fire. Hark!
It was the howl that shriek'd, the fatal bell-man,
Which gives the stern'st good-night—he is about it—
The doors are open; and the surfeited grooms
Do mock their charge with snores. I've drugg'd their possets,
That death and nature do contend about them,
Whether they live or die.

Enter MACBETH.

Macb. Who's there? what ho!
Lady. Alack! I am afraid they have awak'd,
And 'tis not done; th' attempt and not the deed
Confounds us—hark!—I laid their daggers ready—
He could not miss 'em.—Had he not resembled
My father as he slept, I had done't—My husband!
Macb. I've done the deed—didst not thou hear a noise?
Lady. I heard the owl scream and the crickets cry.
Did not you speak?
Macb. When?
Lady. Now.
Macb. As I descended?
Lady. Aye.
Macb. Hark!—Who lies i' th' second chamber?
Lady. Donalbain.

Macb.

Macb. This is a sorry sight! [*Looks on his hands.*
Lady. A foolish thought, to say a sorry sight!
Macb. There's one did laugh in's sleep, and one cry'd,
    Murder!
They wak'd each other, and I stood and heard them;
But they did say their prayers, and addrest them
Again to sleep.
  Lady. There are two lodg'd together.
  Macb. One cry'd *God bless us!* and *Amen* the other,
As they had seen me with these hangman's hands.
List'ning their fear, I could not say *Amen*
When they did say, *God bless us!*
  Lady. Consider it not so deeply.
  Macb. But wherefore could not I pronounce *Amen!*
I had more need of blessing, and *Amen*
Stuck in my throat.
  Lady. These deeds must not be thought on
After these ways—so it will make us mad!
  Macb. Methought I heard a voice cry, *Sleep no more!*
Macbeth doth murder sleep; the innocent sleep,
The death of each day's life, sore labour's bath,
Balm of hurt minds, great nature's second course,
Chief nourisher in life's feast.
  Lady. What do you mean?
  Macb. Still it cry'd, *Sleep no more* (to all the house);
Glamis hath murder'd sleep, and therefore Cawdor
Shall sleep no more; Macbeth shall sleep no more!
  Lady. Who was it that thus cry'd? why worthy Thane,
You do unbend your noble strength, to think
So brain-sickly of things; go, get some water,
And wash this filthy witness from your hand.
Why did you bring these daggers from the place?

They muſt lie there. Go, carry them, and ſmear
The ſleepy grooms with blood.

   Macb. I'll go no more!
I am afraid to think what I have done;
Look on't again I dare not.

   Lady. Infirm of purpoſe!
Give me the daggers!—The ſleeping and the dead
Are but as pictures; 'tis the eye of childhood
That fears a painted devil! If he bleed,
I'll gild the faces of the grooms withal,
For it muſt ſeem their guilt!   [*Knock within.*

   Macb. Whence is that knocking?   [*Starting.*
How is't with me, when every noiſe appals me!
What hands are here? ha! they pluck out mine eyes.
Will all great Neptune's ocean waſh this blood
Clean from my hand?—This my hand will rather
Make the green ocean red.   SHAKSPEARE.

DOCTOR AND GENTLEWOMAN.

   Doct. I have two nights watch'd with you, but can perceive no truth in your report. When was it ſhe laſt walk'd?

   Gent. Since his majeſty went into the field, I have ſeen her riſe from her bed, her night-gown upon her, unlock her cloſet, take forth paper, fold it, write upon't, read it, afterwards ſeal it, and again return to bed; yet all this while in a moſt faſt ſleep.

   Doct. A great perturbation in nature, to receive at once the benefit of ſleep, and do the effects of watching!

In this flumbry agitation, befides her walking, and other actual performances, what (at any time) have you heard her fay?

Gent. That, Sir, which I will not report after her.

Doct. You may to me, and 'tis moft meet you fhould.

Gent. Neither to you, nor any one, having no witnefs to confirm my fpeech.——

Enter Lady MACBETH *with a taper.*

Lo you, here fhe comes! this is her very guife, and, upon my life, faft afleep; obferve her; ftand clofe.

Doct. How came fhe by that light?

Gent. Why, it ftood by her; fhe has light by her continually; 'tis her command.

Doct. You fee her eyes are open.

Gent. Ay, but their fenfe is fhut.

Doct. What is it fhe does now? look how fhe rubs her hands!

Gent. It is an accuftomed action with her to feem thus, wafhing her hands: I have known her continue in this a quarter of an hour.

Lady. Yet here's a fpot!

Doct. Hark, fhe fpeaks! I will fet down what comes from her, to fatisfy my remembrance the more ftrongly.

Lady. Out, damn'd fpot; out, I fay!—One; two; why then 'tis time to do't—hell is mufky. Fie, my Lord, fie; a foldier, and afraid? What need we fear who know it, when none can call our power to account? Yet who would have thought the old man to have had fo much blood in him?

Doct. Do you mark that?

Lady. The Thane of Fife had a wife; where is fhe now? What, will thefe hands ne'er be clean?—No more o'that, o'that, my lord, no more o'that: you mar all with starting!

Doct. Go to, go to; you have known what you should not.

Gent. She has spoke what she should not, I am sure of that: heav'n knows what she has known.

Lady. Here's the smell of blood still: all the perfumes of Arabia will not sweeten this little hand. Oh! oh! oh!

Doct. What a sigh is there! the heart is sorely charg'd.

Gent. I would not have such a heart in my bosom for the dignity of the whole body.

Doct. Well, well, well—

Gent. Pray God it be so, Sir.

Doct. This disease is beyond my practice: yet I have known those which have walkt in their sleep, who have died holily in their beds.

Lady. Wash your hands, put on your night-gown, look not so pale—I tell you yet again, Banquo's buried: he cannot come out of his grave!

Doct. Even so!

Lady. To bed, to bed; there's knocking at the gate! Come, come, come, come, give me your hand: what's done cannot be undone. To bed, to bed, to bed! [*Exit.*

Doct. Will she go to bed?

Gent. Directly.

Doct. Foul whisp'rings are abroad; unnat'ral deeds
Do breed unnat'ral troubles. Infected minds
To their deaf pillows will discharge their secrets.
More needs she the divine than the physician.
Good God, forgive us all! Look after her,
Remove from her the means of all annoyance,
And still keep eyes upon her; so good night!

My mind she's mated, and amaz'd my sight.
I think, but dare not speak.
 Gent. Good night, good doctor. SHAKSPEARE.

MACBETH AND DOCTOR.

 Macb. How does your patient, doctor?
 Doct. Not so sick, my lord,
As she is troubled with thick-coming fancies,
That keep her from her rest.
 Macb. Cure her of that.
Canst thou not minister to minds diseas'd,
Pluck from the memory a rooted sorrow,
Raze out the written troubles of the brain;
And with some sweet oblivious antidote
Cleanse the full bosom of that perilous stuff
Which weighs upon the heart?
 Doct. Therein the patient
Must minister unto himself.
 Macb. Throw physic to the dogs, I'll none of it.

MACBETH. SEYTON.

 Macb. What is that noise? [*A cry within of women.*
 Seyton. It is the cry of women, my good lord.
 Macb. I have almost forgot the taste of fears:
The time has been my senses would have cool'd
To hear a night-shriek, and my fell of hair

Would at a dismal treatise rouse, and stir
As life were in't. I have surfeited with horrors—
Direness familiar to my slaught'rous thoughts
Cannot now start me. Wherefore was that cry?
  Seyton. The queen is dead.
  Macb. She should have dy'd hereafter;
There would have been a time for such a word.
To-morrow, and to-morrow, and to-morrow,
Creeps in this petty space from day to day,
To the last syllable of recorded time;
And all our yesterdays have lighted fools
The way to dusky death. Out, out, brief candle!
Life's but a walking shadow—a poor player,
That struts and frets his hour upon the stage,
And then is heard no more: it is a tale
Told by an idiot, full of sound and fury,
Signifying nothing.
SHAKESPEAR.

WILLIAM AND MARGARET. AN OLD SCOTCH BALLAD.

When all was wrapt in dark midnight,
  And all were fast asleep,
Then in came Marg'ret's grimly ghost
  And stood at William's feet;
Her face was like the April morn,
  Clad in a wintry cloud,
And clay cold was her lily hand
  That held her sable shrowd.

II.

So shall the faireſt face appear
   When youth and years are flown;
Such is the robe that kings muſt wear
   When death has reft their crown.
Her bloom was like the ſpringing flower
   That ſips the ſilver dew,
The roſe was budded in her cheek,
   And opening to the view:

III.

But love had, like the canker-worm,
   Conſum'd her early prime;
The roſe grew pale and left her cheek,
   She dy'd before her time.
Awake, ſhe cry'd, thy true love calls,
   Come from her midnight grave;
Now let thy pity hear the maid
   Thy love refus'd to ſave!

IV.

This is the mirk and fearful hour
   When dreary church-yards yawn,
And injur'd ghoſts come forth to walk,
   And haunt the faithleſs man:
Bethink thee, William, of thy fault,
   Thy pledge and broken oath;
And give me back my maiden vow,
   And give me back my troth.

V.

How could you say my face was fair,
    And yet that face forsake;
How could you win my virgin heart,
    Yet leave that heart to break:
How could you promise love to me,
    And not that promise keep;
Why did you swear mine eyes were bright,
    Yet leave those eyes to weep!

VI.

How could you say my lips were sweet,
    And made the scarlet pale;
And why did I, young witless maid,
    Believe the flattering tale!
That face, alas! no more is fair,
    Those lips no longer red,
Dark are mine eyes, now clos'd in death,
    And every charm is fled.

VII.

The hungry worm my sister is,
    This winding-sheet I wear,
And cold and weary lasts our night,
    Till that last morn appear.
But hark! the cock has warn'd me hence,
    A long and last adieu!
Come see, false man, how low she lies,
    That dy'd for love of you!

VIII.

Now birds did sing, and morning smile,
  And shew her glittering head,
Pale William shook in ev'ry limb,
  Then raving left his bed.
He hy'd him to the fatal place
  Where Marg'ret's body lay,
And stretch'd him on the green grass turf
  That wrapt her breathless clay.

IX.

And thrice he call'd on Marg'ret's name,
  And thrice he wept full sore,
Then laid his cheek to the cold earth,
  And word spoke never more.

SONNET TO SLEEP.

Come, balmy sleep! tir'd nature's soft resort!
  On these sad temples all thy poppies shed;
And bid gay dreams, from Morpheus' airy court,
  Float in light vision round my aching head!—
Secure of all thy blessings, partial power!
  On his hard bed the peasant throws him down;
And the poor sea boy, in the rudest hour,
  Enjoys thee more than he who wears a crown.
Clasp'd in her faithful shepherd's guardian arms,
  Well may the village girl sweet slumbers prove;

And

And they, O gentle sleep! still taste thy charms,
  Who wake to labour, liberty and love.
But still thy opiate aid dost thou deny
  To calm the anxious breast; to close the streaming eye.
                              CHARLOTTE SMITH.

THE FRIAR OF ORDERS GRAY.

IT was a friar of orders gray
  Walk'd forth to tell his beads,
And he met with a lady fair
  Clad in a pilgrim's weeds.

Now Christ thee save, thou reverend friar,
  I pray thee tell to me
If ever at yon holy shrine
  My true love thou didst see.

And how should I know your true love
  From many another one?
O by his cockle, hat, and staff,
  And by his sandal shoon.

But chiefly by his face and mien,
  That were so fair to view;
His flaxen locks that sweetly curl'd,
  And eyne of lovely blue.

O lady, he's dead and gone!
  Lady, he's dead and gone!
And at his head a green grass turf,
  And at his heels a stone.

Within these holy cloisters long
  He languish'd, and he dy'd,
Lamenting of a lady's love,
  And 'plaining of her pride.

Here bore him bare-faced on his bier
  Six proper youths and tall,
And many a tear bedew'd his grave
  Within yon kirk-yard wall.

And art thou dead, thou gentle youth!
  And art thou dead and gone!
And didst thou die for love of me!
  Break, cruel heart of stone!

O weep not, lady, weep not so;
  Some ghostly comfort seek:
Let not vain sorrow rive thy heart,
  Nor tears bedew thy cheek.

O do not, do not, holy friar,
  My sorrow now reprove;
For I have lost the sweetest youth
  That e'er won lady's love!

And now, alas! for thy sad loss
  I'll evermore weep and sigh;
For thee I only wish to live,
  For thee I wish to die.

Weep no more, lady, weep no more,
  Thy sorrow is in vain:
For violets pluck'd the sweetest showers
  Will ne'er make grow again.

Our

Our joys as winged dreams do fly—
   Why then should sorrow last?
Since grief but aggravates the loss,
   Grieve not for what is past!

O say not so, thou holy friar;
   I pray thee, say not so:
For since my true love died for me,
   'Tis meet my tears should flow.

And will he never come again?
   Will he ne'er come again?
Ah! no, he is dead, and laid in his grave,
   For ever to remain.

His cheek was redder than the rose,
   The comliest youth was he:—
But he is dead, and laid in his grave:
   Alas! and woe is me!

Sigh no more, lady, sigh no more;
   Men were deceivers ever:
One foot on sea and one on land,
   To one thing constant never.

Hadst thou been fond he had been false,
   And left thee sad and heavy;
For young men ever were fickle found,
   Since summer trees were leafy.

Now say not so, thou holy friar,
   I pray thee say not so;
My love he had the truest heart—
   O he was ever true!

                             And

And art thou dead, thou much lov'd youth!
   And didſt thou die for me?
Then farewell home; for evermore
   A pilgrim I will be.

But firſt upon my true love's grave
   My weary limbs I'll lay,
And thrice I'll kiſs the green-graſs turf
   That wrapt his breathleſs clay.

Yet ſtay, fair lady; reſt awhile
   Beneath this cloiſter's wall:
See through the hawthorn blows the cold wind,
   Drizzly rain doth fall.

O ſtay me not, thou holy friar,
   O ſtay me not, I pray;
No drizzly rain that falls on me
   Can waſh my fault away.

Yet ſtay, fair lady, turn again
   And dry thoſe pearly tears;
For ſee, beneath this gown of gray,
   Thy own true-love appears!

Here, forc'd by grief and hopeleſs love,
   Theſe holy weeds I ſought:
And here, amid theſe lonely walls,
   To end my days I thought.

But haply, for my year of grace
   Is not yet paſs'd away,
Might I ſtill hope to win thy love,
   No longer would I ſtay.

Now farewell grief, and welcome joy
  Once more unto my heart;
For since I have found thee, lovely youth,
  We never more will part.
          BEAUMONT AND FLETCHER.

THE MOUSE'S PETITION.

Oh! hear a pensive prisoner's prayer,
  For liberty that sighs;
And never let thine heart be shut
  Against the wretch's cries.

  For here forlorn and sad I sit,
Within the wiry grate;
And tremble at th' approaching morn,
Which brings impending fate.

  If e'er thy breast with freedom glow'd,
And spurn'd a tyrant's chain,
Let not thy strong oppressive force
A free-born mouse detain.

  Oh! do not stain with guiltless blood
Thy hospitable hearth;
Nor triumph that thy wiles betray'd
A prize so little worth.

  The scatter'd gleanings of a feast
My frugal meals supply;
And, if thine unrelenting heart
The slender boon deny,

  The cheerful light, the vital air,
Are blessings widely given;
Let nature's commoners enjoy
The common gifts of heaven.

The well taught philosophic mind
To all compassion gives;
Casts round the world an equal eye,
And feels for all that lives.

If mind, as ancient sages taught,
A never dying flame,
Still shifts through matter's varying forms,
In every form the same,

Beware, lest in the worm you crush
A brother's soul you find;
And tremble lest thy luckless hand
Dislodge a kindred mind.

Or if this transient gleam of day
Be all of life we share,
Let pity plead within thy breast
That little all to spare.

So may thy hospitable board
With wealth and peace be crown'd;
And every charm of heart-felt ease
Beneath thy roof be found.

So, when destruction lurks unseen,
Which men, like mice, may share,
May some kind angel clear thy path,
And break the hidden snare.

      MISS AIKIN.

THE DYING KID.

A TEAR bedews my Delia's eye
To think yon playful kid muſt die;
From cryſtal ſpring and flow'ry mead
Muſt in his prime of life recede.

Ere while in ſportive circles round
She ſaw him wheel, and friſk, and bound;
From rock to rock purſue his way,
And on the fearful margin play.

Pleas'd on his various freaks to dwell,
She ſaw him climb my ruſtic cell,
There eye my lawns with verdure bright,
And ſeem all raviſh'd at the ſight.

She tells with what delight he ſtood
To trace his features in the flood,
Then ſkipp'd aloof with quaint amaze,
And then drew near again to gaze.

She tells me how with eager ſpeed
He flew to hear my vocal reed;
And how with critic face profound,
And ſtedfaſt ear, devour'd the ſound.

His ev'ry frolic, light as air,
Deſerves the gentle Delia's care;
And tears bedew her tender eye,
To think the playful kid muſt die.

But knows my Delia, timely wife,
How soon this blameless æra flies?
While violence and craft succeed,
Unfair design, and ruthless deed!

Soon wou'd the vine his wounds deplore,
And yield her purple gifts no more;
Ah! soon eras'd from ev'ry grove,
Were Strephon's name, and Delia's love.

No more these bow'rs might Strephon see
Where first he fondly gaz'd on thee;
No more those beds of flow'rets find,
Which for thy charming brows he twin'd.

Each wayward passion soon would tear
His bosom, now so void of care,
And when they left his ebbing vein,
What but insipid age remain!

Then mourn not the decrees of fate
That gave his life so short a date;
And I will join my tend'rest sighs,
To think that youth so swiftly flies.

      SHENSTONE.

SONNET TO A NIGHTINGALE.

Poor melancholy bird—that all night long
 Tell'st to the moon thy tale of tender wo;
 From what sad cause can such sweet sorrow flow,
And whence this mournful melody of song?

Thy poet's musing fancy would translate
   What mean the sounds that swell thy little breast,
   When still at dewy eve thou leav'st thy nest,
Thus to the listening night to sing thy fate!

Pale sorrow's victims wert thou once among,
   Though now releas'd in woodlands wild to rove?
   Say—hast thou felt from friends some cruel wrong,
Or diedst thou, martyr of disastrous love?
Ah! songstress sad! that such my lot might be,
To sigh and sing at liberty—like thee!
CHARLOTTE SMITH.

SONG FROM THE LAPLAND TONGUE.

   Thou rising sun, whose gladsome ray
Invites my fair to rural play,
Dispel the mist and clear the skies,
And bring my Orra to my eyes.
   Oh! were I sure my dear to view,
I'd climb that pine-tree's topmost bough,
Aloft in air that quivering plays,
And round and round for ever gaze.
   My Orra Moor, where art thou laid?
What wood conceals my sleeping maid?
Fast by the roots enrag'd I'd tear
The trees that hide my promis'd fair.
   Oh! could I ride on clouds and skies,
Or on the raven's pinions rise!
Ye storks, ye swans, a moment stay,
And waft a lover on his way!

My bliſs too long my bride denies,
Apace the waſting ſummer flies:
Nor yet the wintry blaſts I fear,
Not ſtorms or night ſhall keep me here.

What may for ſtrength with ſteel compare?
Oh! love has fetters ſtronger far!
By bolts of ſteel are limbs confin'd,
But cruel love enchains the mind!

No longer then perplex thy breaſt;
When thoughts torment, the firſt are beſt;
'Tis mad to go, 'tis death to ſtay,
Away to Orra, haſte away.

STEELE.

A FRAGMENT.

——— SIR BERTRAND turned his ſteed towards the wolds, hoping to croſs theſe dreary moors before the curfew. But ere he had proceeded half his journey he was bewildered by the different tracks; and not being able, as far as the eye could reach, to eſpy any object but the brown heath ſurrounding him, he was at length quite uncertain which way he ſhould direct his courſe. Night overtook him in this ſituation. It was one of thoſe nights when the moon gives a faint glimmering of light through the thick black clouds of a lowering ſky. Now and then ſhe ſuddenly emerged in full ſplendour from her vail, and then inſtantly retired behind it; having juſt ſerved to give the forlorn Sir Bertrand a wide extended proſpect over the deſolate waſte. Hope and native courage awhile urged him to puſh forwards, but at length the increaſing darkneſs and fatigue of body and mind overcame him; he dreaded moving from the ground he stood on, for fear of unknown pits and bogs; and, alighting from his horse in despair, he threw himself on the ground. He had not long continued in that posture when the sudden toll of a distant bell struck his ears—he started up, and, turning towards the sound, discerned a dim twinkling light. Instantly he seized his horse's bridle, and with cautious steps advanced towards it. After a painful march he was stopped by a moated ditch surrounding the place from whence the light proceeded; and, by a momentary glimpse of moonlight, he had a full view of a large antique mansion, with turrets at the corners, and an ample porch in the centre. The injuries of time were strongly marked on every thing about it. The roof in various places was fallen in, the battlements were half demolished, and the windows broken and dismantled. A drawbridge, with a ruinous gateway at each end, led to the court before the building.—He entered; and instantly the light, which proceeded from a window in one of the turrets, glided along and vanished; at the same moment the moon sunk beneath a black cloud, and the night was darker than ever. All was silent. Sir Bertrand fastened his steed under a shed, and, approaching the house, traversed its whole front with light and slow footsteps.—All was still as death.—He looked in at the lower windows, but could not distinguish a single object through the impenetrable gloom. After a short parley with himself he entered the porch, and, seizing a massy iron knocker at the gate, lifted it up, and hesitating at length struck a loud stroke—the noise resounded through the whole mansion with hollow echoes.—All was still again. He repeated the strokes more boldly and louder—another interval of silence ensued.—A third

time

time he knocked, and a third time all was still. He then fell back to some distance, that he might discern whether any light could be seen in the whole front—it again appeared in the same place, and quickly glided away, as before—at the same instant a deep sullen toll sounded from the turret. Sir Bertrand's heart made a fearful stop—he was a while motionless; then terror impelled him to make some hasty steps towards his steed—but shame stopt his flight; and, urged by honour and a resistless desire of finishing the adventure, he returned to the porch; and, working up his soul to a full steadiness of resolution, he drew forth his sword with one hand, and with the other lifted up the latch of the gate. The heavy door creeking upon its hinges reluctantly yielded to his hand—he applied his shoulder to it and forced it open—he quitted it and stept forward—the door instantly shut with a thundering clap. Sir Bertrand's blood was chilled—he turned back to find the door, and it was long ere his trembling hands could seize it—but his utmost strength could not open it again.— After several ineffectual attempts he looked behind him and beheld, across a hall, upon a large staircase, a pale bluish flame, which cast a dismal gleam of light around. He again summoned forth his courage and advanced towards it—it retired. He came to the foot of the stairs, and, after a moment's deliberation, ascended. He went slowly up, the flame retiring before him, till he came to a wide gallery—the flame proceeded along it, and he followed in silent horror, treading lightly, for the echoes of his footsteps startled him. It led him to the foot of another staircase, and then vanished;—at the same instant another toll sounded from the turret—Sir Bertrand felt it strike upon his heart. He was now in total darkness; and, with his arms extended, began to ascend the second staircase. A

dead

dead cold hand met his left hand, and firmly grasped it, drawing him forcibly forwards—he endeavoured to disengage himself, but could not—he made a furious blow with his sword, and instantly a loud shriek pierced his ears, and the dead hand was left powerless with his—he dropt it, and rushed forwards with a desperate valour. The stairs were narrow and winding, and interrupted by frequent breaches and loose fragments of stone. The staircase grew narrower and narrower, and at length terminated in a low iron grate. Sir Bertrand pushed it open—It led to an intricate winding passage just large enough to admit a person upon his hands and knees. A faint glimmering of light served to shew the nature of the place—Sir Bertrand entered—a deep hollow groan resounded from a distance throughout the vault—he went forwards; and, proceeding beyond the first turning, he discerned the same blue flame which had before conducted him—he followed it. The vault at length suddenly opened into a lofty gallery, in the midst of which a figure appeared, completely armed, thrusting forwards the bloody stump of an arm, with a terrible frown and menacing gesture, and brandishing a sword in his hand. Sir Bertrand undauntedly sprung forwards; and aiming a fierce blow at the figure, it instantly vanished, letting fall a massy iron key. The flame now rested upon a pair of ample folding doors at the end of the gallery. Sir Bertrand went up to it, and applied the key to a brazen lock—with difficulty he turned the bolt—instantly the doors flew open and discovered a large apartment, at the end of which was a coffin rested upon a bier, with a taper burning on each side of it.—Along the room, on both sides, were gigantic statues of black marble, attired in the Moorish habit, and holding enormous sabres in

their

their right hands. Each of them reared his arm and advanced one leg forwards as the knight entered; at the same moment the lid of the coffin flew open, and the bell tolled. The flame still glided forwards, and Sir Bertrand resolutely followed till he arrived within six paces of the coffin. Suddenly a lady in a shroud and black vail rose up in it, and stretched out her arms towards him—at the same time the statues clashed their sabres and advanced. Sir Bertrand flew to the lady, and clasped her in his arms—she threw up her vail and kissed his lips; and instantly the whole building shook as with an earthquake, and fell asunder as with a horrible crash. Sir Bertrand was thrown into a sudden trance, and on recovering found himself seated on a velvet sofa in the most magnificent room he had ever seen, lighted with innumerable tapers, in lustres of pure crystal. A sumptuous banquet was set in the middle. The doors opening to soft music, a lady of incomparable beauty, attired with amazing splendour, entered, surrounded by a troop of gay nymphs more fair than the graces.—She advanced to the knight, and, falling on her knees, thanked him as her deliverer. The nymphs placed a garland of laurel upon his head, and the lady led him to the banquet, and sat beside him. The nymphs placed themselves at the table, and a numerous train of servants entering served up the feast, delicious music playing all the time. Sir Bertrand could not speak for astonishment—he could only return their honours by courteous looks and gestures. After the banquet was finished, all retired but the lady, who, leading back the knight to the sofa, addressed him in these words:

AIKIN's MISCELLANEOUS PIECES.

BOOK IV.

DIALOGUES, CONVERSATIONS, AND FABLES.

LORD AND LADY TOWNLY.

Lord T. How comes it, Madam, that a tradesman dares be clamorous in my house for money due to him from you?

Lady T. You don't expect, my Lord, that I should answer for other people's impertinence?

Lord T. I expect, Madam, you should answer for your own extravagancies that are the occasion of it—I thought I had given you money three months ago to satisfy all these sort of people.

Lady T. Yes; but you see they never are to be satisfied.

Lord T. Nor am I, Madam, longer to be abused thus. What's become of the last five hundred I gave you?

Lady T. Gone.

Lord T. Gone! what way, Madam?

Lady T. Half the town over I believe by this time.

Lord T. 'Tis well; I see ruin will make no impression till it falls upon you.

Lady T. In short, my Lord, if money is always the subject of our conversation I shall make you no answer.

Lord T. Madam, Madam, I will be heard, and make you answer.

Lady T. Make me! Then I must tell you, my Lord, this is a language I have not been used to, and I won't bear it.

Lord T. Come, come, Madam, you shall bear a great deal more before I part with you.

Lady T. My Lord, if you insult me you will have as much to bear on your side I can assure you.

Lord T. Poh! your spirit grows ridiculous——you have neither honour, worth, or innocence to support it.

Lady T. You'll find, at least, I have resentment; and do you look well to the provocation.

Lord T. After those you have given me, Madam, 'tis almost infamous to talk with you.

Lady T. I scorn your imputation, and your menaces; the narrowness of your heart's your monitor; 'tis there, there, my Lord, you are wounded; you have less to complain of than many husbands of an equal rank to you.

Lord T. Why, Madam! do you presume upon your corporal merit that your person's less tainted than your mind? Is it there, there alone, an honest husband can be injured? Have you not every other vice that can debase your birth or stain the heart of woman? Is not your health, your beauty, husband, fortune, family, disclaimed, for nights consumed in riot and extravagance? The wanton does no more; if she conceals her shame does less: and sure the dissolute avowed as sorely wounds my honour and my quiet.

Lady T. I see, my Lord, what sort of wife might please you.

Lord T. Ungrateful woman! could you have seen yourself, you in yourself had seen her.——I am amazed our legislature has left no precedent of a divorce for this more visible injury, this adultery of the mind, as well as that of the person! When a woman's whole heart is alienated to pleasures I have no share in, what is it to me whether a black ace or a powdered coxcomb has possession of it?

Lady T. If you have not found it yet, my Lord, this is not the way to get possession of mine, depend upon it.

Lord T. That, Madam, I have long despaired of: and, since our happiness cannot be mutual, 'tis fit that with our hearts our persons too should separate.—This house you sleep no more in: though your content might grosly feed upon the dishonour of a husband, yet my desires would starve upon the features of a wife.

Lady T. Your style, my Lord, is much of the same delicacy with your sentiments of honour.

Lord T. Madam, Madam, this is no time for compliments——I have done with you,

Lady T. If we had never met, my Lord, I had not broke my heart for it: but have a care; I may not perhaps be so easily recalled as you may imagine.

Lord T. Recalled——Who's there?

Enter Servant.

Desire my sister and Mr. Manly to walk up. [*Exit. Serv.*

Lady T. My Lord, you may proceed as you please; but pray, what indiscretions have I committed, that are not daily practised by a hundred other women of quality?

Lord T. 'Tis not the number of ill wives, Madam, that makes the patience of a husband less contemptible:

and,

and, though a bad one may be the best man's lot, yet he'll make a better figure in the world that keeps his misfortunes out of doors than he that tamely keeps them within.

Lady T. I don't know what figure you may make, my Lord; but I shall have no reason to be ashamed of mine in whatever company I may meet you.

Lord T. Be sparing of your spirit, Madam; you'll need it to support you.——

Enter Lady Grace and Manly.

Mr. Manly, I have an act of friendship to beg of you, which wants more apologies than words can make for it.

Man. Then pray make none, my Lord, that I may have the greater merit in obliging you.

Lord T. Sister, I have the same excuse to entreat of you too.

Lady G. To your request, I beg, my Lord,——

Lord T. Thus then——As you both were present at my ill-considered marriage, I now desire you each will be a witness of my determined separation——I know, Sir, your good-nature and my sister's must be shocked at the office I impose on you; but, as I don't ask your justification of my cause, so I hope you are conscious that an ill woman can't reproach you if you are silent on her side.

Man. My Lord, I never thought till now it could be difficult to oblige you.

Lord T. For you, my Lady Townly, I need not here repeat the provocations of my parting with you——the world I fear is too well informed of them——For the good Lord, your dead father's sake, I will still support you as his daughter——As the Lord Townly's wife you have had every thing a fond husband could bestow; and (to our mutual shame I speak it) more than happy wives desire fire——but those indulgencies must end; state, equipage, and splendour, but ill become the vices that misuse them. ——The decent necessaries of life shall be supplied—— but not one article to luxury; not even the coach that waits to carry you from hence shall you ever use again. Your tender aunt, my Lady Lovemore, with tears, this morning has consented to receive you: where, if time and your condition brings you to a due reflection, your allowance shall be increased——but if you still are lavish of your little, or pine for past licentious pleasures, that little shall be less: nor will I call that soul my friend that names you in my hearing.

Lady G. My heart bleeds for her!   [*Aside.*

Lord T. Oh, Manly, look there! turn back thy thoughts with me, and witness to my growing love. There was a time when I believed that form incapable of vice or of decay; there I proposed the partner of an easy home; there I for ever hoped to find a cheerful companion, an agreeable, intimate, faithful friend, an useful helpmate, and a tender mother——but, oh, how bitter now the disappointment!

Man. The world is different in it's sense of happiness: offended as you are, I know you will still be just.

Lord T. Fear me not.

Man. This last reproach I see has struck her. [*Aside.*

Lord T. No, let me not (though I this moment cast her from my heart for ever) let me not urge her punishment beyond her crimes——I know the world is fond of any tale that feeds it's appetite of scandal: and, as I am conscious severities of this kind seldom fail of imputations too gross to mention, I here, before you both, acquit her of

the

the least suspicion raised against the honour of my bed. Therefore, when abroad her conduct may be questioned, do her fame that justice.

Lady T. Oh, sister! [*Turns to Lady Grace weeping.*

Lord T. When I am spoken of, where without favour this action may be canvassed, relate but half my provocations, and give me up to censure. [*Going.*

Lady T. Support me! save me! hide me from the world! [*Falling on Lady Grace's neck.*

Lord T. [*Returning*]—I had forgot me——You have no share in my resentment; therefore, as you have lived in friendship with her, your parting may admit of gentler terms than suit the honour of an injured husband.
[*Offers to go out.*

Man. [*Interposing.*] My Lord, you must not, shall not leave her thus! One moment's stay can do your cause no wrong! If looks can speak the anguish of her heart, I'll answer with my life there's something labouring in my mind that, would you bear the hearing, might deserve it.

Lord T. Consider! since we no more can meet, press nor my staying to insult her.

Lady T. Yet stay, my Lord—the little I would say, will not deserve an insult; and, undeserved, I know your nature gives it not. But, as you've called in friends to witness your resentment, let them be equal hearers of my last reply.

Lord T. I sha'n't refuse you that, Madam——be it so.

Lady T. My Lord, you ever have complained I wanted love; but as you kindly have allowed I never gave it to another, so when you hear the story of my heart, though you may still complain, you will not wonder at my coldness.

Lady G. This promises a reverse of temper. [*Apart.*

Man. This, My Lord, you are concerned to hear.

Lord T. Proceed—I am attentive.

Lady T. Before I was your bride, my Lord, the flattering world had talked me into beauty; which, at my glass, my youthful vanity confirm'd. Wild with that fame, I thought mankind my slaves: I triumphed over hearts, while all my pleasure was their pain; yet was my own so equally insensible to all, that, when a father's firm commands enjoined me to make choice of one, I even there declined the liberty he gave, and to his own election yielded up my youth————His tender care, my Lord, directed him to you————Our hands were joined—but still my heart was wedded to its folly! My only joy was power, command, society, profuseness, and to lead in pleasures: the husband's right to rule I thought a vulgar law, which only the deformed or meanly-spirited obeyed! I knew no directors but my passions; no master but my will! Even you, my Lord, some time o'ercome by love, was pleased with my delights; nor then foresaw this mad misuse of your indulgence————And, though I call myself ungrateful while I own it, yet as a truth it cannot be denied————that kind indulgence has undone me; it added strength to my habitual failings, and in a heart thus warm, in wild unthinking life, no wonder if the gentler sense of love was lost.

Lord T. Oh, Manly! where has this creature's heart been buried? [*Apart.*

Lady T. What I have said, my Lord, is not my excuse but my confession; my errors (give 'em, if you please, a harder name) cannot be defended! No! What's in its nature wrong no words can palliate, no plea can alter! What then remains in my condition but resignation to your pleasures? Time only can convince you of my future conduct.

conduct: therefore, till I have lived an object of forgiveness, I dare not hope for pardon——The penance of a lonely contrite life were little to the innocent; but to have deserved this separation will strew perpetual thorns upon my pillow.

Lady G. Oh, happy, heavenly hearing!

Lady T. Sister, farewell! [*Kissing her.*] Your virtue needs no warning from the shame that falls on me: but, when you think I have atoned my follies past, persuade your injured brother to forgive them.

Lord T. No, Madam! Your errors thus renounced this instant are forgotten! So deep, so due a sense of them, has made you what my utmost wishes formed, and all my heart has sighed for.

BETWEEN COLONEL RIVERS AND HIS DAUGHTER, ON HER INTENDED ELOPEMENT.

Miss Riv. If my father should not forgive me after all, I shall never forgive myself. But I wonder where Sir Harry can be all this time; I wish he was come. Oh, here he comes; I'll run and meet him. [*Runs and meets her father.* Ah! my father!

Col. Riv. Yes, Theodora, your poor abandoned miserable father.

Miss Riv. Oh! Sir!

Col. Riv. Little, Theodora, did I imagine I should ever have cause to lament the hour of your birth, and less did I imagine, when you arrived at an age to be perfectly acquainted with your duty, you would throw every sentiment of duty off.—In what, my dear, has your unhappy father

father been culpable, that you cannot bear his society any longer? what has he done to forfeit either your esteem or affection? From the moment of your birth to this unfortunate hour he has laboured to promote your happiness. But how has his solicitude on that account been rewarded? You now fly from those arms which have cherished you with such tenderness, when gratitude, generosity, and nature, should have twined you round my heart.

Miss Riv. Dear Sir!

Col. Riv. Look back, infatuated child, upon my whole conduct since your approach to maturity: have not I contracted my own enjoyments on purpose to enlarge yours, and watched your very looks to anticipate your inclinations? Have I ever, with the obstinacy of other fathers, been partial in favour of any man to whom you made the slightest objection? or have I ever shewn the least design of forcing your wishes to my own humour or caprice? on the contrary, has not the engagement I have entered into been carried on seemingly with your own approbation?

Miss Riv. Indeed, Sir, I am so ashamed of myself!

Col. Riv. How then, Theodora, have I merited a treatment of this nature? you have understanding, my dear, though you want filial affection; and my arguments must have weight with your reason, however my tranquillity may be the object of your contempt. I loved you, Theodora, with the warmest degree of tenderness, and flattered myself the proofs I every day gave of that tenderness had made my peace of mind a matter of some importance to my child. But, alas! a paltry compliment from a coxcomb undoes the whole labour of my life; and the daughter whom I looked upon as the support of my declining years betrays me in the unsuspecting hour of security,

curity, and rewards with her person the assassin who stabs me to the heart.

Miss Riv. Oh, my dear father! hear me, Sir, hear me, I beseech you!

Col. Riv. I do not come here, Theodora, to stop your flight, or put the smallest impediment in the way of your wishes. Your person is your own, and I scorn to detain even my daughter by force where she is not bound to me by inclination.—Since therefore neither duty nor discretion, a regard for my peace, nor a solicitude for your own welfare, are able to detain you,—go to this man, who has taught you to obliterate the sentiments of nature, and gained a ready way to your heart, by expressing a contempt for your father.—Go to him boldly, my child, and laugh at the pangs which tear this unhappy bosom. Be uniformly culpable, nor add the baseness of a despicable flight to the unpardonable want of filial affection. [*Going.*

Miss Riv. I feel the justness of his reproach, and am now the most miserable creature in the world. [*Aside.*

Col. Riv. [*Returning.*] One thing more, Theodora, and then farewell for ever.—Though you come here to throw off the affection of a child, I will not quit this place before I discharge the duty of a parent, even to a romantic extravagance, and provide for your welfare while you plunge me into the most poignant of all distress.—In the doating hours of paternal blandishment I have often promised you a fortune of twenty thousand pounds whenever you changed your situation. This promise was indeed made when I thought you incapable either of ingratitude or dissimulation, and when I fancied your person would be given where there was some reasonable pros-

pect

pect of your happiness; but still it was a promise, and shall be faithfully discharged. Here then in this pocket book are notes for that sum.—Take it—but never see me more. Banish my name eternally from your remembrance; and, when a little time shall have removed me from a world which your conduct has rendered insupportable, boast an additional title to your husband's regard, by having shortened the life of your miserable father.

[*Exit.*

Miss Riv. How could I be such a monster, such an unnatural monster, as ever to think of leaving him!—The universe should not bribe me now to go off with Sir Harry. What a wretched creature must she be who can dream of happiness while she wounds the bosom of a father! I'll immediately seek his forgiveness, and assure him of my repentance and determined resolution not to interrupt his felicity by my future conduct.

FALSE DELICACY.

BEVIL AND INDIANA.

Bev. Madam, your most obedient——I am afraid I broke in upon your rest last night——'twas very late before we parted; but 'twas your own fault; I never saw you in such an agreeable humour.

Ind. I am extremely glad we were both pleased; for I thought I never saw you better company.

Bev. Me, Madam! you rally; I said very little.

Ind. But I am afraid you heard me say a great deal;
and

and when a woman is in the talking vein the moſt agreeable thing a man can do, you know, is to have patience to hear her.

Bev. Then its pity, Madam, you ſhould ever be ſilent, that we might be always agreeable to one another.

Ind If I had your talent or power to make my actions ſpeak for me, I might indeed be ſilent, and yet pretend to ſomething more than the agreeable.

Bev. If I might be vain of any thing in my power, Madam, it is that my underſtanding, from all your ſex, has marked you out as the moſt deſerving object of my eſteem.

Ind. Should I think I deſerve this it were enough to make my vanity forfeit the very eſteem you offer me.

Bev. How ſo, Madam?

Ind. Becauſe eſteem is the reſult of reaſon, and to deſerve it from good ſenſe the height of human glory.—Nay, I would rather a man of honour ſhould pay me that than all the homage of a ſincere and human love.

Bev. You certainly diſtinguiſh right, Madam; love often kindles from external merit only———

Ind. But eſteem riſes from a higher ſource, the merit of the ſoul———

Bev. True—And great ſouls only can deſerve it.
[*Bowing reſpectfully.*

Ind. Now I think they are greater ſtill that can ſo charitably part with it.

Bev. Now, Madam, you make me vain, ſince the utmoſt pride and pleaſure of my life is that I eſteem you ——as I ought. But, Madam, we grow grave, methinks —let's find ſome other ſubject.——Pray how did you like the opera laſt night?

Ind.

Ind. First give me leave to thank you for my tickets.

Bev. O! your servant, Madam——

Enter Servant.

Serv. Sir, here's Signor Carbonelli says he waits your commands in the next room.

Bev. Apropos! you were saying yesterday, Madam, you had a mind to hear him——will you give him leave to entertain you now?

Ind. By all means,—desire the gentleman to walk in.

[*Exit Servant.*

After a Sonata is play'd Bevil waits on the Master to the door, &c.

Bev. You smile, Madam, to see me so complaisant to one whom I pay for his visit: now I own I think it not enough barely to pay those whose talents are superior to our own (I mean such talents as would become our condition, if we had them); methinks we ought to do something more than barely gratify them for what they do at our command only because their fortune is below us.

Ind. You say I smile: I assure you it was a smile of approbation; for indeed I cannot but think it the distinguishing part of a gentleman to make his superiority of fortune as easy to his inferiors as he can.————Now, once more to try him.—[*Aside.*] I was saying just now, I believe, you would never let me dispute with you, and I dare say it will always be so: however, I must have your opinion upon a subject which created a debate between my aunt and me just before you came hither; she would needs have it that no man ever does any extraordinary kindness or service for a woman but for his own sake.

Bev. Well, Madam, indeed I can't but be of her mind.

Ind. What, though he would maintain and support her without demanding any thing of her on her part?

Bev. Why, Madam, is making an expense in the service of a valuable woman (for such I must suppose her) though she should never do him any favour, nay, though she should never know who did her such service, such a mighty heroic business?

Ind. Certainly! I should think he must be a man of an uncommon mould.

Bev. Dear Madam, why so? 'tis but at best a better taste in expense—to bestow upon one, whom he may think one of the ornaments of the whole creation—to be conscious that from his superfluity an innocent, a virtuous spirit, is supported above the temptations and sorrows of life! that he sees satisfaction, health, and gladness, in her countenance, while he enjoys the happiness of seeing her (as that I will suppose too, or he must be too abstracted, too insensible). I say if he is allowed to delight in that prospect, alas! what mighty matter is there in all this?

Ind. No mighty matter in so disinterested a friendship.

Bev. Disinterested! I can't think him so! your hero, Madam, is no more than what every gentleman ought to be, and I believe very many are.—He is only one who takes more delight in reflexions than in sensations; he is more pleased with thinking than eating; that's the utmost you can say of him.———Why, Madam, a greater expense than all this men lay out upon an unnecessary stable of horses.

Ind. Can you be sincere in what you say?

Bev. You may depend upon it if you know any such man he does not love dogs inordinately.

Ind. No, that he does not.

Bev.

Bev. Nor cards, nor dice.

Ind. No.

Bev. Nor bottle companions.

Ind. No.

Bev. Take my word then if your admired hero is not liable to any of these kind of demands there's no such pre-eminence in this as you imagine; nay, this way of expense you speak of is what exalts and raises him that has a taste for it: and at the same time his delight is incapable of satiety, disgust, or penitence.

Ind. But still I insist his having no private interest in the action makes it prodigious, almost incredible.

Bev. Dear Madam, I never knew you more mistaken: why, who can be more an usurer than he who lays out his money in such valuable purchases? If pleasure be worth purchasing, how great a pleasure is it to him who has a true taste of life to ease an aching heart, to see the human countenance lighted up into smiles of joy on the receipt of a bit of ore, which is superfluous, and otherwise useless in a man's own pocket? What could a man do better with his cash? This is the effect of a humane disposition where there is only a general tie of nature and common necessity. What then must it be when we serve an object of merit, of admiration!

Ind. Well! the more you argue against it the more I shall admire the generosity.   Conscious Lovers.

ORLANDO AND ROSALIND.

Ros. I will speak to him like a saucy lacquey, and under that habit play the knave with him.—Do you hear, forester?

Orla.

Orla. Very well; What would you?

Ros. I pray you what is't o'clock?

Orla. You should ask me what time o'day; there's no clock in the forest.

Ros. Then there is no true lover in the forest; else sighing every minute, and groaning every hour, would detect the lazy foot of time as well as a clock.

Orla. And why not the swift foot of time? had not that been as proper?

Ros. By no means, Sir: time travels in divers paces with divers persons: I'll tell you who time ambles withal, who time trots withal, who time gallops withal, and who he stands still withal?

Orla. I prithee whom doth he trot withal?

Ros. Marry, he trots hard with a young maid between the contract of her marriage and the day it is solemnized: if the interim be but a se'nnight, time's pace is so hard that it seems the length of seven years.

Orla. Who ambles time withal?

Ros. With a priest that lacks Latin, and a rich man that hath not the gout; for the one sleeps easily because he cannot study; and the other lives merrily because he feels no pain; the one lacking the burden of lean and wasteful learning, the other knowing no burden of heavy tedious penury: these time ambles withal.

Orla. Whom doth he gallop withal?

Ros. With a thief to the gallows: for though he go as softly as foot can fall he thinks himself too soon there.

Orla. Who stays it still withal?

Ros. With lawyers in the vacation; for they sleep between term and term, and then they perceive not how time moves.

M   *Orla.*

Orla. Where dwell you, pretty youth?

Rof. With this shepherdess, my sister; here in the skirts of the forest, like fringe upon a petticoat.

Orla. Your accent is something finer than you could purchase in so removed a dwelling.

Rof. I have been told so of many: but, indeed, an old religious uncle of mine taught me to speak, who was in his youth an inland man; one that knew courtship too well, for there he fell in love. I have heard him read many lectures against it; and I thank God I am not a woman to be touch'd with so many giddy offences as he hath generally tax'd their whole sex withal.

Orla. Can you remember any of the principal evils that he laid to the charge of women?

Rof. There were none principal; they were all like one another, as halfpence are: every one fault seeming monstrous, till his fellow fault came to match it.

Orla. I prithee recount some of them.

Rof. No; I will not cast away my physic but on those that are sick. There is a man haunts the forest that abuses our young plants with carving Rosalind on their barks; hangs odes upon hawthorns, and elegies on brambles; all forsooth deifying the name of Rosalind: if I could meet that fancy-monger I would give him some good counsel, for he seems to have the quotidian of love upon him.

Orla. I am he that is so love-shak'd; I pray you tell me your remedy.

Rof. There is none of my uncle's marks upon you: he taught me how to know a man in love; in which cage of rushes I am sure you are not prisoner.

Orla. What were his marks?

Rof. A lean cheek, which you have not; a blue eye and sunken, which you have not; an unquestionable spirit, which you have not; a beard neglected, which you have not:—but I pardon you for that. Then your hose should be ungartered, your bonnet unbanded, your sleeve unbuttoned, your shoe untied, and every thing about you demonstrating a careless desolation. But you are no such man; you are rather point-device in your accoutrements; as loving yourself, than seeming the lover of any other.

Orla. Fair youth, I would I could make thee believe I love.

Rof. Me believe it! you may as soon make her that you love believe it; which I warrant she is apter to do than to confess she does; that is one of the points in the which women still give the lie to their consciences. But, in good sooth, are you he that hangs the verses on the trees wherein Rosalind is so admired?

Orla. I swear to thee, youth, by the white hand of Rosalind, I am that he, that unfortunate he.

Rof. But are you so much in love as your rhymes speak?

Orla. Neither rhyme or reason can express how much.

Rof. Love is merely a madness; and, I tell you, deserves as well a dark house and a whip as madmen do: and the reason why they are not so punished and cured, is, that the lunacy is so ordinary that the whippers are in love too: yet I profess curing it by counsel.

Orla. Did you ever cure any so?

Rof. Yes, one; and in this manner. He was to imagine me his love, his mistress; and I set him every day to woo me: at which time would I, being but a moonish youth, grieve, be effeminate, changeable, longing, and

liking,

liking; proud, fantastical, apish, shallow, inconstant, full of tears, full of smiles; for every passion something, and for no passion truly any thing, as boys and women are for the most part cattle of this colour: would now like him, now loath him; then entertain him, then forswear him; now weep for him, then spit at him; that I drave my suitor from his mad humour of love to a living humour of madness; which was to forswear the full stream of the world, and to live in a nook merely monastic: and thus I cur'd him; and this way will I take upon me to wash your liver as clear as a sound sheep's heart, that there shall not be one spot of love in't.

Orla. I would not be cured, youth.

Ros. I would cure you, if you would but call me Rosalind, and come every day to my cot and woo me.

Orla. Now, by the faith of my love, I will; tell me where it is?

Ros. Go with me to it and I will shew it you; and, by the way, you shall tell me where in the forest you live: will you go?

Orla. With all my heart, good youth.

Ros. Nay, nay, you must call me Rosalind.—Come, sister, will you go? [*Exeunt.*

SHAKSPEARE.

PROSPERO AND MIRANDA.

Mira. If by your art, my dearest father, you have
Put the wild waters in this roar, allay them:
The sky, it seems, would pour down stinking pitch,
But that the sea, mounting to th' welkin's cheek,
Dashes the fire out. Oh! I have suffer'd

With

With those that I saw suffer: a brave vessel
(Who had no doubt some noble creatures in her)
Dash'd all to pieces. Oh, the cry did knock
Against my very heart: poor souls, they perish'd!
Had I been any god of pow'r I would
Have sunk the sea within the earth; or ere
It should the good ship so have swallow'd and
The freighting souls within her.

   Prof. Be collected;
No more amazement; tell your piteous heart
There's no harm done.

   Mira. O wo the day!

   Prof. No harm,
I have done nothing but in care of thee,
Of thee my dear one, thee my daughter, who
Art ignorant of what thou art, nought knowing
Of whence I am; nor that I'm more better
Than Prospero, master of a full poor cell,
And thy no greater father.

   Mira. More to know
Did never meddle with my thoughts.

   Prof. 'Tis time
I should inform thee further. Lend thy hand,
And pluck my magic garment from me. So!

                                [*Lays down his mantle.*

Lie there my art. Wipe thou thine eyes, have comfort.
The direful spectacle of the wreck, which touch'd
The very virtue of compassion in thee,
I have with such provision in mine art
So safely order'd, that there's no soul,
No, not so much perdition as an hair,
Betid to any creature in the vessel

Which thou heard'st cry, which thou saw'st sink: sit down,
For thou must now know farther.

   Mira. You have often
Begun to tell me what I am, but stopt
And left me to a bootless inquisition;
Concluding—stay, not yet——

   Prof. The hour's now come,
The very minute bids thee ope thine ear;
Obey, and be attentive. Canst remember
A time before we came unto this cell?
I do not think thou canst; for then thou wast not
Out three years old.

   Mira. Certainly, Sir, I can.

   Prof. By what? by any other house, or person?
Or any thing the image, tell me, that
Hath kept in thy remembrance.

   Mira. 'Tis far off:
And rather like a dream than an assurance
That my remembrance warrants. Had I not
Four or five women once that tended me?

   Prof. Thou hadst, and more, Miranda: but how is it
That this lives in thy mind? what seest thou else
In the dark backward and abysm of time?
If thou remember'st ought ere thou cam'st here,
How thou cam'st here thou may'st.

   Mira. But that I do not.

   Prof. 'Tis twelve years since, Miranda; twelve years
         since
Thy father was the duke of Milan, and
A prince of power.

   Mira. Sir, are not you my father?

   Prof. Thy mother was a piece of virtue, and

She

She said thou wast my daughter; and thy father
Was duke of Milan, and his only heir
A princess, no worse issu'd.

Mira. O the heavens:
What foul play had we that we came from thence;
Or blessed was't we did?

Prof. Both, both, my girl:
By foul play, as thou say'st, were we heav'd thence,
But blessedly help'd hither.

Mira. O my heart bleeds
To think o'th' teene that I have turn'd you to,
Which is from my remembrance. Please you farther.

Prof. My brother, and thy uncle, call'd Anthonio—
I pray thee mark me;—that a brother should
Be so perfidious! he whom next thyself
Of all the world I lov'd; and to him put
The manage of my state! as, at that time,
Through all the signories it was the first;
And Prospero the prime duke, being so reputed
In dignity; and for the liberal arts
Without a parallel; those being all my study:
The government I cast upon my brother,
And to my state grew stranger; being transported
And wrapt in secret studies. Thy false uncle—
Dost thou attend me?

Mira. Sir, most heedfully.

Prof. Being once perfected how to grant suits,
How to deny them; whom t' advance, and whom
To plash for over-topping; new created
The creatures that were mine; I say or chang'd 'em,
Or else new form'd 'em; having both the key
Of officer and office, set all hearts

To what tune pleas'd his ear, that now he was
The ivy which had hid my princely trunk,
And fuckt my verdure out on't.——Thou attend'ft not!

 Mira. Good Sir, I do.

 Prof. I pray thee mark me—
I thus neglecting worldly ends, all dedicated
To closeness and the bettering of my mind,
With that which, but by being so retired
O'er-priz'd all popular rate, in my false brother
Awak'd an evil nature; and my trust,
Like a good parent, did beget of him
A falsehood in it's contrary, as great
As my trust was; which had indeed no limit,
A confidence *sans* bound. He being thus lorded,
Not only with what my revenue yielded,
But what my power might else exact; like one,
Who, loving an untruth, and telling 't oft,
Makes such a sinner of his memory,
To credit his own lie, he did believe
He was indeed the duke; from substitution,
And executing th' outward face of royalty,
With all prerogative. Hence his ambition growing—
Dost thou hear child?

 Mira. Your tale, Sir, would cure deafness.

 Prof. To have no screen between this part he play'd,
And him he play'd it for, he needs will be
Absolute Milan. Me, poor man!—my library
Was dukedom large enough; of temporal royalties
He thinks me now incapable, confederates
(So dry he was for sway) wi' th' king of Naples
To give him annual tribute, do him homage;
Subject his coronet to his crown; and bend

The dukedom, yet unbow'd, (alas, poor Milan!)
To moſt ignoble ſtooping!

Mira. O the heavens!

Proſ. Mark the condition, and th' event; then tell me
If this might be a brother?

Mira. I ſhould ſin,
To think but nobly of my grandmother;—
Good wombs have bore bad ſons.

Proſ. Now the condition:
This king of Naples, being an enemy
To me inveterate, hears my brother's ſuit;
Which was, that he, in lieu o' th' premiſes,
Of homage, and I know not how much tribute,
Should preſently extirpate me and mine
Out of the dukedom; and confer fair Milan,
With all the honours, on my brother. Whereon
A treacherous army levy'd, one mid-night
Fated to th' purpoſe, did Anthonio open
The gates of Milan; and, i' th' dark of darkneſs,
The miniſters for th' purpoſe hurry'd thence
Me, and thy crying ſelf.

Mira. Alack, for pity!
I, not remembering how I cry'd out then,
Will cry it o'er again; it is a hint
That wrings mine eyes to't.

Proſ. Hear a little further,
And then I'll bring thee to the preſent buſineſs,
Which now's upon's, without the which this ſtory
Were moſt impertinent.

Mira. Why did they not
That hour deſtroy us?

Proſ. Well demanded, wench;

My tale provokes that queſtion. They durſt not
(So dear the love my people bore me) ſet
A mark ſo bloody on the buſineſs, but
With colours fairer painted their foul ends.
In few, they hurry'd us aboard a bark;
Bore us ſome leagues to ſea; where they prepar'd
A rotten carcaſs of a boat, not rigg'd,
Nor tackle, ſail, nor maſt; the very rats
Inſtinctivly had quit' it; there they hoiſt us
To cry to the ſea that roar'd to us; to ſigh
To th' winds, whoſe pity, ſighing back again,
Did us but loving wrong.

 Mira. Alack! what trouble
Was I then to you!

 Prof. O! a cherubim
Thou waſt, that did preſerve me: thou didſt ſmile,
Infuſed with a fortitude from heav'n,
(When I have brack'd the ſea with drops full ſalt,
Under my burden groan'd) which rais'd in me
An undergoing ſtomach, to bear up
Againſt what ſhould enſue.

 Mira. How came we aſhore?

 Prof. By providence divine.
Some food we had, and ſome freſh water, that
A noble Neapolitan, Gonzalo,
Out of his charity (being then appointed
Maſter of this deſign) did give us, with
Rich garments, linens, ſtuffs, and neceſſaries
Which ſince have ſteeded much. So of his gentleneſs,
Knowing I lov'd my books, he furniſh'd me
From my own library with volumes that
I prize above my dukedom.

           Mira.

Mira. Would I might
But ever see that man!
  Prof. Now I arise:——
Sit still and hear the last of our sea sorrow.
Here in this island we arriv'd, and here
Have I, thy school-master, made thee more profit
Than other princes can, that have more time
For vainer hours, and tutors not so careful.
  Mira. Heav'ns thank you for't! and now, I pray you,
    Sir,
(For still 'tis beating in my mind) your reason
For raising this sea-storm?
  Prof. Know thus far forth;
By accident most strange, bountiful fortune
(Now my dear lady) hath mine enemies
Brought to this shore: and by my prescience
I find, my zenith doth depend upon
A most auspicious star; whose influence
If now I court not, but omit, my fortunes
Will ever after droop——Here cease more questions;
Thou art inclin'd to sleep. 'Tis a good dulness,
And give it way; I know thou canst not chuse.
                             IBID.

PROSPERO, MIRANDA, FERDINAND, AND ARIEL SING-
          ING INVISIBLE.

  Fer. WHERE should this music be, in air or earth?
It sounds no more: and sure it waits upon
Some god o' th' island. Sitting on a bank,
Weeping against the king my father's wreck,

This music crept by me upon the waters,
Allaying both their fury and my passion
With its sweet air; thence I have follow'd it,
Or it hath drawn me rather——but 'tis gone.
No, it begins again.

Ariel's Song.

Full fathom five thy father lies,
   Of his bones are coral made:
Those are pearls that were his eyes;
   Nothing of him that doth fade
But doth suffer a sea-change,
   Into something rich and strange.
Sea-nymphs hourly ring his knell.
   Hark! now I hear them, ding-dong bell.

Fer. The ditty does remember my drown'd father.
This is no mortal business; nor no sound
That the earth owns; I hear it now above me.
   Prof. The fringed curtains of thine eyes advance,
And say what thou seest yond.
   Mira. What is't, a spirit?
Lord, how it looks about! believe me, sir,
It carries a brave form. But 'tis a spirit.
   Prof. No, wench, it eats and sleeps, and has such senses
As we have, such. This gallant which thou seest
Was in the wreck; and, but he's something stain'd
With grief, (that's beauty's canker) thou might'st call him
A goodly person. He hath lost his fellows,
And strays about to find 'em.
   Mira. I might call him
A thing divine; for nothing natural
I ever saw so noble.

Prof.

Prof. It goes on I see, [*Aside*]
As my soul prompts it. Spirit, fine spirit, I'll free thee
Within two days for this.

Fer. Most sure the goddess
On whom these airs attend! vouchsafe my pray'r
May know, if you remain upon this island;
And that you will some good instruction give,
How I may bear me here: my prime request
(Which I do last pronounce) is (O, you wonder!)
If you be maid or no?

Mira. No wonder, sir,
But certainly a maid.

Fer. My language! heav'ns!
I am the best of them that speak this speech,
Were I but where 'tis spoken.

Prof. How? the best?
What wert thou if the king of Naples heard thee?

Fer. A single thing, as I am now, that wonders
To hear thee speak of Naples. He does not hear me;
And that he does, I weep: myself am Naples,
Who with mine eyes (ne'er since at ebb) beheld
The king my father wreck'd.

Mira. Alack, for mercy!

Fer. Yes, faith, and all his lords: the Duke of Milan
And his brave son being twain.

Prof. The Duke of Milan,
And his more braver daughter, could control thee,
If now 'twere fit to do't:———at the first sight
They have chang'd eyes: (delicate Ariel,
I'll set thee free for this.) A word, good sir;
I fear you've done yourself some wrong: a word.——

Mira. Why speaks my father so ungently? this
Is the third man that e'er I saw; the first

That

That e'er I sigh'd for. Pity move my father
To be inclin'd my way!

Fer. O! if a virgin,
And your affection not gone forth, I'll make you
The queen of Naples.

Prof. Soft, sir; one word more,
They're both in either's power: but this swift business
I must uneasy make, lest too light winning
Make the prize light. Sir, one word more; (I charge thee
That thou attend me:)——[*To Ariel,*] thou dost here usurp
The name thou ought'st not, and hath put thyself
Upon this island, as a spy to win it
From me, the lord on't.

Fer. No, as I'm a man.

Mira. There's nothing ill can dwell in such a temple.
If the ill spirit have so fair an house
Good things will strive to dwell with't.

Prof. Follow me.——
Speak you not for him: he's a traitor. Come,
I'll manacle thy neck and feet together;
Sea-water shalt thou drink; thy food shall be
The fresh brook muscles, wither'd roots, and husks,
Wherein the acorn cradled.—Follow.

Fer. No;
I will resist such entertainment till
Mine enemy has more power.

[*He draws, and is charmed from moving.*]

Mira. O dear father,
Make not too rash a trial of him; for
He's gentle though not fearful.

Prof. What I say,
My foot my tutor? put thy sword up, traitor,

Who

Who mak'ſt a ſhew but dar'ſt not ſtrike; thy conſcience
Is all poſſeſs'd with guilt: come from thy ward,
For I can here diſarm thee with this ſtick,
And make thy weapon drop.

 Mira. Beſeech you, father.

 Proſ. Hence: hang not on my garment.

 Mira. Sir, have pity;
I'll be his ſurety.

 Proſ. Silence: one word more
Shall make me chide thee, if not hate thee.
What, an advocate for an impoſtor? huſh!
Thou think'ſt there are no more ſuch ſhapes as he,
Having ſeen but him and Caliban; fooliſh wench!
To th' moſt of men this is a Caliban,
And they to him are angels.

 Mira. My affections
Are then moſt humble: I have no ambition
To ſee a goodlier man.

 Pro. Come on, obey:
Thy nerves are in their infancy again,
And have no vigour in them.

 Fer. So they are:
My ſpirits, as in a dream, are all bound up.
My father's loſs, the weakneſs which I feel,
The wreck of all my friends, and this man's threats,
To whom I am ſubdu'd, are but light to me,
Might I but through my priſon once a day
Behold this maid: all corners elſe o' th' earth
Let liberty make uſe of; ſpace enough
Have I in ſuch a priſon.

 Proſ. It works: come on.
Thou haſt done well, fine Ariel, follow me. [*To Ariel.*]
Hark, what thou elſe ſhalt do me.

         Mira.

Mira. Be of comfort,
My father's of a better nature, sir,
Than he appears by speech: this is unwonted
Which now came from him.

Prof. Thou shalt be as free
As mountain winds: but then exactly do
All points of my command.

Ari. To th' syllable.

Prof. Come, follow; speak not for him.

IBID.

FERDINAND BEARING A LOG.

Fer. There be some sports are painful, but their
    labour
Delight in them sets off: some kinds of baseness
Are nobly undergone, and most poor matters
Point to rich ends. This my mean task wou'd be
As heavy to me as 'tis odious, but
The mistress which I serve quickens what's dead,
And makes my labours pleasures: O, she is
Ten times more gentle than her father's crabbed;
And he's compos'd of harshness. I must move
Some thousands of these logs, and pile them up,
Upon a sore injunction. My sweet mistress
Weeps when she sees me work, and says such baseness
Had never like executor; I forget,
Nay, these sweet thoughts do ev'n refresh my labour,
Least busy when I do it.

Enter MIRANDA; *and* PROSPERO *at a distance unseen.*

Mira. Alas! now, pray you,
Work not so hard; I would the lightning had

Burnt

Burnt up those logs that you're enjoin'd to pile:
Pray set it down and rest you; when this burns
'Twill weep for having wearied you: my father
Is hard at study; pray now rest yourself;
He's safe for these three hours.

Fer. O, most dear mistress,
The sun will set before I shall discharge
What I must strive to do.

Mira. If you'll sit down
I'll bear your logs the while. Pray give me that,
I'll carry't to the pile.

Fer. No, precious creature,
I'd rather crack my sinews, break my back,
Than you should such dishonour undergo
While I sit lazy by.

Mira. It would become me
As well as it does you; and I should do it
With much more ease; for my good will is to it,
And yours it is against.

Pros. Poor worm! thou art infected, and
This visitation shews it.

Mira. You look wearily.

Fer. No, noble mistress; 'tis fresh morning with me
When you are by at night. I do beseech you
(Chiefly that I may set it in my prayers),
What is your name?

Mira. Miranda. O my father,
I've broke your hest to say so!

Fer. Admir'd Miranda!
Indeed, the top of admiration, worth
What's dearest to the world: full many a lady
I've ey'd with the best regard, and many a time

Th'

Th' harmony of their tongues hath into bondage
Brought my too diligent ear! for sev'ral virtues
Have I lik'd sev'ral women, never any
With so full soul, but some defect in her
Did quarrel with the noblest grace she ow'd,
And put it to the foil. But you, O you,
So perfect, and so peerless, are created
Of ev'ry creature's best.

 Mira. I do not know
One of my sex; no woman's face remember,
Save from my glass my own; nor have I seen
More that I may call men than you, good friend,
And my dear father; how features are abroad
I'am skilless of; but, by my modesty,
(The jewel in my dower) I would not wish
Any companion in the world but you;
Nor can imagination form a shape
Besides yourself to like of. But I prattle
Something too wildly, and my father's precepts
I do forget.

 Fer. I am, in my condition,
A prince, Miranda; I do think a king;
(I would not so!) and would no more endure
This wooden slavery than I would suffer
The flesh-fly blow my mouth. Hear my soul speak;
The very instant that I saw you did
My heart fly to your service, there resides
To make me slave to it, and for your sake
Am I this patient log-man.

 Mira. Do you love me?

 Fer. O heav'n, O earth, bear witness to this sound,
And crown what I profess with kind event,

If I speak true; if hollowly, invert
What best is boaded me to mischief! I,
Beyond all limit of what else i' th' world,
Do love, prize, honour you.

 Mira. I am a fool
To weep at what I'm glad of.

 Prof. Fair encounter
Of two most rare affections! heav'ns rain grace
On that which breeds between 'em.

 Fer. Wherefore weep you?

 Mira. At mine unworthiness, that dare not offer
What I desire to give; and much less take
What I shall die to want;—but this is trifling;
And all the more it seeks to hide itself
The bigger bulk it shews. Hence, bashful cunning,
And prompt me plain and holy innocence!
I am your wife if you will marry me;
If not I'll die your maid: to be your fellow
You may deny me; but I'll be your servant
Whether you will or no.

 Fer. My mistress, my dearest,
And I thus humble ever.

 Mira. My husband then?

 Fer. Ay, with a heart so willing
As bondage e'er of freedom; here's my hand.

 Mira. And mine, with my heart in't. And now farewell
Till half an hour hence.

PROSPERO AND ARIEL.

 Prof. Now does my project gather to a head;
My charms crack not; my spirits obey, and time
Goes upright with his carriage: how's the day?

           Ari.

Ari. On the sixth hour, at which time, my lord,
You said our work should cease.

Prof. I did say so
When first I rais'd the tempest: say, my spirit,
How fares the king and's followers?

Ari. Confin'd
In the same fashion as you gave in charge;
Just as you left them, all your prisoners, sir,
In the lime-grove which weather-fends your cell.
They cannot budge till you release. The king,
His brother and yours, abide all three distracted;
And the remainder mourning over them,
Brim-full of sorrow and dismay; but chiefly
Him that you term'd the good old lord Gonzalo,
His tears run down his beard, like winter-drops
From eaves of reeds; your charm so strongly works 'em
That if you now beheld them your affections
Would become tender.

Prof. Do'st thou think so, spirit?

Ari. Mine would, sir, were I human.

Prof. And mine shall.
Hast thou, which art but air, a touch, a feeling
Of their afflictions, and shall not myself,
One of their kind, that relish all as sharply,
Passion'd as they, be kindlier mov'd than thou art?
Though with their high wrongs I'm struck to th' quick,
Yet, with my nobler reason, 'gainst my fury
Do I take part; the rarer action is
In virtue than in vengeance; they being penitent,
The sole drift of my purpose doth extend
Not a frown further; go, release them, Ariel;
My charms I'll break, their senses I'll restore,
And they shall be themselves.

Ari.

Ari. I'll fetch them, sir.

Prof. Ye elves of hills, brooks, standing lakes and
   groves,
And ye that on the sands with printless foot
Do chase the ebbing Neptune, and do fly him
When he comes back; you demi puppets, that
By moon-shine do the green sour ringlets make,
Whereof the ewe not bites; and you whose pastime
Is to make midnight mushrooms, that rejoice
To hear the solemn curfew, by whose aid
(Weak ministers tho' ye be) I have be-dimm'd
The noon-tide sun, call'd forth the mutinous winds,
And 'twixt the green sea and the azur'd vault
Set roaring war; to the dread rattling thunder
Have I giv'n fire, and rifted Jove's stout oak
With his own bolt: the strong-bas'd promontory
Have I made shake, and by the spurs pluck'd up
The pine and cedar: graves at my command
Have wak'd their sleepers; op'd, and let them forth
By my so potent art. But this rough magic
I here abjure; and when I have requir'd
Some heav'nly music, which ev'n now I do,
(To work mine end upon their senses, that
This airy charm is for) I'll break my staff;
Bury it certain fathoms in the earth;
And, deeper than did ever plummet sound,
I'll drown my book.

            IBID.

MIRANDA,

MIRANDA, FERDINAND, &c.

Mira. Sweet lord, you play me falſe.

Fer. No, my dear love,
I would not for the world.

Mira. Yes, for a ſcore of kingdoms you ſhall wrangle,
And I will call it fair play.

Alon. If this prove
A viſion of the iſland, one dear ſon
Shall I twice loſe.

Seb. A moſt high miracle!

Fer. Though the ſeas threaten they are merciful;
I've curs'd them without cauſe.   [*Fer. kneels.*

Alon. Now all the bleſſings
Of a glad father compaſs thee about!
Ariſe, and ſay how thou cam'ſt here.

Mira. O wonder!
How many goodly creatures are there here?
How beauteous mankind is! O brave new world,
That has ſuch people in't.

Proſ. 'Tis new to thee.

Alon. What is this maid with whom thou waſt at play?
Your eld'ſt acquaintance cannot be three hours!
Is ſhe the goddeſs that hath ſever'd us,
And brought us thus together?

Fer. Sir, ſhe's mortal;
But by immortal providence ſhe's mine.
I choſe her when I could not aſk my father
For his advice, nor thought I had one: ſhe
Is daughter to this famous duke of Milan,
Of whom ſo often I have heard renown,

But

But never saw before; of whom I have
Receiv'd a second life, and second father
This lady makes him to me.

Alon. I am hers;
But, oh, how oddly will it sound that I
Must ask my child forgiveness!

Prof. There, sir, stop;
Let us not burthen our remembrance with
An heaviness that's gone.

Gon. I've inly wept,
Or should have spoke ere this. Look down, ye gods,
And on this couple drop a blessed crown:
For it is you that hath chalk'd forth the way
Which brought us hither.

— — — — —
— — — — —

Prof. Our revels now are ended: these our actors,
As I foretold you, were all spirits, and
Are melted into air, into thin air;
And, like the baseless fabric of this vision,
The cloud-capt tow'rs, the gorgeous palaces,
The solemn temples, the great globe itself,
Yea, all which it inherit, shall dissolve;
And, like this unsubstantial pageant faded,
Leave not a wreck behind! we are such stuff
As dreams are made on, and our little life
Is rounded with a sleep.
IBID.

IMOGEN AND PISANIO.

Imo. I would thou grew'st unto the shores o' th' haven,
And question'dst every sail: if he should write,

And I not have it, 'twere as a paper lost
With offer'd mercy in it. What was the last
That he spoke with thee?

Pis. 'Twas, his queen, his queen!

Imo. Then wav'd his handkerchief?

Pis. And kiss'd it, madam.

Imo. Senseless linen, happier therein than I:
And that was all?

Pis. No, madam; for so long
As he could mark me with his eye, or I
Distinguish him from others, he did keep
The deck, with glove, or hat, or handkerchief,
Still waving, as the fits and stirs of's mind
Could best express how slow his soul sail'd on,
How swift his ship.

Imo. Thou should'st have made him ev'n
As little as a crow, or less, ere left
To after-eye him.

Pis. Madam, so I did.

Imo. I would have broke mine eye-strings; crackt
'em, but
To look upon him; till the diminution,
From space, had pointed him sharp as my needle;
Nay, follow'd him till he had melted from
The smallness of a gnat to air; and then
Have turn'd mine eye, and wept—but, good Pisanio,
When shall we hear from him?

Pis. Be assur'd, madam,
With his next 'vantage.

Imo. I did not take my leave of him, but had
Most pretty things to say: ere I could tell him
How I would think on him at certain hours,
Such thoughts, and such; or I could make him swear

The

The she's of Italy should not betray
Mine interest, and his honour; or could charge him
At the sixth hour of morn, at noon, at midnight,
T' encounter me with orisons, (for then
I am in heav'n for him) or ere I could
Give him that parting kiss which I had set
Betwixt two charming words, comes in my father,
And, like the tyrannous breathing of the north,
Shakes all our buds from blowing.
SHAKSPEARE.

IMOGEN IN BOY'S CLOTHES.

Imo. I see a man's life is a tedious one:
I've tir'd myself; and for two nights together
Have made the ground my bed. I should be sick,
But that my resolution helps me. Milford,
When from the mountain top Pisanio shew'd thee,
Thou wast within a ken. Oh Jove, I think
Foundations fly the wretched, such I mean
Where they should be reliev'd Two beggars told me
I could not miss my way. Will poor folks lie
That have affliction on them, knowing 'tis
A punishment, or trial? yet no wonder,
When rich ones scarce tell true. To lapse in fulness
Is sorer than to lie for need; and falsehood
Is worse in kings than beggars. My dear lord!
Thou'rt one o' th' false ones; now I think on thee
My hunger's gone; but e'en before I was
At point to sink for food. But what is this?
[*Seeing the cave.*
Here is a path to't—'tis some savage hold;

'Twere best not call; I dare not call; yet famine,
Ere it clean o'erthrow nature, makes it valiant.
Plenty and peace breed cowards, hardiness ever
Of hardiness is mother.   Ho! who's here?
If any thing that's civil, speak; if savage,
Take or yield food.—No answer? then I'll enter.
Best draw my sword; and, if mine enemy
But fear the sword like me, he'll scarcely look on't.
Grant such a foe, good heav'ns!   [*She goes into the cave.*

Enter Bellarius, Guiderius, *and* Arviragus.

Bel.   You, Paladour, have prov'd best woodman, and
Are master of the feast; Cadwal and I
Will play the cook and servant, 'tis our match:
The sweat of industry would dry, and die,
But for the end it works to.   Come, our stomachs
Will make what's homely savoury; weariness
Can snore upon the flint when resty sloth
Finds the down pillow hard.   Now peace be here,
Poor house, that keep'st thyself!

Guid.   I'm thoroughly weary.

Arv.   I'm weak with toil, yet strong in appetite.

Guid.   There is cold meat i'th'cave, we'll brouze on that
Whilst what we've kill'd be cook'd.

Bel.   Stay, come not in——   [*Looking in.*
But that it eats our victuals, I should think
It was a fairy.

Guid.   What's the matter, sir?

Bel.   By Jupiter, an angel! or, if not,
An earthly paragon.   Behold divineness
No elder than a boy!

Enter

Enter Imogen.

Imo. Good masters, harm me not;
Before I enter'd here I call'd, and thought
T' have begg'd, or bought, what I have took: good troth,
I've stolen nought, nor would not, though I'd found
Gold strew'd o' th' floor. Here's money for my meat:
I would have left it on the board so soon
As I had made my meal, and parted thence
With pray'rs for the provider.

Guid. Money, youth!

Arv. All gold and silver rather turn to dirt!
As 'tis no better reckon'd but of those
Who worship dirty gods.

Imo. I see you're angry:
Know, if you kill me for my fault, I should
Have dy'd had I not made it.

Bel. Whither bound?

Imo. To Milford-haven.

Bel. Say, what is your name?

Imo. Fidele, sir. I have a kinsman who
Is bound for Italy: he embarks at Milford,
To whom being going, almost spent with hunger,
I'm fall'n in this offence.

Bel. Prithee, fair youth,
Think us no churls; nor measure our good minds
By this rude place we live in. Well encounter'd!
'Tis almost night, you shall have better cheer
Ere you depart, and thanks to stay and eat it.
Boys, bid him welcome.

Guid. Were you a woman, youth,
I should woo hard but be your groom in honesty;
I'd bid for you as I would buy.

 Arv. I'll mak't my comfort.
He is a man; I'll love him as my brother;
And such a welcome as I'd give to him,
After long absence, such is yours. Most welcome!
Be sprightly, for you fall 'mongst friends.

 Imo. 'Mongst friends,
If brothers—would it had been as that they   ⎫
Had been my father's sons; then had my price ⎬ *Aside.*
Been less, and so more equal balancing   ⎭
To thee Posthumus.

 Bel. He wrings at some distress.

 Guid. Would I could free't!

 Arv. Or I, whate'er it be,
What pain it cost, what danger; gods!

 Bel. Hark, boys!   [*Whispering.*

 Imo. Great men,
That had a court no bigger than this cave,
That did attend themselves, and had the virtue
Which their own conscience seal'd them, laying by
That nothing-gift of defering multitudes,
Could not out-peer these twain. Pardon me, gods!
I'd change my sex to be companion with them,
Since Leonitus is false.

 Bel. It shall be so:
Boys, we'll go dress our hunt. Fair youth, come in:
Discourse is heavy fasting; when we've supp'd
We'll mannerly demand of thee thy story,
So far as thou wilt speak.

 Guid. I pray draw near.

 Arv. The night to th' owl, and morn to th' lark, less
   welcome!

BELLARIUS

BELLARIUS AND GUIDERIUS.

Enter Arviragus, *with* Imogen *dead, bearing her in his arms.*

Bel. Look, here he comes!
And brings the dire occasion in his arms,
Of what we blame him for.
　Arv. The bird is dead
That we have made so much on! I had rather
Have skipt from sixteen years of age to sixty,
And turn'd my leaping-time into a crutch,
Than have seen this.
　Guid. O sweetest, fairest lily!
My brother wears thee not one half so well
As when thou grew'st thyself.
　Bel. O melancholy!
Who ever yet could found thy bottom? find
The ooze to shew what coast thy sluggish carack
Might eas'liest harbour in?—thou blessed thing!
Jove knows what man thou might'st have made: but ah!
Thou dy'dst, a most rare boy, of melancholy.
Tell me how found you him?
　Arv. Stark, as you see:
Thus smiling, as some fly had tickled slumber,
Not as death's dart, being laugh'd at: his right cheek
Reposed on a cushion.
　Guid. Where?
　Arv. O' the floor:
His arms thus leagu'd; I thought he slept, and put
My clouted brogues from off my feet, whose rudeness
Answer'd my steps too loud.

Guid. Why he but sleeps;
If he be gone he'll make his grave a bed,
With female fairies will his tomb be haunted,
And worms will not come near him.

Arv. With fairest flow'rs,
(Whilst summer lasts and I live here, Fidele)
I'll sweeten thy sad grave. Thou shalt not lack
The flow'r that's like thy face, pale primrose, nor
The azur'd hare-bell, like thy veins; no, nor
The leaf of eglantine, which, not to slander't,
Out-sweeten'd not thy breath. The ruddock would
With charitable bill (oh! bill fore-shaming
Those rich left heirs that let their fathers lie
Without a monument) bring thee all this;
Yea, and furr'd moss besides, when flow'rs are none,
To winter-grown thy corse.

Guid. Prithee have done,
And do not play the wench-like words with that
Which is so serious. Let us bury,
And do not protract with admiration what
Is now due debt. To th' grave.

Arv. Say, where shall's lay him?

Guid. By good Euriphile, our mother.

Arv. Be't so:
And let us, Paladour, though now our voices
Have got the mannish crack, sing him to th' ground
As once our mother: use like note and words,
Save that Euriphile must be Fidele.

Guid. Cadwal,
I cannot sing; I'll weep and word it with thee;
For notes of sorrow out of tune are worse
Than priests and fanes that lie.

Arv.

Arv. We'll speak it then.

Bel. Great griefs I see med'cine the less; for Cloten
Is quite forgot. He was a queen's son, boys;
And, though he came our enemy, remember
He has paid for that. The mean and mighty rotting
Together have one dust; yet reverence
(The angel of the world) doth make distinction
Of place 'twixt high and low. Our foe was princely:
And though you took his life, as being our foe,
Yet bury him as a prince.

Guid. Pray fetch him hither.
Thersites' body is as good as Ajax',
When neither are alive.

Arv. If you'll go fetch him
We'll say our song the whilst.—Brother, begin.

SHAKSPEARE.

DIRGE IN CYMBELINE.

To fair Fidele's grassy tomb
  Soft maids and village hinds shall bring
Each op'ning sweet, of earliest bloom,
  And rifle all the breathing spring.

No wailing ghost shall dare appear
  To vex with shrieks this quiet grove,
But shepherd lads assemble here,
  And melting virgins own their love.

No wither'd witch shall here be seen,
  No goblins lead their nightly crew;
The female fays shall haunt the green,
  And dress thy grave with pearly dew!

The redbreast oft at ev'ning hours
    Shall kindly lend his little aid,
With hoary moss and gather'd flowers,
    To deck the ground where thou art laid.

When howling winds and beating rain
    In tempests shake the sylvan cell;
Oh! midst the chase on every plain,
    The tender thought on thee shall dwell.

Each lonely scene shall thee restore,
    For thee the tear be duly shed;
Belov'd, till life can charm no more,
    And mourn'd, till pity's self is dead.
                            COLLINS.

QUEEN AND LADY.

Queen. What sport shall we devise here in this garden
To drive away the heavy thought of care?
    Lady. Madam, we'll play at bowls.
    Queen. 'Twill make us think the world is full of rubs,
And that my fortune runs against the bias.
    Lady. Madam, we'll dance.
    Queen. My legs can keep no measure in delight
When my poor heart no measure keeps in grief,
Therefore no dancing, girl; some other sport.
    Lady. Madam, we'll tell tales.
    Queen. Of sorrow, or of joy?
    Lady. Of either, madam.
    Queen. Of neither, girl;
For if of joy, being altogether wanting,
It doth remember me the more of sorrow:

Or if of grief, being altogether sad,
It adds more sorrow to my want of joy:
For what I have I need not to repeat;
And of what I want it boots not to complain.
  Lady. Madam, I'll sing.
  Queen. 'Tis well that thou hast cause:
But thou should'st please me better would'st thou weep.
  Lady. I could weep, madam, would it do you good.
  Queen. And I could weep would weeping do me good,
And never borrow any tear of thee. SHAKSPEARE.

CONVERSATION BETWEEN ADAM AND EVE ON GOING TO REST.

Now came still evening on, and twilight grey
Had in her sober livery all things clad;
Silence accompanied; for beast and bird,
They to their grassy couch, these to their nests
Were slunk, all but the wakeful nightingale;
She all night long her amorous descant sung;
Silence was pleas'd: now glow'd the firmament
With living sapphires. Hesperus, that led
The starry host, rode brightest, till the moon,
Rising in cloudless majesty, at length
Apparent queen, unveil'd her peerless light,
And o'er the dark her silver mantle threw,
When Adam thus to Eve. Fair consort, th' hour
Of night, and all things now retir'd to rest,
Mind us of like repose, since God hath set
Labour and rest, as day and night, to men
Successive; and the timely dew of sleep
Now falling with soft slumb'rous weight inclines

Our eyelids: other creatures all day long
Rove idle unemploy'd, and less need rest;
Man hath his daily work of body or of mind
Appointed; which declares his dignity,
And the regard of heav'n on all his ways;
While other animals unactive range,
And of their doings God takes no account.
To-morrow ere fresh morning streak the east
With first approach of light we must be ris'n,
And at our pleasant labour, to reform
Yon flow'ry arbours, yonder alleys green,
Our walk at noon, with branches overgrown,
That mock our scant manuring, and require
More hands than ours to lop their wanton growth;
Those blossoms also, and those dropping gums,
That lie bestrown unsightly and unsmooth,
Ask riddance, if we mean to tread with ease;
Mean while, as nature wills, night bids us rest.
To whom thus Eve, with perfect beauty adorn'd.
My author and disposer, what thou bidst
Unargued I obey; so God ordains;
God is thy law, thou mine; to know no more
Is woman's happiest knowledge and her praise.
With thee conversing I forget all time;
All seasons and their change, all please alike.
Sweet is the breath of morn, her rising sweet,
With charm of earliest birds, pleasant the sun,
When first on this delightful land he spreads
His orient beams, on herb, tree, fruit, and flow'r,
Glist'ring with dew; fragrant the fertile earth
After soft show'rs; and sweet the coming on
Of grateful ev'ning mild; then silent night,
With this her solemn bird, and this fair moon,

And these the gems of Heav'n, her starry train:
But neither breath of morn, when she ascends
With charm of earliest birds; nor rising sun
On this delightful land; nor herb, fruit, flow'r,
Glist'ring with dew; nor fragrance after show'rs;
Nor grateful evening mild; nor silent night
With this her solemn bird; nor walk by moon
Or glit'tring star-light, without thee is sweet.
But wherefore all night long shine these? for whom
This glorious sight, when sleep hath shut all eyes?
To whom our general ancestor reply'd;
Daughter of God and man, accomplish'd Eve,
These have their course to finish round the earth
By morrow evening, and from land to land
In order, though to nations yet unborn,
Minist'ring light prepar'd they set and rise;
Lest total darkness should by night regain
Her old possession, and extinguish life
In nature and in all things, which these soft fires
Not only enlighten, but with kindly heat
Of various influence foment and warm,
Temper or nourish, or in part shed down
Their stellar virtue on all kinds that grow
On earth, made hereby apter to receive
Perfection from the sun's more potent ray.
These then, though unbeheld in deep of night,
Shine not in vain; nor think, though men were none,
That heav'n would want spectators, God want praise:
Millions of spiritual creatures walk the earth
Unseen, both when we wake and when we sleep:
All these with ceaseless praise his works behold
Both day and night. How often from the steep

Of echoing hill or thicket have we heard
Celestial voices to the midnight air,
Sole, or responsive to each other's note,
Singing their great Creator? oft in bands
While they keep watch, or nightly rounding, walk
With heav'nly touch of instrumental sounds:
In full harmonic number join'd, their songs
Divide the night, and lift our thoughts to Heaven.
Thus, taking hand in hand, alone they pass'd
On to their blissful bower.

MILTON.

THE CAMELION; A FABLE.

Oft has it been my lot to mark
A proud, conceited, talking spark,
With eyes that hardly serv'd at most
To guard their master 'gainst a post;
Yet round the world the blade has been,
To see whatever could be seen:
Returning from his finish'd tour,
Grown ten times perter than before;
Whatever word you chance to drop,
The travell'd fool your mouth will stop:
" Sir, if my judgment you'll allow—
" I've seen—and sure I ought to know."
So begs you'd pay a due submission,
And acquiesce in his decision.
 Two travellers of such a cast,
As o'er Arabia's wilds they past,
And on their way in friendly chat
Now talk'd of this, and then of that,

Discours'd

Discours'd a while, 'mongst other matter,
Of the camelion's form and nature.
"A stranger animal," cries one,
"Sure never liv'd beneath the sun:
"A lizard's body, lean and long,
"A fish's head, a serpent's tongue;
"Its tooth with treble claw disjoin'd;
"And what a length of tail behind!
"How slow its pace! and then its hue—
"Who ever saw so fine a blue?"
"Hold there," the other quick replies,
"'Tis green,—I saw it with these eyes,
"As late with open mouth it lay,
"And warm'd it in the sunny ray;
"Stretch'd at its ease the beast I view'd,
"And saw it eat the air for food."
"I've seen it, sir, as well as you,
"And must again affirm it blue:
"At leisure I the beast survey'd,
"Extended in the cooling shade."
"'Tis green, 'tis green, sir, I assure ye"—
"Green!" cries the other in a fury—
"Why, sir, d'ye think I've lost my eyes?"
"'Twere no great loss," the friend replies;
"For, if they always serve you thus,
"You'll find 'em but of little use."
So high at last the contest rose,
From words they almost came to blows:
When luckily came by a third—
To him the question they referr'd;
And begg'd he'd tell 'em, if he knew,
Whether the thing was green or blue.

"Sir,"

"Sirs," cries the umpire, "cease your pother,
"The creature's neither one nor t'other.
"I caught the animal last night,
"And view'd it o'er by candle-light:
"I mark'd it well—'twas black as jet—
"You stare—but, sirs, I've got it yet,
"And can produce it."—"Pray, sir, do;
"I'll lay my life the thing is blue."
"And I'll be sworn that, when you've seen
"The reptile, you'll pronounce him green."

"Well then, at once, to ease the doubt,"
Replies the man, "I'll turn him out:
"And, when before your eyes I've set him
"If you dont find him black I'll eat him."
  He said; then full before their sight
Produc'd the beast, and lo!——'twas white.
Both star'd—the man look'd wond'rous wise—
"My children," the Camelion cries,
(Then first the creature found a tongue)
"You all are right, and all are wrong:
"When next you talk of what you view
"Think others see as well as you:
"Nor wonder if you find that none
"Prefers your eyesight to his own."

MERRICK.

THE SPARROW AND DIAMOND.

I.

I LATELY saw what now I sing,
　　Fair Lucia's hand display'd,—
This finger grac'd a diamond ring,
　　On that a sparrow play'd.

II.

II.

The feather'd plaything she caress'd,
   She stroak'd its head and wings;
And while it nestled on her breast
   She lisp'd the dearest things.

III.

With chisel bill a spark ill set
   He loosen'd from the rest,
And swallow'd down to grind his meat,
   The easier to digest.

IV.

She seiz'd his bill with wild affright,
   Her diamond to descry:
'Twas gone! she sicken'd at the sight,
   Moaning her bird would die.

V.

The tongue-ty'd knocker none might use,
   The curtains none undraw,
The footmen went without their shoes,
   The street was laid with straw.

VI.

When physic ceas'd to spend its store
   To bring away the stone,
Dicky, like people given o'er,
   Picks up when left alone.

VII.

His eyes dispell'd their sickly dews,
   He peck'd behind his wing;
Lucia, recov'ring at the news,
   Relapses for the ring.

VIII.

Mean while within her beauteous breast
   Two different passions strove;
When av'rice ended the contest,
   And triumph'd over love.

IX.

Poor little, pretty, fluttering thing,
   Thy pains the sex display,
Who only to repair a ring
   Could take thy life away!

X.

Drive av'rice from your breasts, ye fair,
   Monster of foulest mien!
Ye would not let it harbour there,
   Could but its form be seen.

XI.

It made a virgin put on guile,
   Truth's image break her word,
A Lucia's face forbear to smile,
   A Venus kill her bird.

THE MONKIES; A TALE.

Whoe'er with curious eye has rang'd
   Through Ovid's tales has seen
How Jove, incens'd, to monkies chang'd
   A tribe of worthless men.
Repentant, soon th' offending race
   Entreat the injur'd pow'r
To give them back the human face,
   And reason's aid restore.

Jove,

Jove, sooth'd at length, his ear inclin'd,
 And granted half their pray'r;
But t'other half he bid the wind
 Disperse in empty air.
Scarce had the thund'rer giv'n the nod
 That shook the vaulted skies,
With haughtier air the creatures strode,
 And stretch'd their dwindled size.
The hair in curls luxuriant now
 Around their temples spread;
The tail that whilom hung below
 Now dangled from the head.
The head remains unchang'd within,
 Nor alter'd much the face;
It still retains its native grin,
 And all its old grimace.
Thus, half transform'd, and half the same,
 Jove bade them take their place,
(Restoring them their ancient claim)
 Among the human race.
Man with contempt the brute survey'd,
 Nor would a name bestow,
But women lik'd the motly breed,
 And call'd the thing a beau!
        MERRICK.

THE NIGHTINGALE AND GLOW-WORM; A FABLE.

THE prudent nymph, whose cheeks disclose
The lily and the blushing rose,
From public view her charms will screen,
And rarely in the crowd be seen;

This simple truth shall keep her wise,
" The fairest fruits attract the flies."

 One night a glow-worm, proud and vain,
Contemplating her glitt'ring train,
Cry'd, Sure there never was in nature
So elegant, so fine a creature!
All other insects that I see,
The frugal ant, industrious bee,
Or silk-worm, with contempt I view;
With all that low mechanic crew
Who servilely their lives employ
In bus'ness, enemy to joy.
Mean, vulgar herd! ye are my scorn,
For grandeur only I was born,
Or sure am sprung from race divine,
And plac'd on earth to live and shine.
Those lights that sparkle so on high
Are but the glow-worms of the sky:
And kings on earth their gems admire,
Because they imitate my fire!

 She spoke. Attentive on a spray
A nightingale forebore his lay;
He saw the shining morsel near,
And flew, directed by the glare;
A while he gaz'd with sober look,
And thus the trembling prey bespoke:—

 Deluded fool, with pride elate,
Know 'tis thy beauty brings thy fate:
Less dazzling long thou might'st have lain
Unheeded on the velvet plain:
Pride, soon or late, degraded, mourns,
And beauty wrecks whom she adorns.

MOORE.

THE GOOSE AND THE SWANS; A FABLE.

I HATE the face, however fair,
That carries an affected air.
The lisping tone, the shape constrain'd,
The study'd look, the passion feign'd,
Are fopperies which only tend
To injure what they strive to mend.
With what superior grace enchants
That face which nature's pencil paints!
Where eyes, unexercis'd in art,
Glow with the meaning of the heart!
Where freedom and good humour sit,
And easy gaiety and wit!
Though perfect beauty be not there,
The master lines the finish'd air;
We catch from ev'ry look delight,
And grow enamour'd at the sight:
For beauty, though we all approve,
Excites our wonder more than love;
While the agreeable strikes sure,
And gives the wounds we cannot cure.
Why then, my Amoret, this care,
That forms you in effect less fair?
If nature on your cheek bestows
A bloom that emulates the rose,
Or from some heav'nly image drew
A form Apelles never knew,
Your ill-judg'd aid will you impart,
And spoil by meretricious art?
Or had you, nature's error, come
Abortive from the mother's womb,

Your forming care she still rejects,
Which only heightens her defects.
When such, of glitt'ring jewels proud,
Still press the foremost in the crowd,
At ev'ry public shew are seen,
With look awry and aukward mien,
The gaudy dress attracts the eye,
And magnifies deformity.
Nature may underdo her part,
But seldom wants the help of art;
Trust her, she is your surest friend,
Nor made your form for you to mend.

 A goose, affected, empty, vain,
The shrillest of the cackling train,
With proud and elevated crest,
Precedence claim'd above the rest.
Says she, I laugh at human race
Who say geese hobble in their pace;
Look here!—the sland'rous lie detect;
Not haughty man is so erect!
That peacock yonder! lord, how vain
The creature's of his gaudy train!
If both were stript, I'd pawn my word
A goose would be the finer bird.
Nature, to hide her own defects,
Her bungled work with fin'ry decks;
Were geese set off with half that shew,
Would men admire the peacock?—No.

 Thus vaunting, cross the mead she stalks,
The cackling breed attend her walks;
The sun shot down his noon-tide beams,
The swans were sporting in the streams;

Their snowy plumes and stately pride
Provok'd her spleen. Why there, she cry'd,
Again, what arrogance we see!—
Those creatures! how they mimic me!
Shall ev'ry fowl the waters skim
Because we geese are known to swim!
Humility they soon shall learn,
And their own emptiness discern.
So saying, with extended wings,
Lightly upon the wave she springs;
Her bosom swells, she spreads her plumes,
And the swan's stately crest assumes.
Contempt and mockery ensu'd,
And bursts of laughter shook the flood.

A swan, superior to the rest,
Sprung forth and thus the fool address'd:
Conceited thing, elate with pride!
Thy affectation all deride:
These airs thy aukwardness impart,
And shew thee plainly as thou art.
Among thy equals of the flock
Thou hadst escap'd the public mock,
And, as thy parts to good conduce,
Been deem'd an honest hobbling goose.

Learn hence to study wisdom's rules;
Know foppery's the pride of fools;
And, striving nature to conceal,
You only her defects reveal.

Moore.

THE PIN AND THE NEEDLE: A FABLE.

A PIN, who long had serv'd a beauty
Proficient in the toilet's duty,
Had form'd her sleeve, confin'd her hair,
Or giv'n her knot a smarter air,
Now nearest to her heart was plac'd,
Now in her mantua's tail disgrac'd:
But could she partial fortune blame
Who saw her lover serv'd the same?
At length from all her honour's cast,
Though various turns of life she pass'd;
Now glitter'd on a taylor's arm;
Now kept a beggar's infant warm;
Now, rang'd within a miser's coat,
Contributes to his yearly groat;
Now rais'd again from low approach
She visits in the doctor's coach;
Here, there, by various fortune tost,
At last in Gresham-hall was lost.
Charm'd with the wonders of the show
On every side, above, below,
She now of this or that inquires,
What least was understood admires.
'Tis plain, each thing so struck her mind,
Her head's of virtuoso kind.
   'And pray what's this, and this, dear sir?'
'A needle,' says th' interpreter.
She knew the name, and thus the fool
Address'd her as a taylor's tool.

'A needle

'A needle with that filthy stone,
'Quite idle, all with rust o'ergrown!
You better might employ your parts,
And aid the sempstress in her arts.
'But tell me how that friendship grew
'Between that paltry flint and you?'—
  'Friend,' says the needle, 'cease to blame;
'I follow real worth and fame.
'Know'st thou the loadstone's power and art,
'That virtue virtues can impart;
'Of all his talents I partake,
'Who then can such a friend forsake?
''Tis I direct the pilot's hand
'To shun the rocks and treacherous sand;
'By me the distant world is known,
'And either India is our own.
'Had I with milliners been bred,
'What had I been?—The guide of thread,
'And drudg'd as vulgar needle do,
'Of no more consequence than you.'

GAY.

THE TWO BEES: A FABLE.

On a fine morning in May two bees set forward in quest of honey; the one wise and temperate, the other careless and extravagant: they soon arrived at a garden enriched with aromatic herbs, the most fragrant flowers, and most delicious fruits. They regaled themselves for a time on the various dainties that were spread before them; the one loading his thigh at intervals with

provisions

provisions for the hive against the distant winter; the other revelling in sweets, without regard to any thing but his present gratification. At length they found a wide-mouthed phial that hung beneath the bough of a peach-tree filled with honey ready tempered, and exposed to their taste in the most alluring manner. The thoughtless epicure, spite of all his friend's remonstrances, plunged headlong into the vessel, resolving to indulge himself in all the pleasures of sensuality. The philosopher, on the other hand, sipped a little with caution; but being suspicious of danger flew off to fruits and flowers, where, by the moderation of his meals, he improved his relish for the true enjoyment of them. In the evening, however, he called upon his friend to inquire whether he would return to the hive, but found him surfeited in sweets which he was as unable to leave as to enjoy. Clogged in his wings, enfeebled in his feet, and his whole frame totally enervated, he was but just able to bid his friend adieu, and to lament with his latest breath that, ' though a taste of pleasure might ' quicken the relish of life, an unrestrained indulgence is ' inevitable destruction.'

INDIRECT DISPUTES.

Amongst the vulgar, where the men vent their passions by swearing, and the women by scolding or crying, their quarrels are generally soon made up; nor does any danger remain after reconciliation. But in higher life, where such efforts are restrained by good breeding, where people have learned to disguise, not to subdue, their passions, an inveterate rancour often lies corroding in the breast,

breast, and generally produces all the effects of inexorable malice.

People consider not that by family repartees and oblique reflections on each side the very inmost secrets of their lives are disclosed to their common acquaintance; and that they oftentimes inconsiderately lay open to their worst enemies faults and imperfections in themselves and their relations which they would take pains to conceal from their dearest friends.

To give you a full idea of what I mean, I send you an account of a conversation which passed between two sisters I yesterday breakfasted with. Miss Harriet the elder sister was about the age of nineteen, and Miss Fanny the youngest not quite seventeen. Their parents are able amply to provide for them; and have spared no cost in masters of every kind, in order to give them all fashionable female accomplishments. Ever since they have quitted the nursery they have been indulged in seeing their own company in Miss Harriet's dressing-room, which is finished and adorned with great elegance of taste and profusion of expense. They are both possessed of no small share of beauty, with so much quickness of apprehension and ready wit as might, if rightly applied, render them extremely entertaining. Not one real misfortune can they yet have met with to sour their tempers or suppress their vivacity: yet I could plainly see that they were very far from being happy, and that their unhappiness arose from their continual bickerings with each other. After breakfast Miss Fanny took up a volume of Shakspeare's plays that lay in the window, and out of the Midsummer Night's Dream read the following part of a speech which Helena makes to her friend Hermia, in the third act:

'Injurious

'Injurious Hermia, most ungrateful maid!
'Have you contriv'd, have you with these contriv'd
'To bait me with this foul derision?
'Is all the counsel that we two have shared—
'The sisters' vows, the hours that we have spent
'When we have chid the hasty-footed time
'For parting us?—O! and is all forgot?'

Then laying down the book, with the tears half starting from her eyes, she looked earnestly at her sister, and, in a tone more theatrical than I wish to hear off the stage, cried out, 'Oh, wretched Helena! unhappy maid! I wonder not 'that in your circumstances you imagined that every word 'was intended as an insult, since no doubt you have often 'experienced such inhuman treatment.' Miss Harriet with some warmth answered 'You should remember, '*sister*, that Helena was a foolish weak girl, fond of a man 'that despised her; and it was kind of anybody to endea- 'vour to cure her of such a mean-spirited passion.'

Fanny. 'Tis always cruel, *sister*, to insult the wretched.

Harriet. Those that are miserable by their own folly, *Miss Fanny*, will call every thing insult and reproach that tends not to sooth and encourage them in a silly passion.

Fanny. If love is a silly passion, *Miss Harriet*, I know some mighty wise people that have felt its power.

Harriet. I don't say love is a silly passion where it is properly placed: but I know, *Madam*, that a headstrong young girl will always be angry with every one that ad- vises her for her good.

Fanny. And I know also, *Madam*——

As soon as the affectionate name of *sister* was dropped, and the ceremony of *Miss* supplied its place, I even then

began

began to fear left ceremony would also undergo the same fate, and that passion at last would introduce open rudeness; but the word *Madam*, doubly retorted, no sooner reached my ears than, trembling for the event, I interrupted the dialogue by taking my leave; and I doubt not but any one from this sketch may easily be able to paint in what manner these young ladies pass most of their hours together.

ADVENTURER.

A CONVERSATION ON TRUTH.

' YESTERDAY,' said she to them, ' I only mentioned
' to you one fault, though I observed two. You very
' readily guess I mean the lie you both told. Nay, look
' up, I wish to see you blush; the confusion I perceive in
' your faces gives me pleasure, as it convinces me it is not
' a confirmed habit: and indeed, my children, I should be
' sorry such a mean one had taken root in your infant
' minds.

' When I speak of falsehood I mean every kind; what-
' ever tends to deceive, though not said in direct terms.
' Tones of voice, motions of the hand or head, if they
' make another believe what they ought not to believe.
' are lies, and of the worst kind, as the contrivance ag-
' gravates the guilt. I would much sooner forgive a lie
' told directly, when perhaps fear entirely occupied the
' the thoughts, and the presence of God was not felt: it
' is Him you affront by telling an untruth.'

' How so?' inquired Mary.

' Because

'Becaufe you hope to conceal it from every human
'creature: but, if you confider a moment, you muft re-
'collect that the Searcher of hearts reads your very
'thoughts; that nothing is hid from him.

'You would blufh if I difcovered it, yet forfeit His
'favour to fcreen yourfelves from correction or reproof;
'or, what is ftill worfe, to purchafe fome trifling gratifi-
'cation, the pleafure of which would laft but a moment.

'You heard the gentleman who vifited me this morning
'very frequently ufe the word honour. Honour confifts in
'refpecting yourfelf; in doing as you would be done by;
'and the foundation of it is truth.

'When I can depend on the veracity of people, that is
'to fay, am certain they adhere to truth, I rely on them;
'am certain they have courage, becaufe I know they will
'bear any inconvenience rather than tell a lie and defpife
'themfelves. Befides, when you have done right, it is
'not then neceffary to confider what you intend to fay.
'Always determine on every occafion to fpeak the truth,
'and you will never be at a lofs for words. If your
'character for this fcrupulous attention is once fixed, your
'acquaintance will be courted; and thofe who are not
'particularly pleafed with you will refpect your honour-
'able principles.

'It is impoffible to form friendfhips without making
'truth the bafis; it is, indeed, the effence of devotion,
'the employment of the underftanding, and the fupport
'of every other duty.

'I govern my fervants and you by attending ftrictly
'to it, and this obfervance keeps my head clear and my
'heart pure; and I am ever ready to pray to the Author
'of good, the fountain of truth.

'While

'While I am discussing the subject let me point out to
you another branch of this virtue—sincerity; and remember I every day set you an example; for I never, to
please for a moment, pay unmeaning compliments, or
permit any words to drop from my tongue that my heart
does not dictate; and when I relate any matter of fact
I carefully avoid embellishing it, in order to render it a
more entertaining story; not that I think such a practice
absolutely criminal; but, as it contributes insensibly to
wear away a respect for truth, I guard against the
vain impulse, lest I lose the chief strength and even ornament of my mind, and become, like a wave of the sea,
drifted about by every gust of passion.

'You must in life observe the most apparently insignificant duties—the great ones are the pillars of virtue;
but the constant concurrence of trifling things makes it
necessary that reason and conscience should always preside to keep the heart steady. Many people make promises and appointments which they scruple not to break
if some other more inviting pleasure occurs. Always
remember that the slightest duty should be performed
before a mere amusement is pursued; for any neglect
of this kind imbitters pleasure. Nothing can long be
pleasant that is not innocent.' ORIGINAL STORIES.

LYING PUNISHED.

BUT a certain man named Ananias, with Sapphira his wife, sold a possession, and kept back part of the price, his wife also being privy to it, and brought a certain part and laid it at the apostles' feet. But Peter said, Ananias, why hath Satan filled thine heart to lie to the Holy Ghost, and to keep back part of the price of the land? Whiles it remained was it not thine own? and after it was sold was it not in thine own power? why hast thou conceived this thing in thine heart? thou hast not lied unto men but unto God. And Ananias hearing these words fell down and gave up the Ghost: and great fear came on all them that heard these things. And the young men arose, wound him up, and carried him out and buried him.

And it was about the space of three hours after when his wife, not knowing what was done, came in. And Peter answered unto her, Tell me whether ye sold the land for so much? And she said, Yea, for so much. Then Peter said unto her, How is it that ye have agreed together to tempt the Spirit of the Lord? Behold, the feet of them which have buried thy husband are at the door, and shall carry thee out. Then fell she down straightway at his feet, and yielded up the ghost: and the young men came in and found her dead, and carrying her forth buried her by her husband. And great fear came upon all the church, and upon as many as heard these things.

THE ACTS.

BOOK V.

DESCRIPTIVE PIECES.

THE CHARACTER OF QUEEN ELIZABETH.

There are few perfonages in hiftory who have been more expofed to the calumny of enemies and the adulation of friends than Queen Elizabeth; and yet there fcarce is any whofe reputation has been more certainly determined by the unanimous confent of pofterity. The unufual length of her adminiftration, and the ftrong features of her character, were able to overcome all prejudices, and, obliging her detractors to abate much of their invectives, and her admirers fomewhat of their panegyrics, have at laft, in fpite of political factions, and (what is more) of of religious animofities, produced an uniform judgment with regard to her conduct. Her vigour, her conftancy, her magnanimity, her penetration, vigilance, and addrefs, are allowed to merit the higheft praifes, and appear not to have been furpaffed by any perfon who ever filled a throne: a conduct lefs rigorous, lefs imperious, more fincere, more indulgent to her people, would have been requifite to form a perfect character. By the force of her mind she controlled all her more active and strong qualities, and prevented them from running into excess: her heroism was exempt from all temerity, her frugality from avarice, her friendship from partiality, her enterprise from turbulency and a vain ambition. She guarded not herself with equal care or equal success from lesser infirmities; the rivalship of beauty, the desire of admiration, the jealousy of love, and the sallies of anger.

Her singular talents for government were founded equally on her temper and on her capacity. Endowed with a great command over herself, she soon obtained an uncontrolled ascendant over the people; and, while she merited all their esteem by her real virtues, she also engaged their affections by her pretended ones. Few sovereigns of England succeeded to the throne in more difficult circumstances; and none ever conducted the government with such uniform success and felicity. Though unacquainted with the practice of toleration, the true secret for managing religious factions, she preserved her people by her superior prudence from those confusions in which theological controversy had involved all the neighbouring nations; and, though her enemies were the most powerful princes of Europe, the most active, the most enterprising, the least scrupulous, she was able by her vigour to make deep impressions on their state; her own greatness meanwhile remained untouched and unimpaired.

The wise ministers and brave warriors who flourished during her reign share the praise of her success; but, instead of lessening the applause due to her, they make great addition to it: they owed, all of them, their advancement to her choice; they were supported by her constancy; and with all their ability they were never able to acquire any

undue

undue ascendant over her. In her family, in her court, in her kingdom, she remained equally mistress: the force of the tender passions was great over her, but the force of her mind was still superior; and the combat which her victory visibly cost her serves only to display the firmness of her resolution, and the loftiness of her ambitious sentiments.

The fame of this princess, though it has surmounted the prejudices both of faction and bigotry, yet lives still exposed to another prejudice, which is more durable because more natural, and which, according to the different views in which we survey her, is capable either of exalting beyond measure or diminishing the lustre of her character. This prejudice is founded on the consideration of her sex. When we contemplate her as a woman we are apt to be struck with the highest admiration of her qualities and extensive capacity; but we are also apt to require some more softness of disposition, some greater lenity of temper, some of those amiable weaknesses by which her sex is distinguished. But the true method of estimating her merit is to lay aside all these considerations, and to consider her merely as a rational being placed in authority, and intrusted with the government of mankind. We may find it difficult to reconcile our fancy to her as a wife or a mistress; but her qualities as a sovereign, though with some considerable exceptions, are the object of indisputed applause and approbation.

HUME.

THE CHARACTER OF MARY QUEEN OF SCOTS.

To all the charms of beauty, and the utmost elegance of external form, Mary added those external accomplishments which render their impression irresistible. Polite, affable, insinuating, sprightly, and capable of speaking and of writing with equal ease and dignity. Sudden, however, and violent in all her attachments, because her heart was warm and unsuspicious. Impatient of contradiction, because she had been accustomed from her infancy to be treated as a queen. No stranger, on some occasions, to dissimulation, which in that perfidious court where she received her education was reckoned among the necessary arts of government. Not insensible to flattery, or unconscious of that pleasure with which almost every woman beholds the influence of her beauty. Formed with the qualities that we love, not with the talents that we admire, she was an agreeable woman rather than an illustrious queen. The vivacity of her spirit, not sufficiently tempered with sound judgment, and the warmth of her heart, which was not at all times under the restraint of discretion, betrayed her both into errors and into crimes. To say that she was always unfortunate will not account for that long and almost uninterrupted succession of calamities which befell her; we must likewise add, that she was often imprudent. Her passion for Darnly was rash, youthful, and excessive: and though the sudden transition to the opposite extreme was the natural effect of her ill-requited love, and his ingratitude, insolence, and brutality, yet neither these, nor Bothwell's artful address and important services, can justify her attachments to that nobleman. Even the manners of the age, licentious as they were, are no apology for this unhappy passion; nor can they induce us to look on that tragical and infamous scene which followed upon it with less abhorrence. Humanity will draw a veil over this part of her character which it cannot approve,

and

and may, perhaps, prompt some to impute her actions to her situation more than to her disposition; and to lament the unhappiness of the former rather than accuse the perverseness of the latter. Mary's sufferings exceed both in degree and in duration those tragical distresses which fancy has feigned to excite sorrow and commiseration; and while we survey them we are apt altogether to forget her frailties, we think of her faults with less indignation, and approve of our tears as if they were shed for a person who had attained much nearer to pure virtue.

With regard to the queen's person, (a circumstance not to be omitted in writing the history of a female reign,) all contemporary authors agree in ascribing to Mary the utmost beauty of countenance and elegance of shape of which the human form is capable. Her hair was black, though, according to the fashion of that age, she frequently wore borrowed locks, and of different colours. Her eyes were a dark grey, her complexion was exquisitely fine, and her hands and arms remarkably delicate both as to shape and colour. Her stature was of an height that rose to the majestic. She danced, she walked, and rode with equal grace. Her taste for music was just, and she both sung and played upon the lute with uncommon skill. Towards the end of her life she began to grow fat; and her long confinement, and the coldness of the houses in which she was imprisoned, brought on a rheumatism which deprived her of the use of her limbs.

ROBERTSON.

A PORTRAIT OF MANKIND INFLUENCED BY VANITY.

Vanity bids all her sons to be generous und brave, and her daughters to be chaste and courteous. But why do we want her instructions? Ask the comedian, who is taught a part he feels not.

Is it that the principles of religion want strength, or that the real passion for what is good and worthy will not carry us high enough?—God! thou knowest they carry us too high—we want not to be, but to seem.

Look out of your door—take notice of that man; see what disquieting, intriguing, and shifting, he is content to go through, merely to be thought a man of plain dealing—three grains of honesty would save him all this trouble:—alas! he has them not.

Behold a second, under a shew of piety, hiding the impurities of a debauched life;—he is just entering the house of God:—would he were more pure, or less pious! but then he could not gain his point.

Observe a third going almost in the same track; with what inflexible sanctity of deportment he sustains himself as he advances!—every line in his face writes abstinence; every stride looks like a check upon his desires. See, I beseech you, how he is cloaked up with sermons, prayers, and sacraments; and so bemuffled with the externals of religion, that he has no hand to spare for a worldly purpose; he has armour at least, why does he put it on? Is there no serving God without all this? Must the garb of religion be extended so wide to the danger of its rending?

Yes,

Yes, truly, or it will not hide the secret;—and what is that?

—— 'That the saint has no religion at all.'

But here comes Generosity; giving—not to a decayed artist—but to the arts and sciences themselves. See, he 'builds not a chamber in the wall apart for the pro-'phets,' but whole schools and colleges for those who come after. Lord, how they will magnify his name! 'Tis in capitals already; the first, the highest, in the gilded rent-roll of every hospital and asylum.

One honest tear shed in private over the unfortunate is worth it all.

What a problematic set of creatures does dissimulation make us! Who would divine that all the anxiety and concern so visible in the airs of one half of that great assembly should arise from nothing else but that the other half of it may think them to be men of consequence, penetration, parts, and conduct? What a noise among the claimants about it? Behold humility out of mere pride, and honesty almost out of knavery; chastity never once in harm's way; and courage, like a Spanish soldier upon an Italian stage—a bladder full of wind.

Hark! that, the sound of that trumpet;—let not my soldier run;—'tis some good Christian giving alms. O pity, thou gentlest of human passions! soft and tender are thy notes, and ill accord they with so loud an instrument.

STERNE.

THE PLANETARY AND TERRESTRIAL WORLDS COMPARATIVELY CONSIDERED

To us who dwell on its surface, the earth is by far the most extensive orb that our eyes can any where behold: it is also clothed with verdure, distinguished by trees, and adorned with variety of beautiful decorations; whereas to a spectator placed on one of the planets it wears an uniform aspect, looks all luminous, and no larger than a spot. To beings who still dwell at greater distances it entirely disappears. That which we call alternately the morning and evening star, as in one part of the orbit she rides foremost in the procession of night, in the other ushers in and anticipates the dawn, is a planetary world, which, with the four others that so wonderfully vary their mystic dance, are in themselves dark bodies, and shine only by reflection; have fields, and seas, and skies of their own; are furnished with all accommodations for animal subsistence, and are supposed to be the abodes of intellectual life; all which, together with our earthly habitation, are dependant on that grand dispenser of divine munificence, the sun; receive their light from the distribution of his rays, and derive their comfort from his benign agency.

The sun, which seems to perform its daily stages through the sky, is in this respect fixed and immovable; 'tis the great axle of heaven, about which the globe we inhabit and other more spacious orbs wheel their stated courses. The sun, though seemingly smaller than the dial it illuminates, is abundantly larger than this whole earth on which so many lofty mountains rise, and such vast oceans roll. A line extending from side to side through the centre of that resplendent orb would measure more than eight hundred thousand miles: a girdle formed to go round its circumference would require a length of millions. Were its solid contents to be estimated the account would overwhelm our understanding, and be almost beyond the power of language to express. Are we startled at these reports of philosophy?

philosophy? Are we ready to cry out in a transport of surprise, 'How mighty is the Being who kindled such a prodigious fire, and keeps alive from age to age such an enormous mass of flame!' Let us attend our philosophic guides, and we shall be brought acquainted with speculations more enlarged and wonderful.

The sun with all its attendant planets is but a very little part of the grand machine of the universe; every star, though it appears no bigger than the diamond that glitters upon a lady's ring, is really a vast globe, like the sun in size and in glory; no less spacious, no less luminous, than the radiant source of the day: so that every star is not barely a world but the centre of a magnificent system; has a retinue of worlds irradiated by its beams, and revolving round its attractive influence, all which are lost to our sight in unmeasurable wilds of ether. That the stars appear like so many diminutive and scarce distinguishable points is owing to their immense and inconceivable distance. Immense and inconceivable indeed it is, since a ball shot from the loaded cannon, and flying with unabated rapidity, must travel at this impetuous rate almost seven hundred thousand years before it could reach the nearest of these twinkling luminaries. While beholding this vast expanse I learn my own extreme meanness, I would also discover the abject littleness of all terrestrial things. What is the earth, with all her ostentatious scenes, compared with this astonishing grand furniture of the skies? What but a dim speck hardly perceivable in the map of the universe? It is observed by a very judicious writer, that if the sun himself, which enlightens this part of the creation, was extinguished, and all the host of planetary worlds which move about him were annihilated, they would not be missed by

an

an eye that can take in the whole compass of nature, any more than a grain of sand upon the sea-shore. The bulk of which they consist, and the space which they occupy, is so exceedingly little in comparison of the whole, that their loss would leave scarce a blank in the immensity of God's works. If then not our globe only, but this whole system, be so very diminutive, what is a kingdom or a country? What are a few lordships, or the so-much admired patrimonies of those who are styled wealthy? When I measure them with my own little pittance they swell into proud and bloated dimensions: but, when I take the universe for my standard, how scanty is their size, how contemptible their figure! they shrink into pompous nothings.

SPECTATOR.

A DEVOTIONAL PSALM.

The heavens declare the glory of God, and the firmament sheweth his handy-work.

Day unto day uttereth speech, and night unto night sheweth knowledge.

There is no speech nor language where their voice is not heard.

Their line is gone out through all the earth, and their words to the end of the world: in them hath he set a tabernacle for the sun,

Which is as a bridegroom coming out of his chamber, and rejoiceth as a strong man to run a race.

His going forth is from the end of the heaven, and his circuit unto the ends of it: and there is nothing hid from the heat thereof.

The law of the Lord is perfect, converting the soul: the testimony of the Lord is sure, making wise the simple.

The statutes of the Lord are right, rejoicing the heart: the commandment of the Lord is pure, enlightening the eyes.

The fear of the Lord is clean, enduring for ever: the judgments of the Lord are true and righteous altogether.

More to be desired are they than gold, yea, than much fine gold: sweeter also than honey and the honeycomb.

Moreover, by them is thy servant warned: and in keeping of them there is great reward.

Who can understand his errors? cleanse thou me from secret faults.

Keep back thy servant also from presumptuous sins; let them not have dominion over me: then shall I be upright, and I shall be innocent from the great transgression.

Let the words of my mouth, and the meditations of my heart, be acceptable in thy sight, O Lord, my strength and my redeemer.

THE PLEASURES OF THE COUNTRY.

Not rural sights alone, but rural sounds,
Exhilerate the spirits, and restore
The tone of languid nature. Mighty winds,
That sweep the skirt of some far-spreading wood
Of ancient growth, make music not unlike
The dash of Ocean on his winding shore,
And lull the spirit while they fill the mind;
Unnumber'd branches waving in the blast,
And all their leaves fast flutt'ring, all at once.
Nor less composure waits upon the roar

Of diftant floods, or on the fofter voice
Of neighb'ring fountain, or of rills that flip
Through the cleft rock, and, chiming as they fall
Upon loofe pebbles, lofe themfelves at length
In matted grafs, that with a livelier green
Betrays the fecret of their filent courfe.
Nature inanimate employs fweet founds,
But animated Nature fweeter ftill,
To footh and fatisfy the human ear—
Ten thoufand warblers cheer the day, and one
The live long night. Nor thefe alone whofe notes
Nice-finger'd art muft emulate in vain,
But cawing rooks and kites that fwim fublime
In ftill repeated circles fcreaming loud;
The jay, the pie, and ev'n the boding owl
That hails the rifing moon, have charms for me.
Sounds inharmonious in themfelves and harfh,
Yet heard in fcenes where peace for ever reigns,
And only there, pleafe highly for their fake.

God made the country, and man made the town:
What wonder then that health and virtue, gifts
That can alone make fweet the bitter draught
That life holds out to all, fhould moft abound,
And leaft be threaten'd, in the fields and groves?
Poffefs ye, therefore, ye who, borne about
In chariots and fedans, know no fatigue
But that of idlenefs, and tafte no fcenes
But fuch as art contrives; poffefs ye ftill
Your element, there only ye can fhine;
There only minds like yours can do no harm.
Our groves are planted to confole at noon
The penfive wand'rer in their fhades. At eve

The

The moon-beam, sliding softly in between
The sleeping leaves, is all the light they wish,
Birds warbling all the music. We can spare
The splendour of your lamps, they but eclipse
Our softer satellite.

———

Domestic happiness, thou only bliss
Of Paradise that has surviv'd the fall!
Though few now taste thee unimpair'd and pure,
Or, tasting, long enjoy thee, too infirm
Or too incautious to preserve thy sweets
Unmix'd with drops of bitter, which neglect
Or temper sheds into thy chrystal cup,
Thou art the nurse of virtue! In thine arms
She smiles, appearing, as in truth she is,
Heav'n-born, and destin'd to the skies again.
Thou art not known where pleasure is ador'd,
That reeling goddess with the zoneless waist
And wand'ring eyes, still leaning on the arm
Of novelty, her fickle, frail support;
For thou art meek and constant, hating change,
And finding in the calm of truth-tried love
Joys that her stormy raptures never yield.

COWPER.

MEN AND ANIMALS COMPARED.

In comparing the different species of animals we find each of them possessed of powers and faculties peculiar to themselves, and admirably adapted to the particular sphere of action which Providence has allotted them. But, amidst that infinite variety which distinguishes each species, we find

find many qualities in which they are all similar, and some which they have in common.

Man is evidently at the head of the animal creation. He seems not only to be possessed of every source of pleasure in common with them, but of many others to which they are altogether strangers. If he is not the only animal possessed of reason, he has it in a degree so greatly superior as admits of no comparison.

The insensible gradation so conspicuous in all the works of nature fails in comparing mankind with other animals. There is an infinite distance between the faculties of a man and those of the most perfect animal; between intellectual power and mechanic force; between order and design and blind impulse; between reflection and appetite.

One animal governs another only by superior force or cunning; nor can it by any address or train of reasoning secure to itself the protection and good offices of another. There is no sense of superiority or subordination among them.

Their want of language seems owing to their having no regular train or order in their ideas, and not to any deficiency in their organs of speech. Many animals may be taught to speak, but none of them can be taught to connect any ideas to the words they pronounce. The reason therefore why they do not express themselves by combined and regular signs is because they have no regular combination in their ideas.

There is a remarkable uniformity in the works of animals. Each individual of a species does the same things, and in the same manner, as every other of the same species. They seem all to be actuated by one soul. On the contrary, among mankind every individual thinks and acts in a way almost peculiar to himself. The only exception to this uniformity of character in the different species of animals

mals seems to be among those who are most connected with mankind, particularly dogs and horses.

All animals express pain and pleasure by cries and various motions of the body; but laughter and shedding of tears are peculiar to mankind. They seem to be expressions of certain emotions of the soul unknown to other animals, and are scarce ever observed in infants till they are about six weeks old. The pleasures of the imagination, the pleasure arising from science, from the fine arts, and from the principle of curiosity, are peculiar to the human species. But, above all, they are distinguished by the moral sense, and the happiness flowing from religion, and from the various intercourses of social life.

Reason of itself cannot any more than riches be reckoned an immediate blessing to mankind. It is only the proper application of it to render them more happy that can entitle it to that name. Nature has furnished us with a variety of internal senses and tastes unknown to other animals. All these, if properly cultivated, are sources of pleasure, but without culture; most of them are so faint and languid, that they convey no gratification to the mind. This culture is the peculiar province of reason; it belongs to reason to analyze our tastes and pleasures; and, after a proper arrangement of them, according to their different degrees of excellence, to assign to each that degree of cultivation and indulgence which its rank deserves, and no more.

GREGORY.

TENDERNESS FOR ANIMALS.

The heart is hard in nature, and unfit
For human fellowship, as being void
Of sympathy, and therefore dead alike
To love and friendship both, that is not pleas'd

With sight of animals enjoying life,
Nor feels their happiness augment his own.
The bounding fawn that darts across the glade
When none pursues, through mere delight of heart,
And spirits boyant with excess of glee;
The horse as wanton, and almost as fleet,
That skims the spacious meadows at full speed,
Then stops and snorts, and, throwing high his heels,
Starts to the voluntary race again;
The very kine that gambol at high-noon,
The total herd receiving first from one
That leads the dance a summons to be gay,
Though wild their strange vagaries, and uncouth
Their efforts, yet resolv'd with one consent
To give such act and utt'rance as they may
To ecstasy too big to be suppress'd;——
These and a thousand images of bliss,
With which kind nature graces ev'ry scene,
Where cruel man defeats not her design,
Impart to the benevolent, who wish
All that are capable of pleasure pleas'd,
A far superior happiness to theirs,
The comfort of a reasonable joy.

 They love the country, and none else, who seek
For their own sake its silence and its shade.
Delights which who would leave that has a heart
Susceptible of pity, or a mind
Cultur'd and capable of sober thought,
For all the savage din of the swift pack,
And clamours of the field?—detested sport,
That owes its pleasures to another's pain;

That feeds upon the sobs and dying shrieks
Of harmless nature, dumb, but yet endu'd
With eloquence that agonies inspire
Of silent tears and heart-distending sighs?
Vain tears, alas! and sighs that never find
A corresponding tone in jovial souls.
Well—one at least is safe. One shelter'd hare
Has never heard the sanguinary yell
Of cruel man exulting in her woes.
Innocent partner of my peaceful home,
Whom ten long years experience of my care
Has made at least familiar: she has lost
Much of her vigilant instinctive dread,
Not needful here, beneath a roof like mine.
Yes—thou may'st eat thy bread, and lick the hand
That feeds thee; thou may'st frolic on the floor
At evening, and at night retire secure
To thy straw couch, and slumber unalarm'd;
For I have gain'd thy confidence, have pledg'd
All that is human in me to protect
Thine unsuspecting gratitude and love.
If I survive thee I will dig thy grave,
And when I place thee in it sighing say
I knew at least one hare that had a friend.

   I would not enter on my list of friends
(Though grac'd with polish'd manners and fine sense,
Yet wanting sensibility) the man
Who needlessly sets foot upon a worm.
An inadvertent step may crush the snail
That crawls at evening in the public path;
But he that has humanity, forewarn'd,
Will tread aside and let the reptile live.

The creeping vermin, loathsome to the sight,
And charg'd perhaps with venom, that intrudes,
A visiter unwelcome, into scenes
Sacred to neatness and repose, th' alcove,
The chamber, or refectory, may die:
A necessary act incurs no blame.
Not so when, held within their proper bounds,
And guiltless of offence, they range the air,
Or take their pastime in the spacious field:
There they are privileg'd; and he that hunts
Or harms them there is guilty of a wrong,
Disturbs th' economy of Nature's realm,
Who, when she form'd, design'd them an abode.
The sum is this: if man's convenience, health,
Or safety, interfere, his rights and claims
Are paramount, and must extinguish theirs.
Else they are all—the meanest things that are—
As free to live, and to enjoy that life,
As God was free to form them at the first,
Who, in his sov'reign wisdom, made them all.
Ye therefore who love mercy teach your sons
To love it too. The spring-time of our years
Is soon dishonour'd and defil'd in most
By budding ills, that ask a prudent hand
To check them.
         COWPER.

AN EVENING's INVOCATION TO WINTER.

Now stir the fire, and close the shutters fast;
Let fall the curtains, wheel the sofa round;
And, while the bubbling and loud-hissing urn
Throws up a steamy column, and the cups

         That

That cheer but not inebriate, wait on each,
So let us welcome peaceful evening in.
Not such his evening, who with shining face
Sweats in the crowded theatre, and, squeez'd
And bor'd with elbow-points through both his sides,
Out-scolds the ranting actor on the stage.

   Oh winter! ruler of th' inverted year,
Thy scatter'd hair with sleet like ashes fill'd,
Thy breath congeal'd upon thy lips, thy cheeks
Fring'd with a beard white with other snows
Than those of age, thy forehead wrapt in clouds,
A leafless branch, thy sceptre and thy throne
A sliding car, indebted to no wheels,
But urg'd by storms along its slipp'ry way;
I love thee, all unlovely as thou seem'st,
And dreadful as thou art. Thou hold'st the sun
A pris'ner in the yet undawning east,
Short'ning his journey between morn and noon,
And hurrying him, impatient of his stay,
Down to the rosy west; but kindly still
Compensating his loss with added hours
Of social converse and instructive ease,
And gathering at short notice, in one group,
The family dispers'd; and fixing thought,
Not less dispers'd by day-light and its cares.
I crown thee king of intimate delights,
Fire-side enjoyments, home-born happiness,
And all the comforts that the lowly roof
Of undisturb'd retirement and the hours
Of long uninterrupted evening know.
No rattling wheels stop short before these gates;
No powder'd pert proficient in the art

Of sounding an alarm assaults these doors
Till the street rings; no stationary steeds
Cough their own knell, while, heedless of the sound,
The silent circle fan themselves and quake:
But here the needle plies its busy task;
The pattern grows; the well-depicted flow'r,
Wrought patiently into the snowy lawn,
Unfolds its bosom; buds, and leaves, and sprigs,
And curling tendrils, gracefully dispos'd,
Follow the nimble finger of the fair;
A wreath that cannot fade, of flow'rs that blow
With most success when all besides decay.
The poet's or historian's page, by one
Made vocal for th' amusement of the rest;
The sprightly lyre, whose treasure of sweet sounds
The touch from many a trembling chord shakes out;
And the clear voice symphonious, yet distinct,
And in the charming strife triumphant still;
Beguile the night, and set a keener edge
On female industry; the threaded steel
Flies swiftly, and unfelt the task proceeds.
The volume clos'd, the customary rites
Of our last meal commence. A Roman meal,
Such as the mistress of the world once found
Delicious, when her patriots of high note,
Perhaps by moon-light, at their humble doors,
And under an old oak's domestic shade,
Enjoy'd—spare feast, a radish and an egg!
Discourse ensues, not trivial, yet not dull,
Nor such as with a frown forbids the play
Of fancy, or proscribes the sound of mirth;
Nor do we madly (like an impious world,

Who deem religion frenzy, and the God
That made them an intruder on their joys)
Start at his awful name, or deem his praise
A jarring note.

   Is winter hideous in a garb like this?
Needs he the tragic fur, the smoke of lamps,
The pent-up breath of an unsav'ry throng,
To thaw him into feeling; or the smart
And snappish dialogue, that flippant wits
Call comedy, to prompt him with a smile?
The self-complacent actor, when he views
(Stealing a side-long glance at a full house)
The slope of faces from the floor to th' roof
(As if one master-spring controll'd them all)
Relax'd into an universal grin,
Sees not a count'nance there that speaks a joy
Half so refin'd or so sincere as ours.
Cards were superfluous here, with all the tricks
That idleness has ever yet contriv'd
To fill the void of an unfurnish'd brain,
To palliate dullness, and give time a shove.

                                COWPER.

THE EMPRESS OF RUSSIA's PALACE OF ICE.

   Less worthy of applause, though more admir'd,
Because a novelty, the work of man,
Imperial mistress of the fur-clad Russ!
Thy most magnificent and mighty freak,
The wonder of the north. No forest fell
When thou would'st build; no quarry sent it's stones

T' enrich thy walls: but thou didst hew the floods,
And make thy marble of the glassy wave.
In such a palace Aristæus found
Cyrene, when he bore the plaintive tale
Of his lost bees to her maternal ear:
In such a palace poetry might place
The armoury of winter; where his troops,
The gloomy clouds, find weapons, arrowy-fleet,
Skin-piercing volley, blossom-bruising hail,
And snow that often blinds the trav'ller's course,
And wraps him in an unexpected tomb.
Silently as a dream the fabric rose;
No sound of hammer or of saw was there.
Ice upon ice—the well-adjusted parts
Were soon conjoin'd, nor other cement ask'd
Than water interfus'd to make them one.
Lamps gracefully dispos'd, and of all hues,
Illumin'd ev'ry side: a wat'ry light
Gleam'd through the clear transparency, that seem'd
Another moon new risen, or meteor fall'n
From Heav'n to earth, of lambent flame serene.
So stood the brittle prodigy; though smooth
And slipp'ry the materials, yet frost-bound
Firm as a rock. Nor wanted aught within,
That royal residence might well befit,
For grandeur or for use. Long wavy wreaths
Of flow'rs, that fear'd no enemy but warmth,
Blush'd on the pannels. Mirrour needed none
Where all was vitreous; but in order due
Convivial table and commodious seat
(What seem'd at least commodious seat) were there,
Sofa and couch, and high-built throne august.

The

The same lubricity was found in all,
And all was moist to the warm touch; a scene
Of evanescent glory, once a stream,
And soon to slide into a stream again.
Alas! 'twas but a mortifying stroke
Of undesign'd severity, that glanc'd
(Made by a Monarch) on her own estate,
On human grandeur and the courts of kings.
'Twas transient in its nature, as in show
'Twas durable; as worthless, as it seem'd
Intrinsically precious; to the foot
Treach'rous and false; it smil'd, and it was cold.

 Great princes have great playthings! Some have play'd
At hewing mountains into men, and some
At building human wonders mountain-high.
Some have amus'd the dull, sad years of life,
Life spent in indolence, and therefore sad,
With schemes of monumental fame; and sought
By pyramids and mausolæan pomp,
Short-liv'd themselves, t' immortalize their bones.
COWPER.

THE POST BOY.

Hark! 'tis the twanging horn! o'er yonder bridge,
That with its wearisome but needful length
Bestrides the wintry flood, in which the moon
Sees her unwrinkled face reflected bright,
He comes, the herald of a noisy world,
With spatter'd boots, strapp'd waist, and frozen locks,
News from all nations lumb'ring at his back.

True to his charge, the close-pack'd load behind,
Yet careless what he brings, his one concern
Is to conduct it to the destin'd inn;
And, having dropp'd th' expected bag—pass on.
He whistles as he goes, light-hearted wretch,
Cold and yet cheerful: messenger of grief
Perhaps to thousands, and of joy to some;
To him indiff'rent whether grief or joy.

COWPER.

AN INVOCATION TO THE STARS.

Tell me, ye shining hosts
That navigate a sea that knows no storms,
Beneath a vault unsullied with a cloud,
If, from your elevation, whence ye view
Distinctly scenes invisible to man,
And systems of whose birth no tidings yet
Have reach'd this nether world, ye spy a race
Favour'd as our's—transgressors from the womb,
And hasting to a grave, yet doom'd to rise,
And to possess a brighter heav'n than yours?
As one who, long detain'd on foreign shores,
Pants to return, and, when he sees afar
His country's weather-bleach'd and batter'd rocks
From the green wave emerging, darts an eye
Radient with joy towards the happy land,
So I with animated hopes behold,
And many an aching wish, your beamy fires,
That shew like beacons in the blue abyss,
Ordain'd to guide th' embodied spirit home,
From toilsome life to never-ending rest.

Love

Love kindles as I gaze. I feel desires
That give assurance of their own success,
And that, infus'd from heav'n, must thither tend.
>   COWPER.

WRITTEN AT MIDNIGHT DURING A THUNDER-STORM.

Let coward guilt, with pallid fear,
To shelt'ring caverns fly,
And justly dread the vengeful fate
That thunders through the sky.

Protected by that hand whose law
The threat'ning storms obey,
Intrepid virtue smiles secure,
As in the blaze of day.

In the thick cloud's tremendous gloom,
The lightning's lurid glare,
It views the same all-gracious pow'r
That breathes the vernal air.

Through nature's ever-varying scene,
By different ways pursued,
The one eternal end of heav'n
Is universal good.

With like beneficent effect
O'er-flaming ether glows,
As when it tunes the linnet's voice,
Or blushes in the rose.

By reason taught to scorn those fears
That vulgar minds molest,
Let no fantastic terrors break
My dear Narcissa's rest.

Thy life may all the tend'rest care
Of providence defend;
And delegated angels round
Their guardian wings extend!
When through creation's vast expanse
The last dread thunders roll,
Untune the concord of the spheres,
And shake the rising soul;
Unmov'd may'st thou the final storm
Of jarring worlds survey,
That ushers in the glad serene
Of everlasting day!

MISS CARTER.

ODE ON ŒLUS's HARP.

ETHEREAL race, inhabitants of air,
Who hymn your God amid the secret grove,
Ye unseen beings! to my harp repair,
And raise majestic strains, or melt in love.
Those tender notes, how kindly they upbraid!
With what soft woe they thrill the lover's heart!
Sure from the hand of some unhappy maid,
Who dy'd of love, these sweet complainings part.
But hark! that strain was of a graver tone,
On the deep strings his hand some hermit throws;
Or he the sacred bard, who sat alone
In the drear waste, and wept his people's woes.
Such was the sung which Zion's children sung,
When by Euphrates' stream they made their plaint;
And to such sadly-solemn notes are strung
Angelic harps to sooth a dying saint.

Methinks

Methinks I hear the full celestial choir
Through heav'ns high dome their awful anthem raise;
Now chanting clear, and now they all conspire
To swell the lofty hymn from praise to praise.
   Let me, ye wand'ring spirits of the wind,
Who, as wild fancy prompts you, touch the string,
Smit with your theme, be in your chorus join'd!
For till you cease my muse forgets to sing.

THOMSON.

ON SLAVERY.

   OH for a lodge in some vast wilderness,
Some boundless contiguity of shade,
Where rumour of oppression and deceit,
Of unsuccessful or successful war,
Might never reach me more! My ear is pain'd,
My soul is sick with every day's report
Of wrong and outrage with which earth is fill'd.
There is no flesh in man's obdurate heart—
It does not feel for man. The nat'ral bond
Of brotherhood is sever'd as the flax
That falls asunder at the touch of fire.
He finds his fellow guilty of a skin
Not colour'd like his own, and, having pow'r
T' enforce the wrong, for such a worthy cause
Dooms and devotes him as his lawful prey!
Lands intersected by a narrow frith
Abhor each other. Mountains interpos'd
Make enemies of nations, who had else
Like kindred drops been mingled into one.
Thus man devotes his brother, and destroys;

And, worse than all, and most to be deplor'd,
As human nature's broadest, foulest blot,
Chains him, and tasks him, and exacts his sweat
With stripes that mercy with a bleeding heart
Weeps when she sees inflicted on a beast!
Then what is man? And what man seeing this,
And having human feelings, does not blush
And hang his head, to think himself a man?
I would not have a slave to till my ground,
To carry me, to fan me while I sleep,
And tremble when I wake, for all the wealth
That sinews bought and sold have ever earn'd.
No: dear as freedom is, and in my heart's
Just estimation priz'd above all price,
I had much rather be myself the slave,
And wear the bonds, than fasten them on him.

COWPER.

THE BASTILE.

Then shame to manhood, and opprobrious more
To France than all her losses and defeats,
Old or of later date, by sea or land,
Her house of bondage, worse than that of old
Which God aveng'd on Pharaoh—the Bastile.
Ye horrid tow'rs, th' abode of broken hearts!
Ye dungeons and ye cages of despair,
That monarchs have supplied from age to age
With music such as suits their sov'reign ears—
The sighs and groans of miserable men!
There's not an English heart that would not leap
To hear that ye were fall'n at last; to know

That ev'n our enemies, so oft employ'd
In forging chains for us, themselves were free.
For he who values liberty confines
His zeal for her predominance within
No narrow bounds; her cause engages him
Wherever pleaded—'tis the cause of man!
There dwell the most forlorn of human kind,
Immur'd though unaccus'd, condemn'd untry'd,
Cruelly spar'd, and hopeless of escape!
There, like the visionary emblem seen
By him of Babylon, life stands a stump,
And, filletted about with hoops of brass,
Still lives, though all it's pleasant boughs are gone,
To count the hour-bell and expect a change;
And ever, as the sullen sound is heard,
Still to reflect, that, though a joyless note
To him whose moments all have one dull pace,
Ten thousand rovers in the world at large
Account it music; that it summons some
To the theatre, or jocund feast or ball:
The wearied hireling finds it a release
From labour; and the lover, who has chid
Its long delay, feels every welcome stroke
Upon his heart-strings, trembling with delight—
To fly for refuge from distracting thought
To such amusements as ingenious woe
Contrives, hard-shifting, and without her tools—
To read engraven on the mouldy walls,
In stagg'ring types, his predecessor's tale,
A sad memorial! and subjoin his own—
To turn purveyor to an overgorg'd
And bloated spider, till the pamper'd pest

Is made familiar, watches his approach,
Comes at his call, and serves him for a friend—
To wear out time in numb'ring to and fro
The studs that thick emboss his iron door,
Then downward and then upward, then aslant
And then alternate, with a sickly hope
By dint of change to give his tasteless task
Some relish, till the sum exactly found
In all directions, he begins again—
Oh comfortless existence! hemm'd around
With woes, which who that suffers would not kneel
And beg for exile, or the pangs of death?

 That man should thus encroach on fellow man,
Abridge him of his just and native rights,
Eradicate him, tear him from his hold
Upon th' endearments of domestic life
And social, nip his fruitfulness and use,
And doom him for perhaps an heedless word
To barrenness, and solitude, and tears,
Moves indignation; makes the name of king
(Of king whom such prerogative can please)
As dreadful as the Manichean god,
Ador'd through fear, strong only to destroy!
'Tis liberty alone that gives the flow'r
Of fleeting life its lustre and perfume,
And we are weeds without it. All constraint,
Except what wisdom lays on evil men,
Is evil; hurts the faculties, impedes
Their progress in the road of science; blinds
The eye-sight of discov'ry, and begets,
In those that suffer'd it, a sordid mind
Bestial, a meagre intellect, unfit

To

To be the tenant of man's noble form.
Thee therefore still, blame-worthy as thou art,
With all thy loss of empire, and though squeez'd
By public exigence till annual food
Fails for the craving hunger of the state,
Thee I account still happy, and the chief
Among nations, seeing thou art free,
My native nook of earth! Thy clime is rude,
Replete with vapours, and disposes much
All hearts to sadness, and none more than mine;
Thine unadult'rate manners are less soft
And plausible than social life requires,
And thou hast need of discipline and art
To give thee what politer France receives
From nature's bounty—that humane address
And sweetness, without which no pleasure is
In converse, either starv'd by cold reserve,
Or flush'd with fierce dispute, a senseless brawl;
Yet, being free, I love thee: for the sake
Of that one feature can be well content,
Disgrac'd as thou hast been, poor as thou art,
To seek no sublunary rest beside.

— — — —

But there is yet a liberty unsung
By poets, and by senators unprais'd,
Which monarchs cannot grant, nor all the powers
Of earth and hell confed'rate take away.
A liberty, which persecution, fraud,
Oppression, prisons, have no power to bind;
Which whoso tastes can be enslav'd no more—
'Tis liberty of heart deriv'd from heav'n,

Bought

Bought with His blood who gave it to mankind,
And seal'd it with the same token.

— — — — — —

He is the freeman whom the truth makes free,
And all are slaves beside.

— — — — — —

———————His t' enjoy
With a propriety that none can feel,
But who, with filial confidence inspir'd,
Can lift to heav'n an unpresumptuous eye,
And smiling say—My Father made them all.
Are they not his by a peculiar right,
And by an emphasis of int'rest his,
Whose eye they fill with tears of holy joy,
Whose heart with praise, and whose exalted mind
With worthy thoughts of that unwearied love
That plann'd, and built, and still upholds a world
So cloth'd with beauty, for rebellious man!

COWPER.

ON HUMANITY.

'TWERE well, says one sage erudite, profound,
Terribly arch'd and aquiline his nose,
And overbuilt with most impending brows;
'Twere well, could you permit the world to live
As the world pleases. What's the world to you?
Much. I was born of woman, and drew milk,
As sweet as charity, from human breasts.
I think, articulate, I laugh and weep,

And exercise all functions of a man.
How then shall I and any man that lives
Be strangers to each other? Pierce my vein,
Take of the crimson stream meand'ring there,
And catechise it well; apply your glass,
Search it, and prove now if it be not blood
Congenial with thine own; and if it be
What edge of subtlety canst thou suppose
Keen enough, wise and skilful as thou art,
To cut the link of brotherhood, by which
One common Maker bound me to the kind.

COWPER.

POVERTY AND LUXURY CONTRASTED

Where then, ah! where shall poverty reside,
To 'scape the pressure of contiguous pride?
If to some common's fenceless limits stray'd
He drives his flock to pick the scanty blade,
Those fenceless fields the sons of wealth divide,
And ev'n the bare-worn common is deny'd.

If to the city sped—What waits him there?
To see profusion that he must not share;
To see ten thousand baneful arts combin'd
To pamper luxury, and thin mankind;
To see each joy the sons of pleasure know
Extorted from his fellow-creature's woe.
Here, while the counter glitters in brocade,
There the pale artist plies the sickly trade;
Here, while the proud their long-drawn pomps display,
There the black gibbet glooms beside the way.

The dome where pleasure holds her midnight reign,
Here, richly deckt, admits the gorgeous train;
Tumultuous grandeur crowds the blazing square,
The rattling chariots clash, the torches glare.
Sure scenes like these no troubles e'er annoy!
Sure these denote one universal joy!
Are these thy serious thoughts?—Ah, turn thine eyes
Where the poor houseless shiv'ring female lies:
She once, perhaps, in village plenty blest,
Has wept at tales of innocence distrest;
Her modest looks the cottage might adorn,
Sweet as the primrose peeps beneath the thorn;
Now lost to all; her friends, her virtue fled,
Near her betrayer's door she lays her head;
And, pinch'd with cold, and shrinking from the show'r,
With heavy heart deplores that luckless hour,
When idly first, ambitious of the town,
She left her wheel and robes of country brown.

 To thine, sweet auburn, thine, the lovliest train,
Do thy fair tribes participate her pain?
E'en now, perhaps, by cold and hunger led,
At proud men's doors they ask a little bread!

 Ah, no, to distant climes, a dreary scene,
Where half the convex world intrudes between,
Through torrid tracts with fainting steps they go,
Where wild Altama murmurs to their woe.
Far different there from all that charm'd before,
The various terrors of that horrid shore;
Those blazing suns that dart a downward ray,
And fiercely shed intolerable day;
Those matted woods where birds forget to sing,
But silent bats in drowsy clusters cling;

Those pois'nous fields with rank luxuriance crown'd,
Where the dark scorpion gathers death around;
Where at each step the stranger fears to wake
The rattling terrors of the vengeful snake;
Where crouching tigers wait their hapless prey,
And savage men more murd'rous still than they;
While oft in whirls the mad tornado flies,
Mingling the ravag'd landscape with the skies.
Far diff'rent these from ev'ry former scene,
The cooling brook, the grassy-vested green,
The breezy covert of the warbling grove,
That only shelter'd thefts of harmless love.

Good heaven! what sorrows gloom'd that parting day,
That call'd them from their native walks away;
When the poor exiles, every pleasure past,
Hung round the bowers, and fondly look'd their last,
And took a long farewell, and wish'd in vain
For seats like these beyond the western main;
And, shudd'ring still to face the distant deep,
Return'd and wept, and still return'd to weep!
The good old sire the first prepar'd to go
To new found worlds, and wept for other's woe;
But for himself, in conscious virtue brave,
He only wish'd for worlds beyond the grave.
His lovely daughter, lovlier in her tears,
The fond companion of his hapless years,
Silent went next, neglectful of her charms,
And left a lover's for her father's arms.
With louder plaints the mother spoke her woes,
And blest the cot where ev'ry pleasure rose;
And kist her thoughtless babes with many a tear,
And claspt them close in sorrow doubly dear;

While

Whilft her fond hufband ftrove to lend relief
In all the filent manlinefs of grief.

O, luxury! thou curft by heaven's decree,
How ill exchang'd are things like thefe for thee!
How do thy potions, with infidious joy,
Diffufe their pleafures only to deftroy!
Kingdoms by thee, to fickly greatnefs grown,
Boaft of a florid vigour not their own.
At ev'ry draught more large and large they grow—
A bloated mafs of rank unweildy woe!
'Till fapp'd their ftrength, and every part unfound,
Down, down they fink, and fpread a ruin round.
GOLDSMITH.

A CHARACTER.

Oh! born to footh diftrefs, and lighten care;
Lively as foft, and innocent as fair;
Bleft with that fweet fimplicity of thought
So rarely found, and never to be taught;
Of winning fpeech, endearing, artlefs, kind,
The lovlieft pattern of a female mind;
Like fome fair fpirit from the realms of reft,
With all her native heaven within her breaft;
So pure, fo good, fhe fcarce can guefs at fin,
But thinks the world without like that within;
Such melting tendernefs, fo fond to blefs,
Her charity almoft becomes excefs!
Wealth may be courted, wifdom be rever'd,
And beauty prais'd, and brutal ftrength be fear'd;
But goodnefs only can affection move;
And love muft own its origin to love.
MISS AIKIN.
A CHARACTER.

A CHARACTER.

Of gentle manners, and of taste refin'd,
With all the graces of a polish'd mind:
Clear sense and truth still shone in all she spoke,
And from her lips no idle sentence broke.
Each nicer elegance of art she knew;
Correctly fair, and regularly true.
Her ready fingers ply'd with equal skill
The pencil's task, the needle, or the quill.
So pois'd her feelings, so compos'd her soul,
So subject all to reason's calm control,
One only passion, strong, and unconfin'd,
Disturb'd the balance of her even mind:
One passion rul'd despotic in her breast,
In every word, and look, and thought confest:
But that was love, and love delights to bless
The generous transports of a fond excess.

Miss Aikin.

A COMPARISON.

The lapse of time and rivers is the same,
Both speed their journey with a restless stream;
The silent pace with which they steal away
No wealth can bribe, no pray'rs persuade to stay,
Alike irrevocably both when past,
And a wide ocean swallows both at last.
Though each resemble each in ev'ry part,
A difference strikes at length the musing heart;

Streams never flow in vain, where streams abound,
How laughs the land with various plenty crown'd!
But time, that should enrich the noble mind,
Neglected leaves a dreary waste behind.
                                        COWPER.

A COMPARISON.

Sweet stream that winds through yonder glade,
Apt emblem of a virtuous maid—
Silent and chaste she steals along
Far from the world's gay busy throng,
With gentle yet prevailing force
Intent upon her destin'd course,
Graceful and useful all she does,
Blessing and blest where'er she goes,
Pure bosom'd as the wat'ry glass,
And Heav'n reflected in her face.   COWPER.

ON A LADY's WRITING.

Her even lines her steady temper show,
Neat as her dress, and polish'd as her brow;
Strong as her judgment, easy as her air;
Correct though free, and regular though fair:
And the same graces o'er her pen preside
That form her manners and her footsteps guide.
                                        MISS AIKIN.

FEMALE AMUSEMENTS.

But if the rougher sex by this fierce sport
Is hurried wild, let not such horrid joy
E'er stir the bosom of the British fair;
Far be the spirit of the chase from them!

Uncomely

Uncomely courage, unbecoming skill,
To spring the fence, to rein the prancing steed;
The cap, the whip, the masculine attire,
In which they roughen to the sense, and all
The winning softness of their sex is lost!
THOMSON.

TRUE GAIETY.

Whom call we gay? That honour has been long
The boast of mere pretenders to the name.
The innocent are gay—The lark is gay,
That dries his feathers, saturate with dew,
Beneath the rosy cloud, while yet the beams
Of day-spring overshoot his humble nest.
The peasant too, a witness of his song,
Himself a songster, is as gay as he.
  Domestic happiness, thou only bliss
Of Paradise that has surviv'd the fall!
Though few now taste thee unimpair'd and pure,
Or, tasting, long enjoy thee; too infirm
Or too incautious to preserve thy sweets
Unmixt with drops of bitter, which neglect
Or temper sheds into the crystal cup,
Thou art the nurse of virtue!
COWPER.

TO STELLA VISITING ME IN MY SICKNESS.

Pallas, observing Stella's wit
Was more than for her sex was fit,
And that her beauty, soon or late,
Might breed confusion in the state,

In high concern for human-kind,
Fix'd honour in her infant mind.
But (not in wranglings to engage
With such a stupid vicious age)
If honour I would here define,
It answers faith in things divine.
As nat'ral life the body warms,
And scholars teach the soul informs,
So honour animates the whole,
And is the spirit of the soul.
Those num'rous virtues which the tribe
Of tedious moralists describe,
And by such various titles call,
True honour comprehends them all.
Let melancholy rule supreme,
Choler preside, or blood, or phlegm,
It makes no diff'rence in the case,
Nor is complexion honour's place.
In points of honour to be try'd,
All passions must be laid aside;
Ask no advice but think alone,
Suppose the question not your own:
How shall I act? is not the case,
But—How would Brutus in my place?
In such a case would Cato bleed?
And how would Socrates proceed?
Drive all objections from your mind,
Else you relapse to human-kind;
Ambition, avarice, and lust,
And factious rage, and breach of trust,
And flatt'ry tipt with nauseous fleer,
And guilty shame, and servile fear,

Envy,

Envy, and cruelty, and pride,
Will in your tainted heart preside.
  Heroes and heroines of old
By honour only were enroll'd
Among their brethren in the skies,
To which (tho' late) shall Stella rise.
Ten thousand oaths upon record
Are not so sacred as her word.
The world shall in its atoms end
Ere Stella can deceive a friend.
By honour seated in her breast
She still determines what is best.
What indignation in her mind
Against enslavers of mankind!
Base kings and ministers of state
Eternal objects of her hate!
  She thinks that nature ne'er design'd
Courage to man alone confin'd.
Can cowardice her sex adorn,
Which most exposes ours to scorn?
She wonders where the charm appears
In Florimel's affected fears;
For Stella never learn'd the art,
At proper times to scream and start,
Nor calls up all the house at night,
And swears she saw a thing in white:
Doll never flies to cut her lace,
Or throw cold water in her face,
Because she heard a sudden drum,
Or found an earwig in a plum!
Her hearers are amaz'd from whence
Proceeds that fund of wit and sense;

                              Which,

Which, tho' her modesty would shroud,
Breaks, like the sun, behind a cloud,
While gracefulness its art conceals,
And yet thro' ev'ry motion steals.

    Say, Stella! was Prometheus blind,
And forming you mistook your kind?
No; 'twas for you alone he stole
The fire that forms a manly soul;
Then, to complete it ev'ry way,
He moulded it with female clay:
To that you owe the nobler flame,
To this the beauty of your frame.

    How would ingratitude delight,
And how would censure glut her spight,
If I should Stella's kindness hide
In silence, or forget with pride!
When on my sickly couch I lay,
Impatient both of night and day;
Lamenting in unmanly strains,
Call'd ev'ry pow'r to ease my pains;
Then Stella ran to my relief
With cheerful face, and inward grief;
And tho' by heav'ns severe decree
She suffers hourly more than me,
No cruel master could require
From slaves employ'd for daily hire
What Stella, by her friendship warm'd,
With vigour and delight perform'd.
My sinking spirits now supplies
With cordials in her hands and eyes;
Now with a soft and silent tread,
Unheard, she moves about my bed:

I see

I see her taste each nauseous draught,
And so obligingly am caught,
I bless the hand from whence they came,
Nor dare distort my face for shame.
    Best pattern of true friends, beware!
You pay too dearly for your care,
If, while your tenderness secures
My life, it must endanger your's;
For such a fool was never found
Who pull'd a palace to the ground
Only to have the ruins made
Materials for an house decay'd.   SWIFT.

DORINA, LUCY. A CONVERSATION.

Lucy. I THOUGHT my aunt was here?

Dor. She is this instant gone, and ordered me to tell you, that, if you learned all your lessons well, she would carry you to the opera.

Lucy. To-night?

Dor. Yes.

Lucy. Is it not the new opera?—Well, I am delighted! Oh, that I had known this sooner!

Dor. Why?

Lucy. Because my hair is most shockingly dressed.— And my new gown—I shall not have that till to-morrow! This is provoking you'll allow.

Dor. Are you not always sure to please, dressed in any way?

Lucy. Oh, I was only joking—I place so little value on all these things.—Do you think this dress prettily trimmed?

Dor. 'Tis charming.

Lucy. Yes, but it is rather faded. I like the rose-colour better, which I wore yesterday. What do you think?

Dor. That whatsoever you wear always appears to me the prettiest.

Lucy. I should have time to dress again before dinner.

Dor. But our lessons?

Lucy. True.—Come, come; I will remain as I am, for it will be so much trouble saved, and I abhor dressing amazingly.—Well, what shall we do?

Dor. Why, your dancing-master is coming, and when you have danced we will draw, and then play on the harpsichord.

Lucy. Oh! as for dancing to-day, that's impossible; I slept ill, and am so languid I am not able to stand on my legs.

Dor. Sit down then. *(She reaches a seat, Lucy sits down and stretches herself with a careless air.)*

Lucy. I really have a dreadful weariness about me.

Dor. Indeed, you look sadly.

Lucy. But seriously, do you think me altered?

Dor. Extremely.

Lucy. Perhaps that is owing to the shocking figure they have made of me.—Oh, it is a settled point, I will certainly dress my hair again for the opera.—Does not my aunt give a breakfast this morning?

Dor. Yes; there is a reading.

Lucy. Oh! when I am married I shall have readings and breakfasts too!—those breakfasts are charming!

Dor. Yes, they take up all the time from noon till four o'clock.

Lucy.

Lucy. And public places, suppers, balls! this is called enjoying life. How happy my aunt is! well, I shall have my turn.

Dor. In the mean time, you should endeavour to gain accomplishments: if we grow weary of public places, fatigued with balls, and disgusted with the gay world, it is then charming to have resources within ourselves.

Lucy. But observe my aunt; she has retained her full relish for youthful amusements; why should not I have the same constancy? Why should I by laborious application bring on certain *ennui*, that I may acquire distant resources, of which, perhaps, I shall never stand in need?

Dor. But does not your aunt herself daily lament the careless education she has received? She gives herself up to dissipation more from custom than taste.

Lucy. To be sure she yawns at the play, has the vapours after all her breakfasts, and her head constantly aches after the opera or masquerade. Yes, this is true—I am very sensible that accomplishments and education may be of some use—then, to be considered as an illiterate woman is humiliating, and repugnant to my inclinations, I must confess. *(She falls into a reverie.)*

Dor. You are pensive.

Lucy. Yes, I feel some efforts of reason which made me sorrowful; you have just said things which have struck me. Why, my dear friend, did you not always speak in this manner?

Dor. I am unwilling either to grieve or contradict you.

Lucy. Do you think that, by taking no more trouble than I give myself, I may, in time, have the least appearance of talents?—the appearance—that is all I wish.

Dor. And do you not pass for having them already?

Lucy. Yes; but, between ourselves, I know nothing.

Dor. Oh, there you are too modest: you play very prettily on the harpsichord.

Lucy. Alas! only three or four lessons, which I know by heart.

Dor. Drawing goes on very well; your last head is charming!

Lucy. Thanks to you.

Dor. No, really, I have scarcely retouched it.

Lucy. But of history and geography, for instance, I know nothing.

Dor. You know the titles of many books: this is quite sufficient for the world; boldly assert that you have read them all. Then, always have a book in your work bag, and on your toilette; affirm that you are passionately fond of reading, and you will soon pass for the best informed woman existing.

Lucy. This is an odd way of being learned, and suits me very well. Come, I'll adopt it; and then my dear friend will always stay with me, and correct my drawings, and my pictures too, when I paint; so this again is a certain accomplishment.

Dor. Come, mademoiselle, I promise you shall possess all those which are usual in the world. True and great talents are so uncommon in ladies of your rank!

Lucy. The very reason why it is so flattering to possess them.—Toinetta will really have that gratification: well, I should like to resemble her.

Dor. This is an odd wish indeed!

Lucy. I love Toinetta, and am not jealous of her superiority; but I see it, and there are moments in which it hurts me.

Dor.

Dor. Surely this is being equally blind respecting her and yourself. You have an excellent understanding and the readiest parts; while Toinetta is a girl capable enough of application, but in fact extremely shallow, notwithstanding her sly look and dry ironical manner.

Lucy. No, do not deceive yourself. Toinetta unites understanding with simplicity and mildness of countenance.

Dor. You are extremely capable of judging, but you are so indulgent!—Indeed, this corresponds with the comparison I always make between you and Toinetta; she displeases me extremely.

Lucy. I am sorry, for I love her.

Dor. Still, she has a certain vulgarity, a roughness in her disposition, which can never sympathize with yours.

Lucy. True, she speaks rather bluntly, and sometimes offends me; but I forgive her: what is extraordinary, her sincerity displeases me; were Toinetta less frank, she would undoubtedly be more agreeable; yet, perhaps, I should repose less confidence in her; I cannot guess why, but methinks the more she contradicts me, the more I am attached to her.

Dor. In this case, mademoiselle, I, who love you to an excess which does not allow me to contradict you in the slightest degree, am very unfortunate.

Lucy. For that reason, my dear friend, I like you still better than Toinetta; you appear by far the more amiable. I should wish to consult her sometimes; but it is with you I would pass my life.

Dor. Well, I am contented with my lot, but nevertheless I fear it is not the most permanent.

Lucy. Ah! believe me, my attachment to you is as

lasting as it is tender. But who comes to interrupt us? Oh, Toinetta. MADAME GENLIS.

DORINA, TOINETTA, LUCY.

Lucy runs in, and throws her port-folio on the table.

Lucy. I am quite out of breath.—Bless me, what a party there is in the saloon! Oh, Dorina, I have just seen the prettiest dress!

Dor. Whose was it?

Lucy. Madam de Bercy's: it is only a polonese, but it is trimmed with peach flowers, and in so tasty, so elegant a style—then, peach flowers are what one has never seen before—oh, it is charming!—Madam de Bercy has so much fancy!

Dor. It is only to be wished she were a little handsomer.

Lucy. She is much admired.

Dor. Yes: but it is said she paints white.

Lucy. Indeed!

Dor. Oh, I do not believe it—nevertheless, her forehead is very shining.

Lucy. Hah, hah! that is comical enough; so, then, when people have shining foreheads—

Toi. You are to conclude they paint white. The rule is worth remembering.—Your great uncle, for instance, certainly paints white!

Lucy. What nonsense!

Toi. Nay, then the rule must be false: for his forehead is much more shining than madam de Bercy's.

Dor. (*To Lucy.*) What did they say to your drawings?

Lucy.

Lucy. They thought them charming, especially the old man's head.

Toi. Oh, but mademoiselle Dorina drew that entirely.

Dor. No, indeed, I only sketched it, and put a few finishing strokes.

Toi. True, you only did the outlines and finished it.

Lucy. (*With a forced smile.*) Toinetta does not spoil me!

Toi. To flatter is to deceive; and how can we deceive those we love?

Lucy. In this manner, Toinetta, you shall always have free leave to tell me what you please.

Dor. Is madam de Surville here?

Lucy. Yes, with her daughter, who is more stiff and dressed out than ever.

Dor. Mademoiselle Flora: Oh, I suppose she is very proud of being present at a reading party!

Lucy. Yes, I will answer for that. She is so pedantic, though only two years older than I am.

Toi. It is said she is quite a prodigy of knowledge.

Dor. (*Ironically.*) A prodigy!—and pray who tells her so?

Toi. Not the person by whom she is educated, but all who know her. For my part, I can assure you she is very modest, for she never speaks of herself, and always endeavours to stamp a value on the merit of others.

Dor. To be sure, she takes particular notice of mademoiselle Toinetta, and every time she comes here, commends her extraordinary talents.

Toi. No, mademoiselle, she never commends me in a ridiculous or extravagant manner; she has too good an understanding to be obliging at the expense of truth; but she always gives me cause to admire her indulgence.

Lucy. My dear Toinetta, I think mademoiselle Flora

a girl who abounds with merit, but I cannot help saying she has the misfortune to be a pedant.

Dor. (*Laughing.*) Yes, yes, pedant is the very word, it is admirably hit off. And a pedant at sixteen!—All this promises charms in future.

Toi. (*To Lucy.*) But, mademoiselle, may I venture to ask in what she is a pedant?

Lucy. In what? why in every thing.

Toi. But have the goodness to name some instances of it.

Lucy. Oh, I will name a thousand.

Toi. One only, if you please.

Lucy. Why, she looks pedantic, has a certain manner of screwing up her mouth, and of coming into a room. Now, do you wish to see her?—here she is.

Dor. (*Laughing.*) Ah! it is the very thing, the very thing; it is she herself! Once more I beg—Oh, this is charming!

Lucy. And then when she sits down, it is thus—on the edge of her chair—looking solemn, turning about as stiff as a poker, and now and then a little cough.

Dor. Oh, the little cough is delightful! it is her's exactly.—Bless me! I think I see her—only she indeed has not that shape, that countenance.

Lucy. (*Laughing.*) Toinetta is displeased, she does not laugh.

Toi. I hear, I see, and am instructed. I had quite a different idea of pedantry; I thought it chiefly consisted in seeking occasions to set one's self off, in making quotations, and deciding boldly. But your definition is much more simple—To have delicate lungs, and sit on the edge of a chair, is what makes a pedant: I will remember this.

Lucy.

Lucy. *(Laughing.)* Really Toinetta is piqued. Well, Toinetta, since you are so much attached to mademoiselle de Surville, I promise you I will not mimic her any more; it will be difficult for me to refrain, but I pledge my word. Come, pout no longer.

Toi. But tell me, mademoiselle, what has she done to incur your hatred?

Lucy. I do not hate her.

Toi. Yet you say every thing you can against her; and indeed, if you will speak sincerely, you must confess that you exaggerate her little foibles; what more could hatred do?

Lucy. But do you think this, Toinetta? What you say makes me uneasy. However, I do not attack her reputation.

Toi. Were you capable of that enormity, could you fully it? is not mademoiselle de Surville a model of sweetness, modesty, and merit? and were any one to say the contrary, would it be attended to?

Lucy. *(To Dorina.)* Really, my dear friend, she frightens me.——Alas, is what I have done so very criminal?

Dor. How childish, to censure you for an innocent joke, which can only appear dangerous in the eyes of mademoiselle Toinetta! And pray what mighty harm do you do by ridiculing mademoiselle Flora? she has only to return it, you will not be offended.

Lucy. By no means; on the contrary, I should be delighted. Yes, I wish she would return it, for then we should be even; and I know not why, but this raillery now oppresses me, spite of myself.

Toi. As for mademoiselle de Surville, be assured she pardons you with all her heart.

Lucy. How does she know that I mimic her?

Toi. Several persons have informed her of it: she told me you did, and I could not deny it.

Lucy. Well!

Toi. She laughed heartily.

Lucy. She laughed, did she?

Dor. She forced a laugh, I fancy.

Toi. And then she reproached herself for having laughed, saying, the subject rather called for compassion. " This poor young woman (added she), who thinks she is only exciting mirth, gives people but a bad opinion of her heart and understanding; since those, who seem to be amused by what she does, judge of this trivial fault with as much rigour as if she were arrived at maturer years."

Lucy. Does she say so?—does she think so?

Toi. Oh, she is truth itself.

Lucy. I must have an explanation with her.—I will justify myself, or, at least, make reparation for my fault. Do you think she imagines I have a bad heart, Toinetta?

Dor. Come, come, let us end this conversation, it absolutely is devoid of common sense. We must go to dinner, and not lose a moment, for we still have all our lessons to learn before the opera. *(To Lucy.)* Come, mademoiselle —what are you musing upon?

Lucy. I am extremely melancholy—I have no appetite, I will have no dinner.

Dor. But, if you are really ill, you must go to bed; you will lose the opera.

Lucy. Well, I will sit down to table. Toinetta, give me your arm. *(She goes out with Toinetta.)*

Dor.

Dor. (*Looking at them as they go out.*) You spoil all my work, mademoiselle Toinetta, but I will be even with you. [*She goes out.*

IBID.

LUCY, DORINA.

Dor. Oh, mademoiselle, you have captivated every body; nothing is talked of in the saloon but your talents, your charms.—Bless me! from whence proceeds this melancholy thoughtful air? why, what is the matter?

Lucy. If you knew what I have heard, and what chance has revealed to me!

Dor. How!

Lucy. After having played on the harpsichord and sung, I went down into the garden; and in passing along the great covered walk I heard my name mentioned. I stopped; the trees concealed me.

Dor. You overheard the conversation, then?

Lucy. Without designing it, and even spite of myself: I lost not one word.

Dor. Well, what was said of you?

Lucy. All the bitterest things which the most satyrical censure could suggest; in short, I heard those very ladies, who had just loaded me with encomiums in the saloon, defame and ridicule me in the most unmerciful manner. Nevertheless, one person singly took my part; and that in the strongest and most generous terms. You will never guess her name!

Dor. I long to know it.

Lucy. It was mademoiselle de Surville.

Dor. Indeed!—but are you quite certain she had not a glimpse of you across the walk?

Lucy. Oh, perfectly certain; she was on the opposite side. I own this kindness on her part humbled as much as it affected me, and gave birth to a painful something, which the malice of the others did not produce; their dissimulation excited my contempt rather than any angry emotions: but mademoiselle de Surville's generosity put me out of humour with myself; and in proportion as she spoke I felt my tears flow. Surely it is much more oppressive to see ourselves convicted of injustice, than to experience that of others!

Dor. Mademoiselle Flora's behaviour was undoubtedly very proper; yet, believe me, the desire of appearing in an advantageous light to the other ladies, and of affecting a good disposition, had some share in it.

Lucy. If so, she still retains the merit of having seized the true means to render herself valuable, and that is a great matter.

Dor. Come, mademoiselle, we must nevertheless think of learning our lessons. What shall we begin with?

Lucy. I know not. I feel a despondency, a melancholy to-day, which I never felt before.

IBID.

PORTRAIT OF A MODERN FINE LADY.

NOTHING perhaps can form a more ludicrous contrast to every thing just and graceful in nature than she whose sole object in life is to pass for a FINE LADY. The attentions she every where and uniformly pays, expects, and even exacts, are tedious and fatiguing. Her various movements, postures, and attitudes, are all adjusted and exhibited by rule. Some, by a happy fluency of the most

elegant

elegant language, have the art of imparting a momentary dignity and grace to the mereſt trifles: and ſhe, ſtudious only to mimic ſuch peculiarities as are moſt admired in others, affects a loquacity peculiarly flippant and teaſing, as the ſubject is conſtantly ſcandal, routs, finery, fans, china; lovers, lap-dogs, or ſquirrels. Her amuſements, like thoſe of a magpie, are only hopping over the ſame ſpots, prying into the ſame corners, and devouring the ſame ſpecies of prey. The ſimple and beautiful delineations of nature, in her countenance, her geſtures and her whole deportment, are habitually deranged, diſtorted or concealed, by the whimſical adoption of whatever grimace or deformity is moſt in vogue. She accuſtoms her face to a ſimper, which every ſeparate feature in it belies; ſpoils, perhaps, a blooming complexion with a profuſion of artificial colouring, murders the moſt exquiſite ſhape, or hides it by loads of uſeleſs drapery; and has her head, air, ſhoulders, arms, and even her feet, converted by art and affectation into what is called the TASTE, the TON, or the FASHION.

She little conſiders all the while to what a torrent of ridicule and ſarcaſm this mode of conduct expoſes her; or how exceedingly cold and hollow muſt that ceremony be which is not the language of a warm heart; how inſipid thoſe ſmiles which indicate no internal pleaſantry; how aukward thoſe graces which ſpring not from habits of good-nature and benevolence. Thus pertneſs ſucceeds to delicacy, aſſurance to modeſty, and all the vagaries of flirting to the ſenſibilities of an ingenuous mind. Deſtined as ſhe is in common with her ſex, and fitted by the peculiar liberality of nature to poliſh and conſole ours, a woman of this deſcription never exerts a

thought

thought beyond the requisitions of the TON, the obsequies of rank, family parade, or personal decoration. With her, punctilio is politeness, dissipation life, and levity spirit. The miserable and contemptible drudge of every tawdry innovation in dress or ceremony, she incessantly mistakes extravagance for taste, finery for elegance, and fashion for whatever strikes her as most incongruous to simplicity and nature. By strutting forward in this manner, the abject puppet of every insignificant and preposterous farce to which the fashionable world give a temporary sanction and celebrity, her whole care and attention are engrossed by circumstance and shew. To her the delicious recollections of an open, artless, and worthy life, are not half so charming as the various tiresome insipidities and inquietudes of a giddy one. Every idea of substantial felicity is habitually absorbed in the flattering and frantic intoxications of female vanity.

It is not therefore intrinsic merit, but a tinselled exterior, which attracts her esteem; and she values neither candour of mind nor modesty of carriage when opposed to frippery or parade. Her favourite examples are not those of acknowledged sincerity, who speak as they feel, and act as they think, but such only as are calculated to dazzle her fancy, amuse her senses, or humour her whims. Her only study is how to glitter or shine, how to captivate and gratify the gaze of the multitude, or how to swell her own pomp and importance. To this interesting object all her assiduities and time are religiously devoted. This makes her the willing slave of every novelty which levity, extravagance, or luxury introduces; invariably recommending that superfluity in dress and equipage on which she builds her own distinction, and fondly attached to the

mechanical

mechanical practice of every punctilio or artifice which folly suggests, or prudery imposes.

ADDRESS TO MOTHERS.

STELLA's BIRTH-DAY.

ALL travellers at first incline
Where'er they see the fairest sign;
And if they find the chambers neat,
And like the liquor and the meat,
Will call again, and recommend
The Angel inn to ev'ry friend.
What though the painting grows decay'd,
The house will never lose its trade!
Nay, though the treach'rous tapster Thomas
Hangs a *new* angel two doors from us,
As fine as dauber's hands can make it,
In hopes that strangers may mistake it,
We think it both a shame and sin
To quit the true old Angel inn.
   Now this is Stella's case in fact;
An angel's face a little crack'd;
(Could poets, or could painters, fix
How angel's look at thirty-six!)
This drew us in at first to find
In such a form an angel's mind;
And ev'ry virtue now supplies
The fainting rays of Stella's eyes.
See at her levee crowding swains,
Whom Stella freely entertains
With breeding, humour, wit and sense;
And puts them but to small expense:

Their

Their mind so plentifully fills,
And makes such reasonable bills,
So little gets for what she gives,
We really wonder how she lives!
And, had her stock been less, no doubt
She must have long ago run out.
Then who can think we'll quit the place,
When Doll hangs out a newer face;
Or stop and light at Chloe's head,
With scraps and leavings to be fed?
  Then, Chloe, still go on to prate
Of thirty-six, and thirty-eight;
Pursue your trade of scandal-picking,
Your hints, that Stella is no chicken:
Your innuendoes, when you tell us
That Stella loves to talk with fellows:
And let me warn you to believe
A truth for which your soul should grieve;
That should you live to see the day
When Stella's locks must all be grey,
When age must print a furrow'd trace
On ev'ry feature of her face;
Though you, and all your senseless tribe,
Could art, or time, or nature bribe
To make you look like beauty's queen,
And hold for ever at fifteen;
No bloom of youth can ever blind
The cracks and wrinkles of your mind;
All men of sense will pass your door,
And crowd to Stella at fourscore.

SWIFT.

ORNAMENTS.

ORNAMENTS.

The world is still deceived by ornament.
In law, what plea so tainted and corrupt,
But, being season'd with a gracious voice,
Obscures the show of evil? In religion,
What damned error but some sober brow
Will bless it, and approve it with a text,
Hiding the grossness with fair ornament?
There is no vice so simple but assumes
Some mark of virtue on its outward parts.
How many cowards, whose hearts are all as false
As stairs of sand, wear yet upon their chins
The beards of Hercules and frowning Mars;
Who, inward search'd, have livers white as milk!
And these assume but valour's excrement
To render them redoubted. Look on beauty,
And you shall see 'tis purchas'd by the weight,
Which therein works a miracle in nature,
Making them lightest that wear most of it.
So are those crisped, snaky, golden locks,
Which make such wanton gambols with the wind
Upon supposed fairness, often known
To be the dowry of a second head,
The scull that bread them in the sepulchre.
Thus ornament is but the gilded shore
To a most dangerous sea; the beauteous scarf
Veiling an Indian beauty: in a word,
The seeming truth which cunning time puts on
T' entrap the wisest.

SHAKSPEARE.

BOOK VI.

DEVOTIONAL PIECES,

AND

REFLECTIONS ON RELIGIOUS SUBJECTS.

It is observed by a late most amiable and elegant writer that religion may be considered in three different views. As a system of opinions, its sole object is truth; and the only faculty that has any thing to do with it is reason, exerted in the freest and most dispassionate inquiry. As a principle regulating our conduct, religion is a habit, and, like all other habits, of slow growth, and gaining strength only by repeated exertions. But it may likewise be considered as a taste, an affair of sentiment and feeling; and in this sense it is properly called devotion. Its seat is in the imagination and the passions, and it has its source in that relish for the sublime, the vast, and the beautiful, by which we taste the charms of poetry and other compositions that address our finer feelings; rendered more lively and interesting by a sense of gratitude for personal benefits. It is in a great degree constitutional, and is by no means found in exact proportion to the virtue of a character.

Miss Aikin.

The general opinion of mankind, that there is a strong connection between a religious disposition and a feeling heart, appears from the universal dislike which all men have to infidelity in the fair sex. We not only look on it as removing the principal security we have for their virtue, but as the strongest proof of their want of that softness and delicate sensibility of heart, which peculiarly endears them to us, and more effectually secures their empire over us than any quality they can possess.

GREGORY.

Be punctual in the stated performance of your private devotions morning and evening. If you have any sensibility or imagination, this will establish such an intercourse between you and the Supreme Being as will be of infinite consequence to you in life. It will communicate an habitual cheerfulness to your temper, give a firmness and steadiness to your virtue, and enable you to go through all the vicissitudes of human life with propriety and dignity.

I wish you to be regular in your attendance on public worship, and in receiving the communion. Allow nothing to interrupt your public or private devotions except the performance of some active duty in life, to which they should always give place.—In your behaviour at public worship observe an exemplary attention and gravity.

IBID.

There is something peculiarly soothing and comfortable in a firm belief that the whole frame of nature is supported and conducted by an eternal and omnipotent Being, of infinite goodness, who intends, by the whole course of

his

his providence, to promote the greatest good of all his creatures; a belief that we are acquainted with the means of conciliating the Divine favour, and that in consequence of this we have it in our own power to obtain it; a belief that this life is but the infancy of our existence, that we shall survive the seeming destruction of our present frame, and have it in our power to secure our entrance on a new state of eternal felicity. IBID.

Mankind certainly have a sense of right and wrong, independent of religious belief; but experience shews that the allurements of present pleasure, and the impetuosity of passion, are sufficient to prevent men from acting agreeably to this moral sense; unless it be supported by religion, the influence of which upon the imagination and passions, if properly directed, is extremely powerful. IBID.

The examples of Lord Bacon, Mr. Locke, and Sir Isaac Newton, among many other first names in philosophy, are a sufficient evidence that religious belief is perfectly compatible with the clearest and most enlarged understanding. IBID.

Whoso stoppeth his ears at the cry of the poor, he also shall cry himself, but shall not be heard.

Say not unto thy neighbour, Go and come again, and to morrow I will give; when thou hast it by thee.

PROVERBS.

"The best effect of your religion will be a diffusive humanity to all in distress.—Set apart a certain proportion of your income as sacred to charitable purposes. But in this, as well as in the practice of every other duty, carefully avoid ostentation. Vanity is always defeating her own purposes.

Fame

Fame is one of the natural rewards of virtue. Do not pursue her, and she will follow you.

Do not confine your charity to giving money. You may have many opportunities of shewing a tender and compassionate spirit where your money is not wanted.—There is a false and unnatural refinement in sensibility, which makes some people shun the sight of every object in distress. Never indulge this, especially where your friends or acquaintances are concerned. Let the days of their misfortunes, when the world forgets or avoids them, be the season for you to exercise your humanity and friendship. The sight of human misery softens the heart, and makes it better: it checks the pride of health and prosperity; and the distress it occasions is amply compensated by the consciousness of doing your duty and by the secret endearment which nature has annexed to all our sympathetic sorrows.

GREGORY.

PIETY.

On piety humanity is built;
And on humanity much happiness;
And yet still more on piety itself.
A soul in commerce with her God is heaven,
Feels not the tumults and the shocks of life,
The whirls of passions, and the strokes of heart.

YOUNG.

The merciful man doeth good to his own: but he that is cruel troubleth his own flesh.

PROVERBS.

Women too often confine their love and charity to their own families. They fix not in their minds the precedency of moral obligations, or make their feelings give way to duty. Good-will to all the human race should dwell in our bosoms; nor should love to individuals induce us to violate this first of duties, or make us sacrifice the interest of any fellow creature to promote that of another to whom we happen to be more partial. A parent under distressed circumstances should be supported, even though it should prevent our saving a fortune for a child; nay more, should they be both in distress at the same time, the prior obligation should be first discharged.

M. WOLLSTONECRAFT.

A BENEVOLENT mind often suffers more than the object it commiserates, and will bear an inconvenience itself to shelter another from it. It makes allowance for failings, though it longs to meet perfection, which it seems formed to adore. The author of all good continually calls himself a God long-suffering; and those most resemble him who practise forbearance. Love and compassion are the most delightful feelings of the soul, and to exert them to all that breathe is the wish of the benevolent heart.

IBID.

PURE religion, and undefiled before God and the Father, is this—to visit the fatherless and widows in their affliction, and to keep himself unspotted from the world.

ST. JAMES.

ON CHARITY.

THOUGH I speak with the tongues of men and of angels, and have not charity, I am become as sounding brass, or a tinkling cymbal. And though I have the gift of prophecy, and understand all mysteries, and all knowledge;

ledge; and though I have all faith, so that I could remove mountains, and have not charity, I am nothing. And though I bestow all my goods to feed the poor, and though I give my body to be burned, and have not charity, it profiteth me nothing. Charity suffereth long, and is kind; charity envieth not; charity vaunteth not itself, is not puffed up, doth not behave itself unseemly, seeketh not her own, is not easily provoked, thinketh no evil; rejoiceth not in iniquity, but rejoiceth in the truth; beareth all things, believeth all things, hopeth all things, endureth all things. Charity never faileth. But whether there be prophecies, they shall fail; whether there be tongues, they shall cease; whether there be knowledge, it shall vanish away. For we know in part, and we prophesy in part. But when that which is perfect is come, then that which is in part shall be done away. When I was a child I spake as a child, I understood as a child, I thought as a child: but when I became a man I put away childish things. For now we see through a glass darkly; but then face to face: now I know in part; but then shall I know even as also I am known. And now abideth faith, hope, charity, these three; but the greatest of these is charity.

CORINTHIANS.

THE WIDOW's MITE.

And he looked up, and saw the rich men casting their gifts into the treasury, and he saw also a certain poor widow casting in thither two mites. And he said, Of a truth I say unto you, that this poor widow hath cast in more than they

they all: for all these have of their abundance cast in unto the offerings of God, but she of her penury hath cast in all the living that she had.

S. LUKE.

CHRIST's SERMON.

TAKE heed that ye do not your alms before men, to be seen of them; otherwise ye have no reward of your Father which is in heaven. Therefore when thou doest thine alms do not sound a trumpet before thee, as the hypocrites do in the synagogues, and in the streets, that they may have glory of men. Verily I say unto you they have their reward. But when thou doest alms, let not thy left hand know what thy right hand doeth; that thine alms may be in secret; and thy father which seeth in secret himself shall reward thee openly.

Lay not up for yourselves treasures upon earth, where moth and rust doth corrupt, and where thieves break through and steal: but lay up for yourselves treasures in heaven, where neither moth nor rust doth corrupt, and where thieves do not break through nor steal: for where your treasure is there will your heart be also. The light of the body is the eye: if therefore thine eye be single thy whole body shall be full of light; but if thine eye be evil thy whole body shall be full of darkness. If therefore the light that is in thee be darkness, how great is that darkness!

No man can serve two masters: for either he will hate the one, and love the other; or else he will hold to the one, and despise the other. Ye cannot serve God and mammon. Therefore I say unto you, Take no thought for your life, what ye shall eat, or what ye shall drink, nor

yet

yet for your body what ye shall put on: is not the life more than meat, and the body than raiment? Behold the fowls of the air: for they sow not, neither do they reap, nor gather into barns; yet your heavenly Father feedeth them.—Are ye not much better than they? Which of you by taking thought can add one cubit unto his stature? And why take ye thought for raiment? Consider the lilies of the field how they grow; they toil not, neither do they spin; and yet I say unto you, that even Solomon in all his glory was not arrayed like one of these. Wherefore, if God so clothe the grass of the field, which to-day is, and to-morrow is cast into the oven, shall he not much more clothe you, O ye of little faith! Therefore take no thought, saying, What shall we eat, or what shall we drink, or wherewithal shall we be clothed? (for after all these things do the Gentiles seek) for your heavenly Father knoweth that ye have need of all these things. But seek ye first the kingdom of God, and his righteousness, and all these things shall be added unto you. Take therefore no thought for the morrow: for the morrow shall take thought for the things of itself. Sufficient unto the day is the evil thereof.

Judge not, that ye be not judged: for with what judgment ye judge ye shall be judged; and with what measure ye mete, it shall be measured to you again. And why beholdest thou the mote that is in thy brother's eye, but considerest not the beam that is in thine own eye? or how wilt thou say to thy brother, let me pull out the mote out of thine eye; and behold, a beam is in thine own eye? Thou hypocrite, first cast out the beam out of thine own eye; and then shalt thou see clearly to cast out the mote out of thy brother's eye.

Give not that which is holy unto the dogs, neither cast ye your pearls before swine, lest they trample them under their feet, and turn again and rend you.

Ask, and it shall be given you; seek, and ye shall find; knock, and it shall be opened unto you: for every one that asketh receiveth; and he that seeketh findeth; and to him that knocketh it shall be opened. Or what man is there of you, whom if his son ask bread will he give him a stone; or if he ask a fish will he give him a serpent? If ye then, being evil, know how to give good gifts unto your children, how much more shall your Father which is in heaven give good things to them that ask him? Therefore all things whatsoever ye would that men should do to you, do ye even so to them: for this is the law and the prophets.

Enter ye in at the strait gate; for wide is the gate and broad is the way that leadeth to destruction, and many there be which go in thereat: because strait is the gate and narrow is the way which leadeth unto life, and few there be that find it.

Beware of false prophets which come to you in sheep's clothing, but inwardly they are ravening wolves: ye shall know them by their fruits. Do men gather grapes of thorns, or figs of thistles? Even so every good tree bringeth forth good fruit, but a corrupt tree bringeth forth evil fruit. A good tree cannot bring forth evil fruit, neither can a corrupt tree bring forth good fruit. Every tree that bringeth not forth good fruit is hewn down, and cast into the fire. Wherefore by their fruits ye shall know them.

Not every one that saith unto me, Lord, Lord, shall enter into the kingdom of heaven; but he that doeth the will of my Father which is in heaven. Many will say to me in that day, Lord, Lord, have we not prophefied in thy name; and in thy name have caſt out devils; and in thy name done many wonderful works? and then will I profeſs unto them, I never knew you: depart from me, ye that work iniquity. Therefore, whofoever heareth thefe fayings of mine, and doeth them, I will liken him unto a wife man which built his houfe upon a rock: and the rain defcended, and the floods came, and the winds blew, and beat upon that houfe, and it fell not: for it was founded upon a rock. And every one that heareth thefe fayings of mine, and doeth them not, fhall be likened unto a foolifh man which built his houfe upon the fand; and the rain defcended, and the floods came, and the winds blew, and beat upon that houfe; and it fell, and great was the fall of it. And it came to pafs when Jefus had ended thefe fayings, the people were aſtoniſhed at his doctrine. For he taught them as one having authority, and not as the fcribes.

When he was come down from the mountain great multitudes followed him.

S. MATTHEW.

ON CHRISTIAN VIRTUES.

VIRTUE is to be acquired; goodneſs is a gift of nature: therefore, with a great portion of goodneſs, we may err, and commit great faults. The good man is intereſting, the virtuous man eſtimable. Since to be virtuous it is neceſſary continually to ſtruggle to conquer our inclinations, and to triumph over ourfelves, it is evident that we ſhould not make ſuch efforts without the moſt powerful motives. What are the motives which determine the impious to purſue virtue? the fear of public cenfure, the defire of being honoured, the love of glory: these sentiments will produce brilliant actions, but they will never inspire that delicacy, that purity of mind. which belongs to the religious man alone. Human passions decrease with age; time moderates and destroys them. How fragile are virtues when they only arise from the passions! like the flowers of the field which are blasted, or torn up by a storm, so obstacles, reverse of fortune, or only an illness, is often sufficient to destroy them for ever. But the waste of the body, the loss of youth, cannot enfeeble these striking ideas; " I am in the presence of God, who reads in the bottom of my heart every moment of my life: his justice reserves for me eternal rewards or punishments."

Let us again observe, that religion renders every virtue more perfect, and that there are several which religion only can produce; for instance, purity of mind. An atheist never existed, who, born with strong passions, supported irreproachable morals. Is there even one who always shews a proper respect to decency in his writings, discourse and actions? But can it be believed that a person entirely devoid of religion watches attentively over his thoughts, and represses carefully those which wound decency and modesty? The silent flights, the deliriums of the imagination, cause no scandal, do no harm in society, afflict nobody. This is assuredly the case when the liberty of thinking can produce no inconvenience to others; and it would be ridiculous and extravagant to limit it, when neither the immortality of the soul nor even the existence of God is firmly believed in the deistical system; nay, if we suppose God never to be offended by our bad actions, we ought to suppose him still more indifferent about our private thoughts. None but a true Christian can

can possess perfect purity of mind, and consequently he only can be constantly virtuous: he alone finds as great an interest in thinking as in acting well; to do good in secret, as to perform brilliant actions; to repress the wanderings of his imagination, to regulate the emotions of his heart, as to preserve to himself a reputation free from reproach.

With respect to other virtues, they receive new lustre from religion. What is humanity without religion? a natural sentiment, it is true, but which never manifests itself but on occasions which rarely happen: the most dreadful view of human misery is necessary to excite it. Who could then resist the impulse of pity? The irreligious man, if he has sensibility, will aid the unfortunate who implore his assistance.

The Christian does not content himself with comforting the wretches he happens to meet; he goes in search of those who dare not present themselves. Worldly benevolence is never an habitual sentiment, still less a governing propensity; it obtains only momentary sacrifices, and imposes no extraordinary deprivation: it may produce some ostentatious acts, but not such as are surprising and sublime; it is excited merely by present and miserable objects, either by pride or a desire of being distinguished.

Christian charity, equally courageous, active, and tender, is ever anxiously employed with the tender care of comforting the wretched; and discovers obscure corners, inhabited by forsaken mothers, or orphans without support; charity elevating a man above the most natural apprehensions, makes him fear neither contagion nor fatigue; it conducts us to those respectable asylums, where at each step we meet with the distressing sight of pain and death, and makes us penetrate the dark recesses of horrid dungeons, to console oppressed innocence! Even the guilty may reasonably hope for succours; they suffer, which is a sufficient title to consideration. By sacrificing every thing, the pleasures, the superfluities of life, fortune, liberty and health; by devoting themselves, without reserve; to the wants of the unhappy; they neither aspire to the glory, nor the esteem of men; they do better than despise encomiums, they do not believe them due to their actions; they think only of fulfilling their duty.—Beneficence is highly extolled, and Christian charity is seldom mentioned, as no acknowledgments are required, nor loud complainings uttered when men are found ungrateful.

A Christian considers riches as a deposit which providence has confided to him to comfort the unhappy. The philosopher says to the unfortunate, " I give, I sacrifice to you:" the Christian, " I restore to you, I fulfil the obligation imposed on me." The former thinks he creates to himself a sacred debt; the latter believes he acquits the one he owes.—A faithful minister of the Divinity, he desires no acknowledgment, a benefactor never discouraged, but refers all to the first author : he enjoys the sweet pleasure of aiding his fellow-creatures, without its being possible he should ever experience the vain agitations caused by the ingratitude of those he obliges.

The humble Christian conceals the heroic actions inspired by religion but those which cannot be hid; sufficiently prove that reason and philosophy, without the assistance of faith, will never rise to this degree of perfection.

MADAME GENLIS.

MUTUAL

MUTUAL FORBEARANCE.

Then came Peter to him, and said, Lord, how oft shall my brother sin against me, and I forgive him—till seven times? Jesus saith unto him, I say not unto thee, Until seven times; but until seventy times seven. Therefore is the kingdom of heaven likened unto a certain king which would take account of his servants. And when he had begun to reckon, one was brought unto him which owed him ten thousand talents: but, forasmuch as he had not to pay, his lord commanded him to be sold, and his wife and children, and all that he had, and payment to be made. The servant therefore fell down, and worshipped him, saying, Lord, have patience with me, and I will pay thee all. Then the lord of that servant was moved with compassion, and loosed him, and forgave him the debt. But the same servant went out, and found one of his fellow-servants which owed him an hundred pence: and he laid hands on him, and took him by the throat, saying, Pay me that thou owest. And his fellow-servant fell down at his feet, and besought him, saying, Have patience with me, and I will pay thee all. And he would not: but went and cast him into prison, till he should pay the debt. So when his fellow-servants saw what was done, they were very sorry, and came and told unto their lord all that was done. Then his lord, after that he had called him, said unto him, O thou wicked servant, I forgave thee all that debt, because thou desiredst me: shouldest not thou also have had compassion on thy fellow-servant, even as I had pity on thee. And his lord was wroth, and delivered him to the tormentors, till he should pay all that was due unto him. So likewise shall my heavenly Father do also unto you, if ye from your hearts forgive not every one his brother their trespasses.

S. MATTHEW.

ON THE GOVERNMENT OF SERVANTS.

None who pretend to be friends of religion and virtue should ever keep a domestic, however expert in business, whom they know to be guilty of immorality. How unbecoming a serious character is it to say of such an one "he is a bad man but a good servant!" What a preference does it shew of private convenience to the interests of society, which demand that vice should be constantly discountenanced, especially in one's own household; and that the sober, honest, and industrious, should be sure of finding encouragement and reward in the houses of those who maintain respectable characters! Such persons should be invariably strict and peremptory with regard to the behaviour of their servants, in every thing which concerns the general plan of domestic government; but should by no means be severe on small faults, since nothing so much weakens authority as frequent chiding. Whilst they require precise obedience to their rules, they must prove by their general conduct that these rules are the effect, not of humour, but of reason. It is wonderful that those who are careful to conceal their ill-temper from strangers should be indifferent how peevish and even contemptibly capricious they appear before their servants, from whom they can hope for no real respect when their weakness is so apparent. When once a servant can say—

"I cannot

"I cannot do any thing to please my mistress to-day," —all authority is lost.

Those who continually change their servants, and complain of perpetual ill-usage, have good reason to believe that the fault is in themselves, and that they do not know how to govern. Few indeed possess the skill to unite authority with kindness, or are capable of that steady and uniformly reasonable conduct, which alone can maintain a true dignity, and command a willing and attentive obedience.
Mrs. Chapone.

If our servants are profane and immoral for want of our admonitions we shall be called to a strict account: it is unreasonable to complain of their dishonesty and corruption if we take no pains to instruct them, and allow them no time for divine worship: a kind of Sunday-evening-school in every family would be a likely means of reforming many, and is a very necessary succedaneum to Sunday-schools for children; the benefit of which may be rendered ineffectual to the most important purposes of life, if religious instruction ceases as soon as young people are dismissed from the schools.
Mrs. Trimmer.

PROVIDENCE COMPARED TO AN INDULGENT MOTHER.

See a fond mother encircled by her children; with pious tenderness she looks around, and her soul even melts with maternal love! One she kisses on its cheek, and clasps another to her bosom: one she sets upon her knee, and finds a seat upon her foot for another. And while by their actions, their lisping words, and asking eyes, she understands their various numberless little wishes, to these she dispenses a look, and a word to those; and, whether she smiles or frowns: it is all in tender love. Such to us, though infinitely high and awful, is Providence: so it watches over us; comforting these, providing for those, listening to all, and assisting every one; and if sometimes it denies the favour we implore, it denies but to invite our more earnest prayers; or if seeming to deny a blessing, grants one in the refusal.

RICHARDSON.

ST. PAUL's ADDRESS TO THE ATHENIANS.

Now while Paul waited for them at Athens, his spirit was stirred in him, when he saw the city wholly given to idolatry. Therefore disputed he in the synagogue with the Jews and with the devout persons, and in the market daily with them that met with him. Then certain philosophers of the Epicureans and of the Stoics encountered him. And some said, What will this babbler say? other some, He seemeth to be a setter-forth of strange gods! because he preached unto them Jesus, and the resurrection. And they took him and brought him into Areopagus, saying, May we know what this new doctrine whereof thou speakest is? For thou bringest certain strange things to our ears: we would know therefore what these things mean. (For all the Athenians and strangers which were there spent their time in nothing else but either to tell or to hear some new thing).

Then Paul stood in the midst of Mars-hill, and said, Ye men of Athens, I perceive that in all things ye are too superstitious:

superstitious: for, as I passed by and beheld your devotions, I found an altar with this inscription, TO THE UNKNOWN GOD. Whom therefore ye ignorantly worship, him declare I unto you. God that made the world and all things therein, seeing that he is Lord of heaven and earth, dwelleth not in temples made with hands, neither is worshipped with men's hands, as though he needed any thing, seeing he giveth to all life and breath, and all things; and hath made of one blood all nations of men for to dwell on all the face of the earth, and hath determined the times before appointed, and the bounds of their habitation; that they should seek the Lord, if haply they might feel after him, and find him, though he be not far from every one of us: for in him we live, and move, and have our being: as certain also of your own poets have said, for we are also his offspring. Forasmuch then as we are the offspring of God, we ought not to think that the Godhead is like unto gold, or silver, or stone, graven by art and man's device. And the times of this ignorance God winked at; but now commandeth all men every where to repent: because he hath appointed a day in the which he will judge the world in righteousness, by that man whom he hath ordained, whereof he hath given assurance unto all men, in that he hath raised him from the dead.

THE ACTS.

ON PRAYER.

AND when thou prayest thou shalt not be as the hypocrites are: for they love to pray standing in the synagogues, and in the corners of the streets, that they may be seen of men. Verily I say unto you, they have their reward. But thou, when thou prayeſt, enter into thy cloſet, and, when thou haſt ſhut thy door, pray to thy Father which is in ſecret; and thy Father which ſeeth in ſecret ſhall reward thee openly. But when ye pray uſe not vain repetitions, as the heathen do, for they think that they ſhall be heard for their much ſpeaking. Be not ye therefore like unto them: for your Father knoweth what things ye have need of before ye aſk him. After this manner therefore pray ye: Our Father which art in Heaven, Hallowed be thy name; Thy kingdom come, Thy will be done in earth as it is in heaven; Give us this day our daily bread, And forgive us our debts, as we forgive our debtors, And lead us not into temptation, but deliver us from evil: For thine is the kingdom, and the power, and the glory, for ever. Amen.

For, if ye forgive men their trepaſſes, your heavenly Father will alſo forgive you: but if ye forgive not men their treſpaſſes, neither will your Father forgive your treſpaſſes.

Moreover, when ye faſt, be not as the hypocrites, of a ſad countenance: for they diſfigure their faces, that they may appear unto men to faſt. Verily I ſay unto you, they have their reward. But thou, when thou faſteſt, anoint thine head, and waſh thy face; that thou appear not unto men to faſt, but unto thy Father which is in ſecret: and thy Father which ſeeth in ſecret ſhall reward thee openly.

S. Matthew.

Jesus ſaith unto her, Woman, believe me the hour cometh when ye ſhall neither in this mountain, nor yet at Jeruſalem, worſhip the Father. Ye worſhip ye know not what: we know what we worſhip: for ſalvation is of the Jews. But the hour cometh, and now is, when the true
worſhippers

worshippers shall worship the Father in spirit and truth: for the Father seeketh such to worship him. God is a spirit: and they that worship him must worship him in spirit and truth.

S. JOHN.

A PROPHETIC EFFUSION.

COMFORT ye, comfort ye my people, saith your God. Speak ye comfortably to Jerusalem, and cry unto her, that her warfare is accomplished, that her iniquity is pardoned: for she hath received of the Lord's hand double for all her sins.

The voice of him that crieth in the wilderness, Prepare ye the way of the Lord, make straight in the desert a highway for our God. Every valley shall be exalted, and every mountain and hill shall be made low, and the crooked shall be made straight, and the rough places plain: and the glory of the Lord shall be revealed, and all flesh shall see it together: for the mouth of the Lord hath spoken it. The voice said, Cry. And he said, What shall I cry? All flesh is grass; and all the goodliness thereof is as the flower of the field: the grass withereth, the flower fadeth, because the spirit of the Lord bloweth upon it. Surely the people is grass: the grass withereth, the flower fadeth, but the word of our God shall stand for ever.

O Zion, that bringest good tidings, get thee up into the high mountain: O Jerusalem, that bringest good tidings, lift up thy voice with strength, lift it up, be not afraid; say unto the cities of Judah, Behold your God! Behold, the Lord God will come with strong hand, and his arm shall rule for him: behold his reward is with him, and his work before him. He shall feed his flock like a shepherd:

herd: he shall gather the lambs with his arm, and carry them in his bosom, and shall gently lead those that are with young. Who hath measured the waters in the hollow of his hand, and meted out heaven with the span, and comprehended the dust of the earth in a measure, and weighed the mountains in scales, and the hills in a balance? Who hath directed the spirit of the Lord, or, being his counsellor, hath taught him? With whom took he counsel, and who instructed him and taught him in the path of judgment, and taught him knowledge, and shewed to him the way of understanding? Behold, the nations are as a drop of a bucket, and are counted as the small dust of the balance: behold, he taketh up the isles as a very little thing. And Lebanon is not sufficient to burn, nor the beasts thereof sufficient for a burnt offering. All nations before him are as nothing: and they are counted to him less than nothing, and vanity. To whom then will ye liken God? or what likeness will ye compare unto him? The workman melteth a graven image, and the goldsmith spreadeth it over with gold, and casteth silver chains. He, that is so impoverished that he hath no oblation, chooseth a tree that will not rot: he seeketh unto him a cunning workman to prepare a graven image that shall not be moved. Have ye not known? have ye not heard? hath it not been told you from the beginning? have ye not understood from the foundations of the earth? It is he that sitteth upon the circle of the earth, and the inhabitants thereof are as grashoppers; that stretcheth out the heavens as a curtain, and spreadeth them out as a tent to dwell in. That bringeth the princes to nothing; he maketh the judges of the earth as vanity. Yea, they shall not be planted; yea, they shall not be

sown;

sown; yea, their stock shall not take root in the earth: and he shall also blow upon them, and they shall wither, and the whirlwind shall take them away as stubble. To whom then will ye liken me, or shall I be equal? saith the Holy One. Lift up your eyes on high, and behold who hath created these things that bringeth out their host by number: he called them all by names, by the greatness of his might, for that he is strong in power: not one faileth. Why sayest thou, O Jacob, and speakest, O Israel, my way is hid from the Lord, and my judgment is passed over from my God? Hast thou not known? Hast thou not heard, that the everlasting God, the Lord, the creator of the ends of the earth, fainteth not, neither is weary? there is no searching of his understanding. He giveth power to the faint; and to them that have no might he increaseth strength. Even the youths shall faint and be weary, and the young men shall utterly fall: but they that wait upon the Lord shall renew their strength; they shall mount up with wings as eagles; they shall run and not be weary; and they shall walk and not faint.

ISAIAH.

ON PRAYER.

THERE is a constant intercourse kept up with our Creator, when we learn to consider him as the fountain of truth, which our understanding thirsts after; but his goodness brings him more on a level with our bounded capacities—we trace him in every work of mercy, and feel his fatherly care. Every blessing is doubled when we suppose it comes from him, and afflictions almost lose their name when we believe they are sent to corrrect, not crush us.

us.—While we are alive to gratitude and admiration, we must adore God.

The human soul is so framed, that goodness and truth must fill it with ineffable pleasure; and the nearer it approaches to perfection the more earnestly will it pursue them, seeing their beauty.

The Supreme Being dwells in the universe. He is as essentially present to the wicked as to the good; but the latter delight in his presence, and try to please him, while the former shrink from a judge who is of too pure a nature to behold iniquity. They wish for the rocks to cover them, mountains, or the angry sea, to hide them from the presence of that Being—in whose presence only they could find joy. We feel the emotions that attract to goodness; painful ones disturb us, when we resist them. The wiser and the better we are, the more visible, if I may use the expression, is God—for wisdom consists in searching him out—and goodness in endeavouring to copy his attributes.

To attain any thing great, a model must be held up to our understanding, and engage our affections; a view of the disinterested goodness of God is calculated to touch us more than can be conceived by a depraved mind. When the love of God is shed abroad in our hearts, true courage will animate our conduct, as nothing can hurt those who trust in him. If the desire of acting right is ever present with us, if admiration of goodness fills our souls, we may be said to pray constantly. And if we try to do justice to all, and good as far as we can, we prove whose servants we are, and whose laws we transcribe in our lives.

Never be very anxious, when you pray, what words to use: regulate your thoughts; and know that virtue calms

the

the passions, gives clearness to your understanding, and opens it to pleasures that the thoughtless and vicious have not a glimpse of—for you must be acquainted with God to find peace, to rise superior to worldly temptations. Habitual devotion is of the utmost consequence, as what oftenest occupies the thoughts will influence our actions. But, observe what I say, *that* devotion is mockery, selfishness, which does not improve our moral character.

Men of old prayed to the devil, to him sacrificed their children, and committed every kind of barbarity and impurity. We serve a long-suffering God; we must pity the weakness of our fellow-creatures, we must not beg for mercy and not shew it;—we must not acknowledge that we have offended, without trying to avoid doing so in future. We are to deal with our fellow-creatures as we expect to be dealt with. This is practical prayer!—those who enjoy it feel frequently sublime pleasures, and lively hopes animate them in this vale of tears, that seem a foretaste of the felicity they will enjoy when the understanding is enlightened, and the affections regulated.

ORIGINAL STORIES.

Do not err, my beloved brethren. Every good gift, and every perfect gift, is from above, and cometh down from the Father of lights, with whom is no variableness, neither shadow of turning. If any of you lack wisdom, let him ask of God, that giveth to all men liberally, and upbraideth not; and it shall be given him.

S. JAMES.

A PRIVATE

A PRIVATE MORNING PRAYER.

Gracious Creator, support of all those who trust in thee—with humble gratitude do I approach to enjoy the highest privilege of my nature, that of making known my wants, and casting my cares on thee. Thou knowest whereof I am made, and rememberest that I am but dust: self-convicted I prostrate myself before thy throne of grace, and seek not to hide or palliate my faults; be not extreme to mark what I have done amiss—still allow me to call thee Father, and rejoice in my existence, since I can trace thy goodness and truth on earth, and feel myself allied to that glorious Being who breathed into me the breath of life, and gave me a capacity to know and to serve him.

Filled with the idea of thy awful majesty, and impressed by thy love, I think I would rather die than swerve from thy holy law—but I cannot forget my former weakness—and doubt my own resolutions—grant me then thy helping hand lest I fall—and may thy presence never be a terror to me, or ever be forgotten! Pursuing the employments and duties of my station, thou art my guide and stay; may vice never separate me from my God—Oh! let me perceive the light of thy countenance, where only there is fullness of joy!

I laud and magnify thy holy name, for that thou hast made me an intelligent being; and with a trembling heart hope that I shall never abuse the inestimable gift: but that I shall cultivate my talents, and prove that indeed I am an offspring of the Most-High, by conforming to his will, and doing good to my fellow creatures. May universal benevolence expand my heart, and yet may I

endeavour

endeavour studiously to fulfil my private duties; to attain that end may I govern my temper and subdue my passions, and resolutely follow rational pursuits as the way to be useful and virtuous.

Into thy hands do I commit myself this day, and humbly dedicate all my powers to thy service.—Accept, I beseech thee, the imperfect sacrifice of a heart frail but sincere, which glows with a sense of thy goodness whilst my understanding is lost in meditating on thy wisdom, and power. Drawn to thee more by love than fear—I know that all my happiness must proceed from thee—grant that no earthly desire may make me forget this conviction, and may it constantly actuate my conduct; in sorrow and in joy may I recollect that thy favour is the one thing needful, the attainment of virtue the main end of life, and the reward of every suffering. May these sentiments animate every action, left they rise up in judgment against me: and, as the least proof of my love to thee, may I ever anxiously try to be an useful and active member of society, following the example of thy Son, whose delight it was to do thy will. In his name and words I further pray unto thee, first recommending to thy care those I particularly love; bless them, and bless me, also by making me a comfort to them! Our Father, &c.

O.

PRIVATE EVENING PRAYER.

After the active employments of the day I return to thank my heavenly Father for his numberless mercies.—All around me is now still—and the resolutions of the morning come with full force into my mind to humble me before thee, and make me wonder at my own weakness

and

and folly. I have neglected many opportunities of doing good and improving myself; and, not sufficiently attentive to my temper, have given pain to those I ought to have been a comfort to. Particular instances of impatience and want of forbearance strike me at this moment, when I am imploring thee to have mercy on me, and vouchsafe to pardon me, that I may sleep in peace.

Every good and every perfect gift cometh from thee; oh grant me a wise and understanding heart—may a reverential fear of thee ever still the tumult of passion, silence every eager wish, and make me resigned to thy most afflictive dispensations, cheerfully enduring necessary chastisement as a proof of thy love, and a means of calling home my scattered thoughts from deceitful pleasures, and the vain desire of worldly prosperity!—these prospects and hopes now fade before me, and appear insignificant when compared with thy favour, and the heart-felt joy arising from virtue.

Full of these thoughts, I seek repose—the image of death presents itself—but why should I be afraid while I can trust in thee—may I die the death of the righteous, and then I shall wake to a new and glorious day—the cloud will be removed that darkens my view—for thou hast graciously promised to wipe away the tear that sorrow and frailty forces me to shed whilst struggling with my infirmities.

Preserve me from the dangers of the night, if it be thy good pleasure, and bless and guard all those I love. At peace with every human creature, I beg thee to bless the whole world of which I make a part—May thy will be done on earth as it is in heaven!—Glory be to God on high, and on earth peace! Q.

A SOCIAL

A SOCIAL MORNING PRAYER.

ALMIGHTY God, whose watchful eye overlooks all thy works, receive our sincere thanks for thy fatherly care of us the night past, and for every other mercy during life, whatever appearance it might wear. If trials and afflictions should in future be more particularly our lot, oh grant that they may produce the desired effect, and make us humble and patient; resigned to thy will in this world, and in some measure prepared for a better! Do Thou vouchsafe to enlighten our understandings and help our infirmities;—yet may we ever be attentive to our thoughts as well as conduct, conscious that a pure God, who cannot bear even the shadow of iniquity, is constantly about our paths, and spieth out all our ways.

We earnestly desire to be enabled to exert ourselves for the service of our fellow creatures; and let a due sense of our own weakness make us ready to practise charity and forbearance. Teach us with humble awe to imitate the divine pattern thou hast set before us—the qualities thou hast condescended to display to attract our affection and lure us to the paths of virtue, where only true peace and lasting pleasure is to be found; may we emulate them here, that we may more perfectly know thee hereafter the source of true joy.

To these our important petitions we wish to add our requests for more particular favours.—Preserve us, we beseech thee, from the contagion of vice and folly when we enter into the active scenes of the day, and from the bodily dangers to which we are liable; grant us necessary food, and those temporal blessings thou knowest to be the

fittest

fittest for us, and most conducive to our eternal welfare—our attainment of virtuous habits and purity of mind.

Pardon, we entreat thee, our past offences, and grant us thy assistance to fulfil with more steadiness the duties of the present day, for the sake of Jesus Christ, in whose name we presume to pray unto thee, and implore blessings that we can never deserve—but thou art good, therefore thou art to be feared. And ever may the whole host of intelligent beings join to praise him who liveth for ever and ever, King of kings and Lord of lords.

Our Father, &c.

O.

A SOCIAL EVENING PRAYER.

Most adorable God! whose fatherly care is over all thy creatures, we desire to offer unto thee our thankful acknowledgments for thy protection of us through the day past; and for preserving us from many unseen dangers, to which we are at all times subject. By thee we are fed and clothed, and have an habitation to shelter us from the inclemency of the weather; but thy tender affectionate care of us is more particularly displayed in affording us not only the necessaries, but the comforts and conveniencies of life. These are the free gifts of thy love:—Oh teach us to have a due sense of them! that whilst thou preservest our frail bodies our minds may be improved, and the main purpose of life diligently pursued—to attain that end, enable us to resign ourselves cheerfully to thy will, patiently enduring those afflictions which thy wisdom hath appointed for our real benefit.

And, that we may indeed serve thee truly, we beseech thee, O Father of mercies! to look with compassion on the

the weakness and infirmities of our nature, and grant us Thy divine assistance—save us or we perish!—and lead us to discover more and more, by every day's experience, our numberless faults and imperfections: and, that we may be heartily desirous to correct them, make us thoroughly sensible that our true happiness consists in a life of religion and virtue.

To thy care we humbly commit ourselves this night; trusting in Thy protection of us while we sleep: in that helpless state we seem to be more particularly exposed to the dreadful calamities of fire, robbery, or tempest; but, knowing that thy almighty power can defend us from every ill, we now earnestly seek that sure defence:—O grant us a quiet and refreshing sleep, that we may rise in health and safety to fulfil our daily duties, and shew forth thy praise not only with our lips but in our lives.—We wish, while we entreat fresh mercies, to thank thee for the past.—Thou art good, and of thy mercies there is no end! —Blessing, honour, and glory, be ascribed unto thee!—and we thank thee for allowing us to praise thee, and see the hand from which so many blessings flow!

Lord God, our creator and preserver, accept our prayers, which we humbly offer in the name, and through the mediation, of Jesus Christ! *Amen.*

O.

THE MORNING HYMN.

These are thy glorious works, Parent of good,
Almighty, thine this universal frame,
Thus wond'rous fair; thyself how wond'rous then!
Unspeakable, who sitt'st above these heavens

To

To us invisible, or dimly seen
In these thy lowest works; yet these declare
Thy goodness beyond thought and pow'r divine.
Speak, ye who best can tell, ye sons of light—
Angels; for ye behold him, and with songs
And choral symphonies, day without night,
Circle his throne rejoicing; ye in heaven,
On earth, join all ye creatures to extol
Him first, him last, him midst, and without end!
Fairest of stars, last in the train of night,
If better thou belong not to the dawn,
Sure pledge of day, that crown'st the smiling morn
With thy bright circlet, praise him in thy sphere,
While day arises, that sweet hour of prime!
Thou sun, of this great world both eye and soul,
Acknowledge him thy greater, sound his praise
In thy eternal course, both when thou climb'st,
And when high noon hast gain'd, and when thou fall'st.
Moon, that now meet'st the orient sun, now fly'st
With the fix'd stars, fix'd in their orb that flies!
And ye five other wand'ring fires, that move
In mystic dance, not without song, resound
His praise, who out of darkness call'd up light!
Air, and ye elements, the eldest birth
Of Nature's womb, that in quaternion run
Perpetual circle, multiform, and mix
And nourish all things, let your careless change
Vary to our great Maker still new praise!
Ye mists and exhalations, that now rise
From hill or steaming lake, dusky or grey,
Till the sun paint your fleecy skirts with gold,
In honour to the world's great author, rise!

Whether

Whether to deck with clouds th' uncolour'd sky,
Or wet the thirsty earth with falling showers,
Rising or falling still advance his praise.
His praise, ye winds, that from four quarters blow,
Breathe soft or loud; and wave your tops, ye pines,
With every plant in sign of worship wave.
Fountains, and ye that warble as ye flow,
Melodious murmurs, warbling, tune his praise.
Join voices, all ye living souls; ye birds,
That singing up to heaven's gate ascend,
Bear on your wings and in your notes his praise.
Ye that in waters glide, and ye that walk
The earth, and stately tread, or lowly creep;
Witness if I be silent, morn or even,
To hill or valley, fountain, or fresh shade,
Made vocal by my song; and taught his praise.
Hail, universal Lord! be bounteous still
To give us only good; and if the night
Have gather'd ought of evil, or conceal'd,
Disperse it, as now light dispels the dark.
                                        MILTON.

AN ADDRESS TO THE DEITY.

God of my life! and author of my days!
Permit my feeble voice to lisp thy praise;
And, trembling, take upon a mortal tongue
That hallow'd name to harps of seraphs sung.
Yet here the brightest seraphs could no more
Than hide their faces, tremble, and adore.
Worms, angels, men, in ev'ry different sphere
Are equal all, for all are nothing here.

All nature faints beneath the mighty name,
Which Nature's works thro' all her parts proclaim.
I feel that name my inmoſt thoughts control,
And breathe an awful ſtillneſs thro' my ſoul;
As by a charm the waves of grief ſubſide;
Impetuous paſſion ſtops her headlong tide:
At thy felt preſence all emotions ceaſe,
And my huſh'd ſpirit finds a ſudden peace,
Till every worldly thought within me dies,
And earth's gay pageants vaniſh from my eyes;
Till all my ſenſe is loſt in infinite,
And one vaſt object fills my aching ſight.

But ſoon, alas! this holy calm is broke;
My ſoul ſubmits to wear her wonted yoke;
With ſhackled pinions ſtrives to ſoar in vain,
And mingles with the droſs of earth again.
But he, our gracious Maſter, kind as juſt,
Knowing our frame, remembers man is duſt!
His ſpirit, ever brooding o'er our mind,
Sees the firſt wiſh to better hopes inclin'd;
Marks the young dawn of every virtuous aim,
And fans the ſmoking flax into a flame.
His ears are open to the ſofteſt cry,
His grace deſcends to meet the lifted eye;
He reads the language of a ſilent tear,
And ſighs are incenſe from a heart ſincere.
Such are the vows, the ſacrifice I give;
Accept the vow, and bid the ſuppliant live;
From each terreſtrial bondage ſet me free;
Still every wiſh that centers not in thee;
Bid my fond hopes, my vain diſquiets ceaſe,
And point my path to everlaſting peace.

If the soft hand of winning pleasure leads
By living waters, and thro' flow'ry meads,
When all is smiling, tranquil, and serene,
And vernal beauty paints the flattering scene,
Oh! teach me to elude each latent snare,
And whisper to my sliding heart—beware!
With caution let me hear the syren's voice,
And, doubtful, with a trembling heart rejoice.

If friendless in a vale of tears I stray,
Where briars wound, and thorns perplex my way,
Still let my steady soul thy goodness see,
And with strong confidence lay hold on thee;
With equal eye my various lot receive,
Resign'd to die, or resolute to live;
Prepar'd to kiss the sceptre, or the rod,
While God is seen in all, and all in God.

I read his awful name, emblazon'd high
With golden letters on th' illumin'd sky;
Nor less the mystic characters I see
Wrought in each flower, inscrib'd on ev'ry tree;
In every leaf that trembles to the breeze
I hear the voice of God among the trees;
With thee in shady solitudes I walk,
With thee in busy crowded cities talk;
In every creature own thy forming power,
In each event thy providence adore.
Thy hopes shall animate my drooping soul,
Thy precepts guide me, and thy fear control.
Thus shall I rest; unmov'd by all alarms,
Secure within the temple of thine arms,
From anxious cares, from gloomy terrors free,
And feel myself omnipotent in thee.

Then when the last, the closing hour draws nigh,
And earth recedes before my swimming eye;
When trembling on the doubtful edge of fate
I stand, and stretch my view to either state;
Teach me to quit this transitory scene
With decent triumph, and a look serene;
Teach me to fix my ardent hopes on high;
And, having liv'd to thee, in thee to die.

MISS AIKIN.

AN ADDRESS TO THE DEITY.

FATHER of light and life! thou good supreme!
O teach me what is good—teach me thyself!
Save me from folly, vanity, and vice,
From every low pursuit! and feed my soul
With knowledge, conscious peace, and virtue pure;
Sacred, substantial, never-fading bliss!

THOMSON.

CHARACTER OF A GOOD MAN.

THE earth is the Lord's, and the fulness thereof; the world, and they that dwell therein.

For he hath founded it upon the seas, and established it upon the floods.

Who shall ascend into the hill of the Lord? and who shall stand in his holy place?

He that hath clean hands and a pure heart; who hath not lifted up his soul unto vanity, nor sworn deceitfully.

He shall receive the blessing from the Lord, and righteousness from the God of his salvation.

This

This is the generation of them that seek him: that seek thy face, O Jacob.

Lift up your heads, O ye gates, and be ye lift up, ye everlasting doors; and the King of glory shall come in.

Who is this King of glory? the Lord, strong and mighty, the Lord mighty in battle.

Lift up your heads, O ye gates, even lift them up, ye everlasting doors; and the King of glory shall come in.

Who is this King of glory? the Lord of hosts, he is the King of glory.

PSALMS.

AN ADDRESS TO THE DEITY.

O Thou great arbiter of life and death!
Nature's immortal, immaterial sun!
Whose all prolific beam late call'd me forth
From darkness, teeming darkness, where I lay
The worm's inferior, and in rank beneath
The dust I tread on, high to bear my brow;
To drink the spirit of the golden day,
And triumph in existence; and couldst know
No motive but my bliss; and hath ordain'd
A rise in blessing! with the patriarch's joy
Thy call I follow to the land unknown.
I trust in thee, and know in whom I trust;
Or life, or death, is equal, neither weighs!
All weight in this—O let me live to thee!

YOUNG.

DAVID's CONFIDENCE IN GOD's GRACE.

The Lord is my shepherd, I shall not want.

He maketh me to lie down in green pastures; he leadeth me beside the still waters; he restoreth my soul; he leadeth me in the paths of righteousness, for his name's sake.

Yea, though I walk through the valley of the shadow of death, I will fear no evil, for thou art with me, thy rod and thy staff they comfort me.

Thou preparest a table before me, in the presence of mine enemies; thou anointest my head with oil, my cup runneth over.

Surely goodness and mercy shall follow me all the days of my life, and I will dwell in the house of the Lord for ever.

PSALMS.

AN ADDRESS TO THE DEITY.

Thou, who didst put to flight
Primæval silence when the morning stars,
Exulting, shouted o'er the rising ball;
O Thou, whose word from solid darkness struck
That spark, the sun; strike wisdom from my soul;
My soul which flies to thee her trust, her treasure,
As misers to their gold, while others rest.

YOUNG.

THE PRESENCE OF GOD.

When Israel went out of Egypt, the house of Jacob from a people of strange language:

Judah

Judah was his sanctuary, and Israel his dominion.

The sea saw it and fled: Jordan was driven back.

The mountains skipped like rams, and the little hills like lambs. What ailed thee, O thou sea, that thou fleddest? thou Jordan that thou wast driven back?

Ye mountains, that ye skipped like rams? and ye little hills like lambs?

Tremble thou earth at the presence of the Lord, at the presence of the God of Jacob:

Which turned the rock into a standing water, the flint into a fountain of waters.

PSALMS.

THE POWER OF GOD.

Bless the Lord, O my soul. O Lord my God, thou art very great; thou art clothed with honour and majesty.

Who coverest thyself with light as with a garment; who stretchest out the heavens like a curtain;

Who layeth the beams of his chambers in the waters, who maketh the clouds his chariot; who walketh upon the wings of the wind.

Who maketh his angels spirits; his ministers a flaming fire.

Who laid the foundations of the earth, that it should not be removed for ever.

Thou coveredst it with the deep as with a garment: the waters stood above the mountains.

At thy rebuke they fled; at the voice of thy thunder they hasted away.

They go up by the mountains; they go down by the vallies unto the place which thou hast founded for them.

Thou

Thou haſt ſet a bound that they may not paſs over; that they turn not again to cover the earth.

He ſendeth the ſprings unto the vallies, which run among the hills;

They give drink to every beaſt of the field: the wild aſſes quench their thirſt.

By them ſhall the fowls of the heaven have their habitation, which ſing among the branches.

He watereth the hills from his chambers: the earth is ſatisfied with the fruit of thy works.

He cauſeth the graſs to grow for the cattle, and herb for the ſervice of man: that he may bring forth food out of the earth:

And wine that maketh glad the heart of man, and oil to make his face to ſhine, and bread which ſtrengtheneth man's heart.

The trees of the Lord are full of ſap, the cedars of Lebanon which he hath planted;

Where the birds make their neſts: as for the ſtork the fir-trees are her houſe.

The high hills are a refuge for the wild goats, and the rocks for the conies.

He appointed the moon for ſeaſons: the ſun knoweth his going down.

Thou makeſt darkneſs, and it is night: wherein all the beaſts of the foreſt do creep forth.

The young lions roar after their prey, and ſeek their meat from God;

The ſun ariſeth, they gather themſelves together and lay them down in their dens.

Man goeth forth unto his work, and to his labour until the evening.

O Lord,

O Lord, how manifold are thy works! in wisdom hast thou made them all: the earth is full of thy riches.

So is this great and wide sea, wherein are things creeping innumerable, both small and great beasts.

There go the ships: there is that leviathan, whom thou hast made to play therein.

These wait all upon thee: that thou mayest give them their meat in due season.

That thou givest them, they gather: thou openest thine hand, they are filled with good.

Thou hidest thy face, they are troubled; thou takest away their breath, they die and return to their dust.

Thou sendest forth thy spirit, they are created; and thou renewest the face of the earth.

The glory of the Lord shall endure for ever, the Lord shall rejoice in his works.

He looketh on the earth, and it trembleth; he toucheth the hills, and they smoke.

I will sing unto the Lord as long as I live, I will sing praise unto my God while I have my being.

My meditation of him shall be sweet; I will be glad in the Lord.

Let the sinners be consumed out of the earth, and let the wicked be no more. Bless thou the Lord, O my soul. Praise ye the Lord.

PSALMS.

THE GOODNESS OF GOD.

O LORD our Lord, how excellent is thy name in all the earth! who hast set thy glory above the heavens.

Out of the mouth of babes and sucklings hast thou or-
dained

dained strength because of thine enemies, that thou mightest still the enemy and the avenger.

When I consider the heavens, the work of thy fingers: the moon and the stars which thou hast ordained:

What is man that thou art mindful of him? and the son of man that thou visitest him?

For thou hast made him a little lower than the angels, and hast crowned him with glory and honour.

Thou madest him to have dominion over the works of thy hands; thou hast put all things under his feet:

All sheep and oxen, yea, and the beasts of the field;

The fowl of the air, and the fish of the sea; and whatsoever passeth through the paths of the seas.

O Lord our Lord, how excellent is thy name in all the earth!

PSALMS.

REMEMBER now thy Creator in the days of thy youth, while the evil days come not, nor the years draw nigh, when thou shalt say, I have no pleasure in them.

ECCLESIASTES.

THE END.

BOOKS FOR THE USE OF YOUNG PERSONS.
Printed for J. Johnson, St. Paul's Church-yard.

1. SACRED HISTORY, from the creation of the world, selected from the Scriptures, with annotations and reflections suited to the comprehension of young minds; particularly calculated to facilitate the study of the Holy Scriptures in schools and families, and to render this important branch of education easy to the tutor and pleasing to the pupil. 6 vols. dedicated, by permission, to the Queen. Price 21s. bound; by Mrs. Trimmer.

2. A FATHER's INSTRUCTIONS: consisting of Moral Tales, Fables, and Reflections, designed to promote a love of truth, a taste for knowledge, and an early acquaintance with the works of nature, by Thomas Percival, M. D. 4s.

3. MORAL AND LITERARY DISSERTATIONS on, 1. Truth and Faithfulness. 2. On Habit and Association. 3. On Inconsistencies of Expectation in literary Pursuits. 4. On a Taste for the general Beauties of Nature. 5. On a Taste for the Fine Arts, &c. chiefly intended as a Sequel to a FATHER's INSTRUCTIONS. By the same. Price 5s.

4. BIOGRAPHICAL SERMONS: or, a Series of Discourses on the principal Characters in Scripture, viz. Abraham, Jacob, Joseph, Moses, Job, Daniel, St. Peter, St. Paul, and Jesus Christ, by W. Enfield, LL. D. 3s. 6d.

The Author has adopted this mode of address, not merely on account of its novelty, but from an expectation that the interesting scenes, which it has given him an opportunity of describing, will engage the feelings of his readers in favour of virtue; and also with a view to lead young persons into a habit of making useful reflections on the actions and characters of men, whether represented in the pages of Sacred or Civil History, or exhibited in real life.

5. ORIGINAL STORIES, from real Life, with Conversations, calculated to regulate the affections, and form the mind to truth and goodness. On the following subjects:

The Treatment of Animals.---The Ant.---The Bee.---Goodness.---True humanity.---The Lark's Nest.---The Asses.

The Difference between them and Men.---The first Step towards Virtue.---Parental Affection of a Dog.---Brutality punished.

The Story of crazy Robin.---The Man confined in the Bastile.

Anger.---An ungoverned Temper creates its own Misery.---True Greatness of Mind.---History of Jane B------

Lying.---A Definition of Honour.---Truth.---History of Lady L. and Mrs. B.---Virtue the Source of Content.

Anger.---When justifiable.---Folly produces Self-contempt, and the Neglect of others.

Beauty.---Virtue embellishes the Person, gives Grace and Variety to Beauty.---The Tulip and the Rose.---External Ornaments.---Characters.

BOOKS, &c.

Summer Evening's Amusement.---Ridicule of personal Defects censured.---A Storm.---History of a Sailor.

The Inconveniences arising from immoderate Indulgence.---The Marks of Rationality.---The Rights of Society.

The Danger of Delay.---Indolence and social Attentions incompatible.---Virtue is an active Principle, and does not reside in the Imaginations.---Description of a Mansion-House in Ruins.---History of Charles Townley.

Dress.---A Character.---An Example.---Vanity distinguished.---Trifling Omissions undermine Affection.

Behaviour to Servants.---True Dignity of Character.

Employment.---Idleness produces Misery.---The Cultivation of the Fancy raises us above the Vulgar

Innocent Amusements, resulting from the Exercise of Benevolence.---Description of a Welch Castle.---History of a Welch Harper.---Family Pride.

Prayer.---A Moon-light Scene.---Resignation.

The Benefits arising from Devotion.---The History of the Village School mistress.---Fatal Effects of Inattention to Expense, in the History of Mr. C.

A Visit.---Pride---False Pride sometimes useful.

Charity.---The History of Peggy and her Family.---The Sailor's Widow.

Visit to Mrs. B.---Accomplishments render an Individual pleasing--but Virtue only demands Respect, is the one Thing needful.

Bodily Pain first exercises the Faculties.---Fortitude the Basis of Virtue.---The Folly and Selfishness of Irresolution.

Journey to London.

Charity.---Shopping.---The distressed Stationer.---Mischievous Consequences of delaying Payment.---False Sensibility.

Visit to a Poor Family in London.---Idleness the Parent of Vice.---Prodigality and Generosity incompatible.---Benevolent Exertions the first Spring of Comfort and Virtue.---True and false Motives for Saving.---Self-denial noble when it is practised to benefit others.

Mrs. Mason's farewell Advice to her Pupils.---Observations on Letter-writing. Price 3s. bound.

Milton Keynes UK
Ingram Content Group UK Ltd.
UKHW030929171124
451206UK00007B/28